The
GAME
of
DESIRE

Also by Shan Boodram

Laid: Young People's Experiences with Sex in an Easy-Access Culture

The
GAME
of
DESIRE

5 Surprising Secrets to Dating with Dominance—and Getting What You Want

SHAN BOODRAM

DEY ST.
An Imprint of WILLIAM MORROW

THE GAME OF DESIRE. Copyright © 2019 by Shannon Brady. All rights reserved. Printed in the United States of America. No part of this book may be used or reproduced in any manner whatsoever without written permission except in the case of brief quotations embodied in critical articles and reviews. For information, address HarperCollins Publishers, 195 Broadway, New York, NY 10007.

HarperCollins books may be purchased for educational, business, or sales promotional use. For information, please email the Special Markets Department at SPsales@harpercollins.com.

FIRST EDITION

Designed by Joy O'Meara

Library of Congress Cataloging-in-Publication Data has been applied for.

ISBN 978-0-06-295254-7

19 20 21 22 23 LSC 10 9 8 7 6 5 4 3 2 1

For my husband, Jared Brady, who served valiantly as my cheerleader, therapist, confidante, booty call and relentless inspiration during the emotional process of living—then writing—this book.

Contents

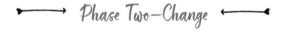

── PROLOGUE ──

*C*ourtney seemed stuck—caught between two thoughts, two versions of herself, but mostly between two colors.

"Should I make the smiley face red or black?" she asked with her marker hovering over a stack of notecards.

I glanced around her office, a place I knew she spent far too much time in, then replied, "The next action card in the routine is the physical challenge, so why not make that one black? Then you can make the smiley face red."

The colors did not matter in the least, and we actually didn't even need to make cue cards, since Courtney had rehearsed the routine until she knew it by heart; but I invited her to use her marker collection because I knew it would calm her nerves. I suspected that she knew this too.

Courtney had gone on at least a dozen dates since we began working together months ago, but this meetup with Derek was special. Derek was her ideal playmate to a *T*: a conscious thinker, a health nut and a hot firefighter who looked like his nickname was Mr. October. She had been crushing on him for awhile but had only mustered the courage and skill set to ask him out a few days ago. The *Derek-type* was exactly what we'd been working toward, and the best part of all was that he wasn't the only high-interest playmate Courtney had lined up. Another man named River, who she'd described as a potential soul mate, was flying in from Dallas in a couple of weeks to see her as well.

"Don't stress out too much about getting this date in the can. Derek is the one who should be scared of you with ya dangerously seductive self!"

Courtney exhaled into a half smile and pressed the cap on her marker as if to say, *Amen*. She handed me the cue cards, then grabbed her purse. "Okay, we should probably head out. He'll be there soon."

I stood in agreement and looked her over one more time. "Do you need to wear a bra?"

We left her office in separate cars and by the time I got to the restaurant, Courtney (and her freed nipples) were already outside on her faux good-news phone call, which was the first technique of the routine. After working with me to fix her struggling love life, Courtney was inspired to begin her own workshop for women, who, like her, had been bullied in high school. The "caller" was a web designer who had agreed to take on her new passion project, pro bono. All of this was true but of course, it didn't *just* happen . . . but it did happen to be something we could use to her advantage because positive first impressions are well worth their weight in gold.

Courtney pointed through the window at a man sitting with his back to us. I nodded then flashed three cards at her for a final reminder: a red smile (make sure this is the first thing he sees), blue connected arrows (touch consensually ASAP) and a newspaper (share good news). I slid into the table behind Derek and a beat later Courtney walked in with a tsunami of positive vibes. She finished up her call, loudly, then approached Derek, who had now gotten to his feet.

"It's so good that we're finally doing this," she said as she hugged him tightly. "I just got some awesome news that I have to share! Maybe you're my new good-luck charm."

I did a fist pump under my table and waved the fourth cue card with the drawing of a keg, a symbol to remind her to be the life of the party. A few minutes later the waiter sauntered over to their table and Courtney cradled her chin in her hands then struck up some small talk.

The waiter took the bait, shifted his body toward her and stood taller. "You've been here before, right? We have some new things on the menu, do you want some recommendations?"

In response to this, Courtney switched her attention back to Derek. "What do you think I should get?" She appraised him and smiled with approval. "I trust you know what you're doing."

When the waiter left, Courtney proceeded to tell Derek about the phone call. He asked a series of rapid-fire follow-ups then surprisingly revealed he too had been severely picked on growing up. They shared a moment, exchanging their high school pitfalls and triumphs that I'm sure would have gone on longer if I weren't there. I held up the fifth card, a squiggly face, and waited for Courtney to find something to disagree with him about. After all, fire isn't created with sunlight alone; to create sparks you must also have friction.

Derek started talking about football and how it helped him gain the confidence he lacked in high school. With this Courtney sat up straighter to investigate. "You're a football guy, eh? Who's your team?"

"Oh, you're a football gal?" said Derek excitedly. He leaned so far over the table, you'd truly think he was holding that damn thing up. "I'm a Rams fan."

Up to that point, Courtney had mirrored his body position, plus she had been giving him the full flirtatious treatment: her speech was slow, her body was in a perfect S formation and she had been picturing him naked to keep her pupils dilated. But the Rams comment changed everything. She sat back to put distance between them, then closed her body by crossing her arms and pointing her feet toward the door. "The Rams, seriously? Just when I thought we could be friends."

For the next few minutes, Courtney scolded him about his bad taste in football. He defended himself and his team, but she was unrelentingly displeased with him. I held the red-smiley-face card up, indicating it was time to turn the disagreement into an opportunity to tease and create their first inside joke. I couldn't hear what she said but I noticed her uncross her arms and poke out that hip again. *You're welcome, Derek,* I thought.

The waiter stopped by, took my order and then stared down at my bright yellow cards. In moments like this I was so glad to live in L.A., a place where too many weird things happen for anyone to really give a damn. He walked away and I flashed the seventh card, which was a picture of a dumbbell that signified it was time to get physical. Courtney glanced down at her Fitbit then back up at Derek.

"Shoot," she murmured.

"What?"

"It's stupid, but me and my friends are doing this twenty-one-day physical challenge that's kind of turned into a competition. This is awkward, but I have to squat now. Will you do it with me?"

"Here? No," he said flatly.

Like the professional that she was, she didn't back down. "Please, just thirty seconds so I don't look like a dork in here alone? We don't even have to get up, we can just hover over our seat."

He shook his head, but this time with a smile that said, *You win.* The two of them scooted back their chairs, then squatted. This technique may sound crazy but let's analyze the genius behind it.

1. Exercise increases the heart rate, which is also the same physiological response you get when you like someone new.
2. "Misbehaving" in a civilized place brings you back to the joys of childhood.
3. Doing something physically exerting while you're inches away from someone you have chemistry with is the closest you're gonna get to sex in public without drawing stares or sirens.

Courtney wavered on her heels then placed her hand on Derek's for balance as they kept their eyes locked on one another. "Okay, done!" she declared.

They both collapsed back and laughed until their breathing returned to normal.

"What other alerts do you have on there?" quizzed Derek.

Once again, Courtney took this as an opportunity to cross the physical barrier. Most women are afraid to introduce touch on their first few dates, which is precisely why I taught Courtney not to be. Everything she had done, from the moment she asked *him* out, was designed to make it abundantly clear she was far from average.

Courtney inspected his watch and turned his wrist over in her hand until it naturally fell into her palm. She held it there for a second then gestured for him to take it back. As he retracted, she let her fingers brush against his. I later learned that our good sport Derek had brushed back.

I held up the card with three Xs on it, a prompt for Courtney to begin mind-fucking Derek. She nodded subtly in a way that looked like she was agreeing with him, even though I was certain the gesture was for me. As they chatted some more, she casually lifted her hand and gripped then stroked her glass up and down then down and back up. She also took every opportunity to expose her neck and draw attention to her mouth. The goal of mind-fucking is to activate someone's sexual responses, without them overtly understanding why they are becoming aroused.

I pulled out the card with the bathroom symbol drawn on it and a few beats later, Courtney excused herself, being mindful to touch Derek's shoulders reassuringly as she left. If you have a hard time introducing touch on dates, the bathroom technique should solve that dilemma by giving you a natural excuse to touch a neutral place. This break also provides a crucial opportunity to freshen up, not just physically, but mentally. Professional sports teams take a halftime break to regroup, so why shouldn't you? I encouraged Courtney and the other women in our group (who you will meet later on) to use this time to recenter themselves by rapping their favorite pump-up verse, reapplying their vaginal fluids (again, more on that later) and most important, to stare at themselves ravenously in the mirror until *they* couldn't resist the woman gazing back.

The waiter approached with my soup and salad, which I had totally forgotten I'd even ordered. I looked up at him apologetically and asked, "Can I get this to go, please?"

I wanted to be gone before Courtney got back to communicate that I had total confidence in her ability to close without prompts. This was the moment the training wheels came off. Before I left, I threw the remaining cue cards in the trash. They were:

- Ask a bold question (*Why are you still single?*).
- Ask a weird and sexy question (*If you were a sexual superhero, what would your special power be?*).
- Leave him with an anecdote or story to think about.
- Get the fuck out of there!

With that last note in mind, I sent Courtney a reminder text once I got back to my car:

Don't let him extend the date beyond dinner, no matter how good things are going

About an hour later, she called and practically yelled, "Girl, that date went so damn smooth. I got a second date *on* the date. Literally while we were eating, he said, I want to see you again!"

"You're officially an indisputable pro now."

She laughed and clapped her hands joyfully. "All thanks to you, Shan. This shit really works."

— INTRODUCTION —

*H*ello luvas!

Be honest: How many of you know an awesome person with a romantic life that could be summed up with these six words: *the short end of the stick*? Perhaps that friend might even be you. I'm not here to judge, but I am here to wake your butt up by letting you know that despising your experiences as a single person is not normal. When people say relationships take work, they are talking about the inevitable misalignments that occur when two (or more) people try to share one life. What they're not talking about is all the unnecessary drama, unreturned texts and lackluster sex that result from picking up floor scraps because you don't feel worthy of joining the dating feast. And believe me, despite the fact that we are statistically in a dating famine—or as *Vanity Fair* dubbed it, a Dating Apocalypse—there is a feast out there of explosive chemistry, conversations until dawn, fairy-tale firsts and finger-licking-good seconds.[1]

In short, I wrote this book to teach each of you how to boldly play the game of desire, and win.

Thankfully, in this game, there really aren't any losers. First of all, the goal here is not to trick or one-up potential mates, but instead to get the best out of everyone in each budding connection. Second, while it's fun to walk into a room feeling like you own it, cool to know how to make people feel excited in your presence, and exciting to be the one deciding if you wanna call someone back, there's also a ton of value in coming up short because that's how you get better and find better matches. With this in mind, the choice to play isn't a question of morality but one of personal endurance: How much longer can you stand to wait for luck to notice you and fix your broken, lonely heart?

In David Brooks's book *The Social Animal,* he states that the recipe for happiness has three parts; two of those three have to do with the quality and quantity of a person's close relationships.[2] I became a sexologist because I couldn't understand why we, as a society, were leaving such a critical component of our well-being up to chance. In other important areas like our career, finances and health, we are taught that if we want to excel we must study, seek out expert guides and practice proven behaviors. As an intimacy educator, I've made it my duty to help people understand that this formula works wonders on the interpersonal side of life too. From my private counseling service, to my YouTube channel, to features on major networks and publications, I've reached millions of people on a topic they've unfortunately barely spoken about in school. I'm a certified sex education counselor in Canada, a certified sexologist in America, Facebook Watch's couples counselor on *Make Up or Break Up,* and MTV's millennial intimacy expert on their "Guide To" series. I've written for *Cosmopolitan,* the TV show *The Bold Type* and *Teen Vogue.* My first book, *Laid: Young People's Experiences with Sex in an Easy-Access Culture,* is still on shelves. I'm a member of the National Coalition of Sexual Health where I've led the execution of a sex education video for new military members and I'm a part of Trojan's Sexual Health Advisory Council. In total, I've worked in the intimacy space for over ten years, and wanna know the one conclusion I've come to?

Most people have no clue what they're doing, no idea what they're doing wrong and thus, absolutely no concept of how to change the direction of their romantic fate.

Yes, women have a ton of advice columns. And yes, we have libraries of self-help books that encourage us to be a bitch, a prude or a vixen; but in my experience of listening to singles, they don't need any more arbitrary tips. They need a clear system to follow that's inclusive, multifaceted and proven.

Before we get into the details of the system I've created, let's first analyze the current conditions of the dating landscape, because once you know where you want to go, it's important to understand what you must get through.

According to the 2014 U.S. Census poll, there are 107 million unmarried Americans over 18, and more than half are women.[3] Jon Birger, author of *Date-onomics,* believes these numbers alone can tell us all we need to know about the current conditions: "Sociologists, psychologists and economists have done a ton of research on sex ratios, and the consensus is clear. When men are in oversupply, the dating culture is more traditional and more monogamous, but when women are in oversupply—as they are today . . . the dating culture is less monogamous and more libertine; women are more likely to be treated as sex objects rather than as romantic love interests."[4]

Birger's assessment is consistent with what I've heard firsthand from the vast majority of singles I've met through my work. In preparation for this project, I asked a pool of three hundred women to describe dating in one sentence and here are some of the most common responses I received:

"Dating is a chore. . . . Most people I meet are disrespectful and just want sex."

"Dating is draining, men are extremely immature and misogynistic."

"Dating is annoying because it feels like I'm starting something that won't finish the way I want it to."

"Dating is confusing because people want all the benefits of a relationship but don't actually want to commit."

In further support of the gender ratio theory, popular dating apps like Bumble, Match and Coffee Meets Bagel have more users that identify as women than men. But somewhat unsurprisingly, according to a study conducted by Hinge, looking to your phone to find a real connection, regardless of your gender, is statistically not the most fruitful route. In fact, only one in five hundred Hinge swipes led to a phone number exchange, and 81 percent of Hinge users have reported they've never found a long-term relationship through a swiping app.[5]

In 2018, HBO put out a documentary called *Swiped: Hooking up in the Digital Age* by Nancy Jo Sales that painted a grim picture of mating for millennials and Gen Z's. Sales said that one of the most disturbing findings of her deep dive was the rampant racism that swipe-right culture seems to normalize by ranking attractiveness solely based on race.[6]

Even more disturbing were the statistics *Swiped* pointed to. According to the U.K.'s National Crime Agency, reports of online-dating-related rape have risen by more than 450 percent in six years.[7] According to the Centers for Disease Control, in 2017, a record-breaking 2.2 million cases of syphilis, gonorrhea and chlamydia were diagnosed in the U.S.[8]

Finally, the culture of dating in a famine has left a massive impact on our general feelings about connection. A Harris Poll conducted in 2016 found that more than 70 percent of those who participated identified themselves as lonely.[9]

LET'S RECAP. TODAY'S SINGLE WOMAN IS IN A MARKET WHERE WOMEN ARE in oversupply, sex is at the forefront, real connections are statistically improbable, reports of sexual assault are rising, sexually transmitted infections are spiking and people think it's okay to talk about race as though they're ordering a pizza.

If reading all of this makes you feel like closing up shop and heading for a life of shoe-crafting solitude in the depths of a forest, I can't say I blame you. But I do dare to challenge you because while, yes, many people are currently struggling, there are the few who've mastered the art of connection, who are thriving. And if in your mind you need to have one million followers or a face sculpted by the gods to be a part of that few, you need this book more than you could possibly know. I say all this as someone who has been through the merciless fires of dating hell, gotten my shit together and then come out not just alive, but ablaze with purpose and gratitude *because* I found (and married) the love of my life.

Some people refer to their life partner as their better half, and in my case, I would boldface, underline and add exclamation marks to that statement. My partner, Jared Brady, is the kind of sweet, empathetic and gentle person I will probably never be. Which is fine, because I'm the smart-ass, analytical and worry-free woman he needs to balance him out. It works in a way that has made every love song literal, every sunset vibrant and every aspect of my life richer. In the most obnoxiously cliché way possible, finding and being in a good relationship is the best thing that's ever happened to me. But, Jared wasn't a fluke or a one-off. He was the better of a lot of bests and the result of years of good decisions and calculated moves. In other words, please believe, before I got to the altar, your girl found and fully enjoyed her time at the feast (*Will Smith voice* *You know what I'm shaying?!*).

That is why this game is worth playing and why I led this journey with Courtney and five others. Through their experience, I hope to empower single women everywhere to have more fun than they can imagine while using tangible tools and a strategy to fulfill their wildest intimate aspirations.

Although we will be moving through this process as a group, everyone's outcome might look different. For sure, a successful long-term monogamous marriage is a beautiful example of love that we all can admire. On the other side of the coin, an incredible, reciprocal one-night stand, where both parties leave feeling better and just as healthy, is also something worth applauding, even if it's not something we would personally do. The goal here is the confidence, acceptance and mutuality that come from feeling desired; the conditions in which this result occurs are far less important.

All right—before I sound any more like a drawn-out infomercial, let's get to why we're all here! Below are the five phases that will serve as our guide as I attempt to lead six short-end-of-the-stick daters to the land of abundant desire.

This book is a detailed account of how I tested this five-phase program on six down-on-love daters—and how you, dear reader, can implement these tools for yourself. Our journey is radical, raw,

Phase One. KNOW who you've become by identifying the core traits of your intimate self. This includes being fully aware of your strengths, weaknesses, blind spots and patterns. This knowledge also needs to be supplemented with advanced feedback from others who know you intimately—be they close friends or exes.

Phase Two. CHANGE the habits and perceptions that are holding you back. This includes changing your appearance, your mind about your limits, faults and even your traumas. Learn the art of seduction, anti-seduction and the habits that may be preventing you from making powerful connections where it matters most. You can become whoever you consistently choose to be. If a component of your reality does not serve your vision of your highest self, it is no longer you.

Phase Three. LEARN from a series of experts (don't worry, I've done a lot of the work here for you!) to fine-tune your external and internal game.

ridiculous, turbulent—and absolutely true. I hope in the upcoming pages you will vicariously learn through these women (whom you will come to know very well) how to overcome any fears, faults, limiting beliefs and insecurities that have been preventing you from discovering your own feast.

All right, let's get started. Now would be an ideal time to tuck away your preconceived notions on the *do's* of dating, and your good-girls-don't guidelines. Because the story of how these women became everything they should be is driven by doing almost everything you've been told you should not!

Become a master at approaching, attracting, flirting and influencing. Decide who you want to attract and learn how to find and entice them.

Phase Four. PRACTICE what you've learned thus far in low-risk environments, including at work, among friends and on casual dates. In addition, test out new hypotheses so you can create your own unique toolbox for making connections at will. Flirting, seducing and influencing should not be reserved for "the one." These are skills that will transform all of your relationships, including the one you have with yourself.

Phase Five. BE the person you've always wanted to be. Enjoy the company of people who better you and bring you joy. Join the feast and empower others, through your exceptional transformation, to do the same. Finally, revisit the other four phases periodically because this work is never done. And once you get into the swing of things where it starts getting *really* fun, you'll realize how great that news is!

— 1 —

I TELL IT LIKE IT IS

*A*t 9:45 A.M. I sat down with two computers, a blank dry erase board and a vat of tea, ready to take on the 254 women whom I was scheduled to interview over the next four days. A week prior, I put out a post looking for incredibly frustrated single women who were local to L.A. I expected to get a trickle of responses, but instead I got a flood of applicants who were ready to devote themselves to my program designed to change their luck. Despite the volume, I sent out an invitation to video interview them all because you can't assess who someone is solely based on their "About Me" section. Even though my application covered everything from their romantic history to their friends' opinions of their chronic singledom, the only way I would truly know if someone was a fit was if we were face-to-face. Or screen-to screen . . . you get the gist.

I was on the hunt for a group that was diverse in ethnicity, body type, personality, dating goals, sexual orientation, and roadblocks. In addition, I had a checklist of criteria that they *had* to hit in order to be selected:

1. They must be in the city for at least 80 percent of the program
   I get that we're in the digital age but to truly analyze the process and results, I needed to observe the finalists without any filters.

2. They must have their shit together

In other words, in accordance with Maslow's Hierarchy of Needs[1], their basic needs had to be met. If their livelihood, health or living situation was in flux, it would be unrealistic to ask them to totally devote themselves to the pursuit of love and belonging.

3. They must work well with others

In my counseling service, it's come one, come all! But this program was extremely unique in that I would be crossing every single professional boundary. Participants would be invited into my home, they would meet my husband, hear my personal secrets and if they wanted to grab a cocktail on social field trips, I didn't plan on stopping them. For this reason, I had a strict policy: if you seemed like a dick, this program wouldn't be a fit.

THE PRINCIPLE OF CREATING THREE SET-IN-STONE STANDARDS IS A PROVEN theory in successful mate selection created by Dr. Ty Tashiro in his book *The Science of Happily Ever After.* Essentially, Tashiro encourages everyone to determine their three "wishes," aka non-negotiables, before beginning their hunt for a love connection.[2] In relation to finding group members, three wishes were sufficient since I wanted to keep my search broad. But when it comes to dating, I disagree with Tashiro and encourage anyone who works with me to choose five wishes, because your effort should amount to more options than that of the average person. We will build what I call your Frozen Five in future chapters.

When I connected with the first woman over Skype, I instantly understood just how much of a challenge narrowing down these applicants would be. Her name was Amanda and she seemed all kinds of great.

"I was able to convince an investor to put half a million into my business, so it's crazy that I can't get a man to text me back."

She was a coffee-drinking, straight-talking entrepreneur who had recently begun to suspect she was the "kind of woman that men only wanted to have sex with." She rarely made eye contact and answered all questions with short, quippy remarks. But behind her icy front, I could see glimpses of a warm heart and a hearty sense of humor. I wondered how many of the men who ghosted her got to spend a full evening with that softer side. Amanda struck me as a cactus woman, someone who uses spikes in order to protect what's precious and vulnerable on the inside. Yes, this method works marvelously in movies, where the plot is set in stone, or small towns, where the options are limited; but in big cities where new prospects are literally a swipe away, most aren't gonna stick around to see what's on the other side of someone's wall of armor. Unless of course they're determined to get something specific, like sex.

I was about to put a circle around her name so we could work on removing those spikes together, but she informed me that she planned on traveling for the summer. This put Amanda in violation of the first of my three standards.

My next call was a massage therapist in her early twenties with a rocking body and an even more rocking personality who described herself as "a sexually liberated millennial that hates that sex is the focus of today's relationships."

That sentence of course caught my interest. The most crucial thing I'd had to realize as a sex-positive advocate who doesn't want to have sex with everyone, is that people are extremely lazy and unimaginative. Most people will define you however you define yourself, without examining the nuances of what you *actually* mean. For example, I'm a sexologist who is not blind to the lightbulbs that spark in people's minds when I share that fun fact. So, if I meet someone new I make a point to emphasize the research-based side of my work. On dates, I used to go the extra mile to ensure all parties were on the same page. Before going out with someone I would communicate verbatim, "I'm looking forward to hanging with you but I'm not going to give you head and we won't be having sex."

I know that sounds cringe-worthy, but I said it and I stuck to it. And you know what? Not one person cancelled plans with me, and despite a few valiant attempts throughout the night to see if I was bluffing, my dates respected my boundaries.

The key to happiness is managing expectations. I could have absolutely taught my second caller this, but she wouldn't be learning it in this group because it wasn't just in the love department that she was in flux: she was flirting with a new career, considering moving back home, at odds with all of her female friends and in between cars. This put her in violation of the second bit of criteria and thus not a match for this project.

Midday I connected with Venus, a thirty-two-year-old bisexual performance artist who embodied all the angst of a frustrated single—exactly what I'd been looking for. "I don't get why it is so hard to get someone to like me like that? I like men, I like women, but who likes me?" she asked intensely.

I paused, unsure if she wanted me to answer, but thankfully, she continued. Venus was willing to try my program because she was fed up that her dates didn't see the greatness she felt she possessed. She had boasted about her accomplishments and all the inner work she had done: therapy, yoga training, nonviolent-communication work, 12 Step, tantra, couples coaching, healthy-relating courses, bodywork, a coaching/leadership program. But she admitted that after all that, she still felt at a loss when it came to making connections.

When I asked what seemed to turn people off, she paused for a long time then came up with, "I tell it like it is."

My gripe with the people who describe honesty as a fault is that I don't think they're being honest with themselves. "Telling it like it is" is often just a spruced-up way of saying, *People think I'm blunt, and insensitive.* It's not that most people are *untruthful;* it's that we have a working filter that makes it easy for us to coexist with others. Honesty to a happy life is not what a bat is to baseball, it's what a putter is to golf: use it gently and thoughtfully when the time is right. To support my theory, Venus also revealed that her problems making connections weren't limited to romantic relationships but also friendships and work partnerships. In short, she was very disagreeable, and despite the fact that we are told that nice people finish last, in healthy relationships, agreeable people finish first.

An agreeable person is usually friendly, empathetic and tactful. Their first instinct is to do what's best overall, not just what feels best to them at the time. Agreeableness is one of the most important traits when it comes to maintaining long-term romantic relationships, but that doesn't mean being disagreeable doesn't have its perks too. An agreeable person accepts the status quo, but the disagreeable challenge customs and thoughts to align with their visions. Therefore, we can deduce that a lot of progress depends on people who are willing to go against the grain. So yes, there are some pros to having a contrary spirit, but excelling at group work ain't one of them.

But I did love her eagerness, so I asked one more vetting question about how she planned to spend her summer.

"I've started a new job that has me tied up quite a bit, but the manager is a spineless narcissist so I'm thinking of either pursuing legal action against him or quitting."

Okay, so definitely not the best fit. This is the perfect example of why set standards are crucial when selecting people to align yourself with (vertically or horizontally). Had I not made up my mind on what I needed, I might have allowed my ego to make an *I'm up for the challenge* judgment call that could have been costly down the line.

The rest of the morning was your average audition-style montage: a lot of people who weren't quite the right fit and a few who *absolutely* were not.

A twenty-five-year-old woman asked, "Why do I keep meeting guys who have been to jail?"

When I proposed that she may have a massive partner selection issue that could be linked with repeating pain from her past, she explained that she wasn't a live-in-the-past kind of person and preferred to only move forward in life. I didn't know how I could teach someone who didn't have an interest in understanding themselves, so I put a line through her name and kept going.

Another woman in her thirties confided, "To be honest I would really like to just have sex and leave it at that. I text this guy I was seeing, *I wanna get naked and sit on you while I jack off.* And a few hours later he responded, *I don't want to be with a chick who uses the term jack off.* So I fired back, *Okay would you have preferred I said, flick my bean?*"

Her issue, while kind of funny, wasn't that difficult to solve. She needed to download any number of hookup apps that are specifically designed for no-strings-attached encounters or simply meet someone at a bar past 2 A.M. But aside from needing the fastest route to the bedroom, she also needed to develop a stronger Spidey sense for when dirty talk was appropriate. I hear complaints all the time from women that men need to work on their dick-pic timing; naturally, there are women who need to learn that art too. *Consent* is more than just a word, it is a complex language that none of us are above learning. So I sent her some app recommendations and a referral to check out *Yes Means Yes* by Jessica Valenti and Jaclyn Friedman, then pressed on.

And then, thankfully, came Maya, a twenty-four-year-old office administrator/aspiring writer with frizzy hair, wire glasses, a gummy smile and a quiet fierceness. When I asked what drew her to apply to my project she said plainly, "It said it teaches people how to date. I don't think I've ever done that before, but I'd like to learn how."

I scanned her application and asked, "It says you date men and women. I'm assuming that means you are bisexual?"

She paused for a second. I thought she was considering how to answer but she was actually considering how to put me in my place. "I identify as pansexual but I am moving away from that label and just embracing the term queer. You should never assume someone's label because it's just as easy to ask."

For those who don't know the difference, a bisexual person is someone who is attracted to cisgender men and women (cisgender meaning they identify with the gender they were assigned at birth). A pansexual person is someone who is attracted to cisgender people, but also people who exist outside of the gender binary—including agender, bigender, gender-fluid, gender non-conforming, intersex, and transgender people.

"Totally understand and I apologize for that," I said before getting back to business. "What did you mean when you said you don't *think* you've ever dated?"

"I mean that I've never had a partner besides one boyfriend in high school, which lasted approximately one month, and I've only had two dating experiences, that didn't go anywhere." Maya spoke so quietly I had to strain to hear. "I feel that I'm at an age where maybe I've missed my chance. I feel a lot of pressure from family and friends, and even though they don't mean anything by it, a lot of the time it consumes me. So many of my friends are in committed relationships and my anxiety holds me back from even beginning one."

In recent years I've tried to learn more about anxiety by listening a lot to those who have it. Anxiety as a disorder is unwarranted fear or distress that interferes with daily life. We all have some level of anxiety. It is an everyday emotion that can be a good thing, because it makes us hyperalert in stressful times. But if anxiety persists when there is no real trigger for our fight-or-flight response, it can cause serious issues both mentally and physically. According to Harvard Health, women make up almost two-thirds of an estimated 40 million adults with excessive anxiety.[3]

"Have you seen someone about your anxiety and depression?"

"Yes," she assured me. "I've been to therapists, but for the most part, I'm over my anxiety being the focus of my life."

I really respected that intention Maya had set and I strongly believed I could help support that effort. I was tempted to extend our conversation a bit longer but alas, my next caller was already waiting. So, I said my goodbyes then drew two circles around her name: the first because she needed to learn from this project and the second because I knew I could learn from being around her.

A few calls later, I connected with a twenty-three-year-old woman who made an excellent point that I want to expand on: "Is there no middle ground between dating assholes while you focus on other areas of your life and meeting the guy you want to spend your life with?"

She was speaking to a unique and conflicted time period I call The Practice Years that exists for most of us between ages sixteen and twenty-five. The problem with this phase is that even though people are biologically driven to look for love, society insists that any focus outside of individual achievement is a waste of energy. This propaganda that relationships are distractions as opposed to a healthy addition to self-discovery causes young people to take on a "motel mentality" in the dating department. Motel daters treat people as if they won't have to deal with the consequences of their actions, they feel no remorse in putting their home training on pause and they have a sense of entitlement that isn't worth the $69 that they have to offer. Worst of all, motel dating is marketed as cool in popular music, movies and macho talk that young men consume. Therefore, the wisest thing to do during The Practice Years is to be meticulous in finding partners who are keen on building healthy relationships where the goal is to leave with a higher understanding of self, instead of a suitcase of stolen towels and toiletries. There are plenty of ethical practice daters, but the younger you are, the harder they are to find, hence why your Frozen Five can be a heart saver. I would have gladly helped the caller on her pursuit, but go figure, she planned on backpacking for half the summer.

Immediately after that I connected with a woman named Jenn who gave me a quote that makes me smile to this day: "I had a friend named Alexa who once showed me a note this guy wrote her: *Some like Coke, some like Pepsi, but I like Lexy because she's so sexy.* I've never felt sexy. I've always wondered if things would be different if I had a better name."

But my favorite quote of all came from a twenty-five-year-old, braces-wearing, pink-and-blue-haired environmental engineer named Deshawn: "I don't mind scary movies but if you want me to freak out, let's small talk. I'd rather be running from Freddy Krueger then be stuck at a dinner party with him."

Deshawn was a young black woman working in STEM (science, technology, engineering and mathematics). According to the National Girls Collaborative Project, minority women make up fewer than one in ten employed scientists and engineers. This is a reality Deshawn said she was aware of from the moment she entered graduate school. So she started finding ways to fit in, and some of those methods had become a big detriment to her social life.

"I'm terrible at flirting, I'm awkward, guys don't approach me, and I get friend-zoned a lot. I live back at home with my mom, I go to work, I attend church on Sundays, I tutor kids in the evenings and hang out with friends occasionally on weekends—that's my life," said Deshawn as she sat in her car, which I noticed was a cute BMW. "It's been a while since I've really felt desired and if I'm totally honest, that probably has a lot to do with my feelings about my body. In the past three years I've gained a lot of weight. I've accepted I'm in the plus-size group, but I have no idea how to dress because it's still so new to me."

Deshawn looked down and frowned but I couldn't help but smile, having found my second participant. Deshawn perfectly exemplified a wonderful woman who felt excluded from the happily-ever-after narrative, and as a result, I could see she had begun excluding herself. That had to change, and I was certain I could help.

When I asked Deshawn what she would magically change about dating if she could, she said, "I would make it easier for people to meet in person and talk to others in public places."

Boom. That was magic I could teach! Without a second thought, I circled her application but then she asked me a question that made me want to star and underline it: "What apparatus do you plan on using to get your intended results for the chosen subjects?"

I smiled widely. Not one person had asked me that question until that point, but in fairness, no one else was a scientist. Now, although I kind of ragged on traditional education earlier, I'd like to tear a page out of my sixth-grade notebook to address Deshawn's query.

The Scientific Method for the Game of Desire

QUESTION

Can someone learn how to be attractive?

HYPOTHESIS

If I expose a group of struggling daters to my five-phase program, then they will become expert seducers and leave my program with the power to attract the love life of their dreams.

TERMINOLOGY

Playmate—a person who you want to have fun with through flirting, seducing and rapport-building.

Low-interest playmate—a person who is missing too many key qualities to be considered a contender for a long-term connection. However, you still enjoy their company and wish to ensure they enjoy yours.

High-interest playmate—a person that qualifies against your frozen five and is a contender for a long-term connection.

Frozen five—five standards that a person must meet in order to be considered a high-interest playmate.

APPARATUS

Phase One—KNOW

1. Have the participants complete a self-summary workbook that will give them the self-insight and language to describe their intimate needs to others.
2. Have the participants reach out to their exes in order to illuminate any problematic behaviors they may not be aware of. Self-insight is an incom-

plete system without feedback from others and it's best to go to a source who knows you but who you truly believe has no stake in deluding you or seeking revenge.

Phase Two—CHANGE

1. Teach the participants, with the help of experts, to maximize and, if necessary, play up their look.
2. Teach the group about seduction and anti-seduction so that they will understand what transformations must come next.
3. Reveal through one-on-one sessions what each of their self-sabotaging qualities are.

Phase Three—LEARN

1. Teach the group what to look for in their search for a long-term lover and how to find that person, especially using online dating.
2. Expose the group to a series of experts who will teach them how to attract, flirt, seduce and protect themselves.

Phase Four—PRACTICE

1. Practice what we've learned thus far in group settings, plus conduct four group experiments that could reveal new tools not currently utilized by the general population.
2. Have participants go on solo dates with a low-interest playmate to continue practicing old techniques while testing out five unique ones.

Phase Five—BE

Participants will choose a high-interest playmate to go on a first date with. They will be coached for the first date but must secure a second on their own without coaching.

MEASUREMENT OF SUCCESS

Their success or failure on the second date with a high-interest playmate will partially serve as their results marker but the overall final goal is in how they feel as opposed to who they're with. Does each woman now feel she has or is highly capable of achieving her dream love life? Dream life?

Day two of interviews, I gave myself a good old-fashioned nine-to-five schedule, but by lunch, the only notable thing I had accomplished was the execution of a lackluster bowl of porridge. The women were great and honest and sweet but not the right fit. The recurring theme was their frustration over being ghosted as well as a half-complacent, half-nonchalant attitude about dating altogether. And while I admired all the queens who were more focused on their grind or families, for the purpose of this project I wanted people who were starved for romance. When I connected with a thirty-year-old property manager from Texas named Courtney, that is the exact sentiment she shared.

"I'm frustrated with the whole dating process!" exclaimed Courtney, who wore glasses, a blazer and a no-nonsense expression. "I'm straightforward and I'm beginning to think men don't appreciate that quality in a woman. Let me make this clear, I'm looking for someone of the opposite sex to build something with and I'm looking for someone who knows what they want too."

Courtney was the first person I spoke with who came to the call ready to take notes, clutching an orange marker and a gray notebook. This was a woman who wanted answers. "All right, I get how you feel about dating, but tell me more about you, Courtney. How would you describe yourself?"

"I'd describe myself as a big woman," she began. "I'm tall, I've got size to me, I've got a big presence and I have big plans—I know this about myself. I just want a partner who knows themself too. I'd also describe myself as someone who holds people accountable for what they say. I let people know out the gate, make sure you mean what you say before you go and open your mouth."

I liked Courtney. She instantly reminded me of myself, but the version that I was before I realized I couldn't actually treat people like they were made up of circuit boards. Like her, I too enjoyed expectations, structure and knowing exactly how things worked best. (This part of my personality is what drove me to study the science of sex and love to begin with!) But I had to also learn that no one wants to feel like they are being categorized and generalized instead of personalized—especially when it comes to matters of the heart.

I also thought Courtney was an interesting candidate because she was walking proof of the massive educational flaw in our society. The skills she had learned in order to thrive as a woman in corporate America were likely the same ones that were sabotaging her love life. When dealing with her tenants she had to be straightforward, stern and inflexible with deadlines, but if one adopts this mind-set when dealing with lovers, it's deadly.

"Just know that if you're looking for someone willing to do what it takes, look no further because I'm hella fed up with the bullshit," she concluded as her office phone began ringing behind her.

"Do you need to get that?" I asked.

"No," she said casually. "I'm on break and I like to wait until one task is completed before I move on to the next."

I put a circle around Courtney's name and confirmed her as the third participant. She was a prime example of someone who had the right intentions and the right ideas but lacked the finesse to get the results she desired. We all know communication is key in successful relationships, but it's important to narrow this statement down. One of my favorite principles is: communication is kind of about what you say, but mostly it's about what you want to accomplish.

For example, if your romantic partner isn't texting you as much as you'd like, you can:

A. tell them that you're not satisfied with their communication skills and warn them to step it up.
B. challenge them to a game—if they think about pizza, they have to text you something that made them smile that day.

In both circumstances the goal is the same. And while A gets to the point, B creates a whole new experience that both parties can feel good about. Courtney occurred to me as the kind of person who chose A. Every time.

BUT FOR EVERY YANG, THERE IS A YIN. AND COURTNEY'S YIN WAS A TWENTY-nine-year-old mother named Pricilla who didn't know how to ask for what she wanted at all.

"I tend to be very quiet and shy," said Pricilla with the soft tone to prove it. "I don't like being the center of attention. I find dating stressful because the process of getting to know people is hard for me. It just takes me a while to come out of my shell."

"What attracted you to this experience?" I asked.

"My ten-year-old son," she began. "One day he says to me, I don't want a stepdad. I asked him why and he said that he's getting older and realized it would probably never happen since I don't date anyone long enough. I was really shocked but also sad that I hadn't been providing healthy relationships for him to model."

Pricilla dropped her head and her long black hair dramatically fell over her eyes. She was classically beautiful, but more specifically she was the new classic. She had her full lips, a full-figured body, full brows and Kim Kardashian-esque makeup—she even had the slight nasal voice to match. If you bumped into her on the street, you'd think she was stuck up, but upon further inspection she seemed beaten down.

Pricilla, who was the oldest of eight siblings, revealed she had a mother who had done just that. "My mother never had a kind word to say. She wasn't really cut out for the role so when she had my sisters, they turned to me as the mother figure. When I really think about it, I was already a mom at my son's age. I've always had to be very empathetic and nurturing. Maybe that's why I'm always trying to fix broken men."

She sounded disappointed in herself and my heart went out to her and the many women I knew just like her. A lot of women—mothers in particular—give without assessing what they have to gain. But in order to curb this bad habit, you must believe that you are precious with something precious to offer. So, I turned that question on Pricilla by asking about her favorite quality.

"My selflessness. I enjoy helping others and making them happy," she replied.

Bingo, I thought. This was the issue Pricilla needed help with. If your favorite thing about yourself is that you're more concerned with the needs of others than your own, what kind of people do you think you'll attract? The answer is, a mix of good-intentioned people grateful to be with a giver, and narcissists who will take until there is nothing left to give. And it didn't sound like Pricilla had any system in place to sort through the two.

This reminded me of a lesson on attraction that I learned as a kid from my dad. Brian Boodram grew up in a small developing country off the coast of South America called Guyana. When my dad was growing up, Guyana was rich in crime and poverty—things he did not miss. But what he did miss was the terrain—80 percent of Guyana is covered by tropical jungle, which made the rain forest his second home, something he was determined to take with him when he moved to Canada. Fast-forward, I essentially grew up with a Disney-movie backyard full of birds, fruits and flowers. My dad loved his self-made jungle, but he quickly learned that what attracted the birds he loved was also of interest to the rodents we all hated. There was nothing he could do to stop them from approaching but he learned how to keep them from returning: he began putting pepper seeds in the feeder and topsoil, since birds and plants don't mind pepper but rats sure do.

Pricilla seemed to be a garden of all fruits, but no pepper.

I GOT THROUGH THE REST OF MY CALLS AND CLOSED THE DOOR TO MY OFFICE feeling satisfied. Pricilla and Courtney were not only two women that this project could help, they were also two women who I knew could help each other.

Day three of my search seemed like it would be a total bust. Aside from a few quotables that emphasized how dire the current dating conditions were, like, "Guys DM me and text me and stuff. I'm assuming that's kind of like dating?" along with "Dating is insanely weird. I either get an inappropriate response like a dick pic or no response at all," none of the applicants were really standing out.

By the time my last call had rolled around I was wiped and elated to find she was a no-show. I went out on my balcony to offset my cabin fever but moments later, I heard the Skype ringtone beckoning me back to my desk. Reluctantly, I got my butt up and connected with Stephanie, a twenty-eight-year-old Ivy League graduate that worked for the court system. And we all know the cliché way that this story ends, right? She was fucking great.

Stephanie revealed very quickly that she was a late bloomer who didn't date or have sex until age twenty-five. When I asked her why she waited she attributed it to an equal mix between her "religious upbringing and crippling insecurities."

"I struggled growing up in my Korean-American community because being open and expressive is just not celebrated," explained Stephanie. "I've often wondered what it would be like if I grew up in a Brazilian family. I wondered if I would be less self-conscious or less, I dunno . . . I'm super-open-minded and I'm open to all walks of life; to me, the weirder the better! But my Korean-American community is super-Christian and not into interracial dating. My parents refused to meet my last boyfriend because he wasn't the right type."

"What is your type?" I asked.

"Typically, I've been attracted to alpha guys who end up being macho assholes. I've come to recognize that when I date, I'm more concerned with keeping something alive instead of seeing if I'm getting any enjoyment out of it. I feel like I did a lot of dating for dating's sake, which again made it really hard to admit when something wasn't serving me or going anywhere."

Stephanie, on the other hand, was a woman who was going places. She had a good job, an impressive academic background, her own car, her own apartment, a beautiful voice, a sweet personality and an open mind. Stephanie was basically the kind of woman this project was made for. During my brainstorming session I described the ideal candidate as:

> Everyone who meets her, platonically, is thrown to hear she struggles romantically because (modesty aside) she's the full package: she's smart, she's fun, she's interesting, and heck yes, she got skills in the bedroom and boardroom! She's the funniest one of all her friends, the career overachiever and the Michelangelo of winged eyeliner. She's read self-help books, has cultural interests, knows what bills are currently being voted on and even knows all the lyrics to Hamilton . . . but despite it all, maintaining romantic attention has been a massive struggle for her.

I doubted she knew all the lyrics to *Hamilton* but in many ways, this was Stephanie. Except, Stephanie had stopped believing that *she* was this person. Between feeling like she was a disappointment and her disappointing launch into adult love, her confidence and sense of direction seemed to be shot. Stephanie seemed to put herself second in fear that she would never be anyone's first pick.

To confirm this, when I asked her what she felt she needed to work on she confessed, "I'm really accommodating. I often just mask my own preferences to the point where I don't have a personality, and that's boring."

This goes back to the age-old question: Why do nice people finish last? My answer is because people don't differentiate *people pleasing* and having a character rooted in confidence and kindness that is *pleasing* to people. Having a character rooted in confidence and kindness means that you find joy in being good to others, which makes it easy to sniff out and discard people who don't have good intentions. People pleasers, on the other hand, are so consumed with their desire to belong that they relinquish their right to be respected. Based on Stephanie's recountings, it was evident why she'd become the nice woman at the back, but I was confident that I could work with her to bring her up to speed. I thanked her for her time and circled her name, then went back to my balcony to remind myself what outside felt like.

I woke up on the final day of interviews, checked my dry erase board and thought *Shit! I already have my five candidates: Maya, Deshawn, Courtney, Pricilla and Stephanie.*

There were still over fifty women I had yet to meet, and aside from my solid five I had plenty of backup options, like a sweet twenty-six-year-old transgender graphic designer with a tiny lisp and huge heart as well as a forty-seven-year-old diplomat who would have been perfect had her job not been so strict. Half of me wanted to say fuck it and cancel all remaining calls but the other half knew that I had to see this phase through to the end. So I adjusted my attitude, made another vat of tea and set an intention to whip through the remaining calls like a telemarketer. Perhaps the storyline of the women I'd already chosen could be combined so that I could make space for someone new?

In light of this, I'd like to retro-apologize to anyone I connected with on the final day of my search. After a few calls I realized I sounded like a wacky casting agent for *Jerry Springer*: "Say, are you a thirtysomething bossy property manager with a ten-year-old son that you wish admired your love life? No? Any chance you're an awkward environmental engineer struggling to accept her weight gain while trying to figure out how to deal with your anxiety so you can start dating in the queer community?"

I tried my best to keep the calls especially short so I wouldn't get too attached to any of the remaining women, which was hard since most were sweet and super-interested. That's why I was intrigued when I connected with Cherise, a thirty-seven-year-old, bald-by-choice, white collar professional. She spoke to me like I was the person at the call center she *had* to tolerate in order to save money on her plan, but I guess in her defense, she really did feel as though she had been cheated in the love department for a long-ass time.

"I haven't been in a relationship in over five years and I haven't met anyone decent in that time either," she said, irritated. "The last guy I kind of dated I met at a music festival among mutual friends. I have no real idea why it ended, it just dropped off like a cliff and I for sure wasn't heartbroken. It was the most un-spark-having-ass dating experience I'd ever been on."

"What drew you to applying to take this summer-long course with me?" I asked Cherise as I had done with everyone else.

She smiled for the first time. "I'm told I'm intimidating, beautiful, strong, bold, smart and it seems all this greatness continues to keep them away."

OH. OKAY.

I'd love to point out just how many times in my four days of casting that I heard the words "I'm too intimidating" (in other words, *me, I'm super fly, too super-duper fly/ I'm Supercalifragilisticexpialidocious*) in answer to the question, "Why are you single?"

Not that this reasoning isn't true, but anecdotally I'd say it's probably *actually* true 5 percent of the time. The other 95, someone is chronically single because they are narcissistic or grim or desperate or clingy or a windbag or conceited or avoidant or unstable or a pleaser or terrible at partner selection. In short, most people who can't find or keep love are in that predicament because they've got some work to do, not because they're too perfect for anyone to work with.

She paused for a while and I considered cutting the call short like I had been doing all day. But then she continued, with tears in her eyes and a voice that was totally different than the one she'd began with: "I'm tired of being looked at but never seen. I want to express that at this point I know I must be doing something wrong and I'm willing to do what it takes to fix it. I'm sick and tired of waiting to be loved."

After we ended our chat, I thought about Cherise for a long, long while. Cherise was also a cactus woman, who failed to see the disconnect between who she presented herself as and who she hoped others would see. But in that final moment of our call I saw her walls come down and it was strikingly beautiful. It was clear that Cherise was going to be a challenge to my third criteria: They must work well with others. But I truly felt up for this one.

After the last call I was a blissful pile of exhaustion and exhilaration, but I remained in my office for a while longer to reflect and clean. I removed the piled-up dishes, candy bar wrappers and tea mugs that kept me afloat throughout my marathon of interviews. Then I cleared my whiteboard, which was littered with notes, to make space for six important names: Deshawn, Courtney, Pricilla, Stephanie, Maya and finally, Cherise.

Six was certainly not my original plan and it put a wrench in my budget, but who doesn't love a wild card?

That night, I had *incredible* celebratory sex with Jared, who had been expertly giving me extra space over the previous four days. I'm an ambivert who needs alone time in order to gain strength to perform extroversion; he understands that and me in a way that I didn't think was possible. And to me that one little word, *understands,* encompasses all the joys of finding your person(s). I was excited, grateful and (I at least thought) prepared to help the six selected women capture that feeling for themselves.

After a great night's rest, I returned to my desk and drafted an email with the subject line: *You Had Me at Hello—Let's Get Started!*

2

SINGLE AND TERRIFIED TO MINGLE

*W*hen the day of our first group meetup arrived, I was one giant cocktail of nerves, adrenaline and spaghetti (I would have chosen a better meal for the big day, but your girl had leftovers to finish).

I thought about what I wanted to wear for the entire week, pivoting between a two-piece power suit and a bodycon dress before I realized I was going about this the wrong way. This experiment was not about impressing others, it was about being seductively comfortable and noticeably impressed with yourself. In order to be successful at that, you must try your hardest to make it appear that you are not trying. This may sound confusing but, in the end, it will make sense: effort needs to be both the primary, and secret, ingredient in your game.

Therefore, when the big day came, I slid into my standard Netflix-and-chill look: horny makeup (which we will cover in Chapter 5), "messy" hair, minimal jewelry and relaxed but still pressed-out clothes.

As scheduled, the first knock came at 11:30 A.M. I opened the door wide with an even wider smile but jerked a touch when I saw Pricilla, the mom of our group. Her makeup was done as though it were 11:30 on a Friday night but her outfit, jeans and an oversize hooded sweatshirt screamed Saturday-morning errands. Perhaps she had gone through the same debate as me but instead of a happy medium she went the mullet route: party up top and bummy on the bottom.

"Great smoky eye," I said as we walked into my living room.

"Thanks," said Pricilla shyly.

"So what's your son up to this weekend?"

"With his dad," she said, as someone simultaneously knocked and pushed open the front door.

I was greeted by the gummy smile of Maya, who wore a T-shirt that had whales and penguins swimming in outer space printed on it. Maya was an interesting character: she didn't do her eyebrows or wear makeup, and if I'd had to guess, all of her clothes had at least two previous owners. But despite her casual casing, she also struck me as the last person I'd want to get on the wrong side of. Among the group, she was the youngest, with the least romantic experience, but based on our brief interactions, I'd also say she was the strongest and the most likely to put you in your place.

Shortly thereafter Stephanie, the late-blooming academic, and Courtney, the stern property manager, arrived. Courtney wore glasses and a yellow tank top that was an exceptional choice against her dark complexion. Stephanie had on jeans, flip-flops and a checkered off-the-shoulder shirt, which—spoiler alert!—was an outfit I saw a lot during our future months together. The colorful-haired scientist Deshawn was running late, and my wildcard addition, Cherise, still hadn't completed the onboarding paperwork so she couldn't attend that day.

"What do you guys have planned for the weekend?" I asked, trying to fill the dead space.

A better icebreaker for nervous guests would have been: *What does an ideal weekend look like for you?* This gives people the opportunity to talk themselves up without any time constraints because maybe they don't plan on being awesome this weekend, but everyone has done something awesome at some point . . . and if they haven't, you've given them the space to make it up.

Right on cue Stephanie remarked, "I don't know yet, I'm kind of boring."

"Yeah, same," echoed the group, as they all avoided eye contact like I was an eclipse.

"Come on, there has to be something going on?" I pressured awkwardly.

Saved by the knock, Deshawn arrived then said her hellos. "Sorry I'm late, did I miss the introductions already?"

"No," I said as I smiled at her and the group. With all parties seated, I launched into a speech welcoming them to the program, which, as I told them, was easily the most exciting (and terrifying) project in my years as an intimacy educator.

"By the time we are done working together, I want you to know how to flirt and connect like you know how to walk and talk," I continued. "I want you to be in the driver's seat of every intimate interaction you have. While this program is about love, dating and romantic connections, what we are trying to accomplish is much bigger than that. You aren't just here to find a boyfriend or girlfriend, you're here to learn how to make powerful and memorable bonds with everyone you choose, effortlessly."

The room was still for a bit, but Deshawn fixed that with a nervous laugh. "Yeah, good luck with the effortless part when it comes to me."

"None of us need luck, we need commitment and the right attitude. Actually, let me ask all of you a question: What kind of person do you think remains in control and on top at all times?"

Deshawn began, "The person with the most knowledge, I think."

Maya continued. "Uh, the person with the most confidence?"

"Maybe the person who is shameless, I don't know if that makes sense or not," said Stephanie.

"The person who works the hardest," said Pricilla.

"I would also say confidence," added Courtney.

I jumped back in. "The correct answer is nobody. You're not here to learn how to be undefeated, you're here to become a champion. And to do that, it's impossible to come out on top every time. And when you don't, you have two choices: you can lose, or you can learn. So yes while ultimately I want you to be winners, to get there you have to commit yourself to being an even better learner."

"What kind of things are we going to be doing?" asked Pricilla as she tugged on the strings of her hoodie. "Like I said in my application, I don't feel comfortable with blind dates."

I softened my tone. "No one has to do anything they don't want to, but I do encourage you to approach this with an open mind. You're not going to get different results by doing the same things."

With a few of the women smiling and nodding, I decided I had done enough talking. I asked them to introduce themselves, and in light of Deshawn's and Pricilla's reactions, I also invited them to share any additional fears they had.

Maya was sitting closest to me and even though her nervous eyes pleaded for me not to, I gestured for her to go first. She sat up straighter but kept her eyes low. "Hey, I'm Maya. I work for a startup company but I'm an aspiring writer and, um, yeah, there's really not much else to say. I am very nervous about this experience but I'm also just a very nervous person. I have no idea how to even begin to process about what's going to happen except that I'm also excited to see who I become at the end of this. I have, like, no experience dating. So this is probably one of the biggest life steps for me, maybe."

Courtney went next without prompting. "I'm Courtney, and I am a property manager for two buildings. Listen, y'all, here's a life hack—be a property manager. You get to live rent-free and you get flexible hours."

Everyone laughed and Courtney smiled then continued. "I'll admit that I'm terrified to hear what people really think of me. Like, I want to hear it, but I don't want to hear it. Does that make sense?"

"Yes!" exclaimed Stephanie. "I feel like Courtney articulated how I feel perfectly. I'm a newer dater. I just started dating, like, three years ago. I've experienced some failures and I think I'm normal and I'm cool and I like me, but I'm also like, well, maybe there's something to be said about the way I am dating or who I am that is impeding me. And maybe whatever that is, is so obvious to everybody else."

I nodded and kept my mouth shut since I had decided not to reveal the step-by-step plan of the program to the group. But between you and me, in the not-so-distant future we would address Stephanie's and Courtney's fear of direct criticism in the most terrifying way possible.

"As for me," continued Stephanie as she exhaled, then looked away, "there isn't a ton to say. I work for the government but I'm not, like, thrilled at my job. My life is pretty basic. I'm trying to lose weight and get myself together. I guess this is a part of that whole process."

My face twisted instinctively. Actually, there *was* a ton to say. Stephanie was an Ivy League grad who worked for the court system. She had a brilliant mind and a wandering spirit that had led her to take up residence in New York, South Korea, London, Switzerland and L.A.—all within the past five years. There were many more fascinating parts to Stephanie than her negative opinion of her body and her body of work.

Pricilla went next. "I'm Pricilla. I'm a hair-transplant technician and I'm also trying to lose weight like Stephanie, but I'm also really excited about what everyone is nervous about because I wanna pinpoint what's wrong so I can fix it. The only thing that would make me nervous would be, like, blind dates."

I asked the obvious: "What's with the big fear of blind dates?"

Pricilla tugged harder on her hoodie's strings until she was practically choking herself. "Blind dates give me anxiety because I feel pressured to be interested or I'll make the other person feel bad."

Pricilla was so self-sacrificing that she seemed guilty any time that she had to take up any attention. But I learned through prying and social media investigating that she had the kind of life worth taking up space to gush about! For example, she easily could have talked about her awesome relationship with her son or the fact that she had worked as an assistant to Steven Seagal. She even lived in Russia for three months, since Mr. Seagal happens to be homies with Vladimir Putin.

Next came Deshawn. "Hello again, everyone. I was born in California, I love Beyoncé and I also work for the government."

I wanted to smack my forehead. Deshawn was technically also a government employee, yes—but she wasn't a pencil pusher, she was an environmental engineer working to end California's water crisis! Clearly, we needed a crash course on the dangers of down-playing. Being humble and undervaluing yourself are not the same thing—and believe me, they yield very different outcomes.

"As per this process? Well, I am most afraid of finding out I'm not, like, cute awkward but really awkward. To backtrack, I grew up knowing that I was weird . . . but, like, normal weird. Then I went to engineering school and I was only around people who are extremely hard to talk to and extremely uncomfortable, so I fear I may have adopted some of those personality traits and now my awkwardness has escalated."

I smiled in acknowledgment and gave her a once-over as I thought about what she had said. Deshawn struck me as sweet and outgoing so I personally would not describe her as socially awkward *but* I could make an argument for her being physically awkward. Her hair sat in a curly coif above her ears and was dyed a combination of colors that seemed to match her braces. She wore an overly loose bright-patterned outfit with the wrong bra, which kept her busy as she pivoted between readjusting her shirt and fold-ing her arms over her chest. She also had a large hoop nose ring and several other piercings in her ears. From my vantage, Deshawn was a visual concoction of too many colors, materials, movement and metal. If I had bumped into Deshawn on the street, I would have assumed she was a quirky teen who was late for her part-time job at Chipotle, not an environmental engineer. That had to change.

I ended the meeting by issuing a multiple-choice form that allowed participants to assess their ability on a scale from one to ten to attract, connect, influence, seduce and flirt. This form provided the framework for what was ahead but also created a marker to assess how far each had come in the end. Predictably, there were a lot of fives and no tens in their submissions. Also, somewhat notably, Courtney scored herself the highest and Pricilla scored herself the lowest. The yang, and the yin.

LATER THAT WEEK, I INVITED THE GROUP OUT TO AN INFORMAL MEETUP AS A new dating app, Crown, was throwing a launch party in West Hollywood. When I arrived at the venue the line to get in practically wrapped around the street, a testament to the dire dating scene in Los Angeles.

Cherise and Pricilla were unable to make this event, which left Courtney, Deshawn, Stephanie, Maya and me standing in a small group on the large rooftop that overlooked the massive city.

After everyone had said their initial hellos and gotten drinks, a lull hung over us that seemed amplified by the bustling mixer happening at our heels. I pointed to a clip in Maya's hair. "Are those lizards?"

She smiled with gums. I looked around at the group; aside from Courtney, who wore a black and white ensemble with black lipstick, no one was really dressed for a singles' party.

"Shan Boody?" asked a man in bright colors.

I nodded.

"I thought I recognized you. I love your work," he said, then looked over my shoulder at the group.

Taking his cue, I introduced him to everyone. "These are my girls Deshawn, Courtney, Stephanie and Maya."

"Hey, wassup, ladies?" he said, smiling and leaning in.

The group smiled back politely, said one word each, then pivoted their bodies away as if they had to get back to some top-secret discussion.

He nodded a few times then said, "Cool, nice to meet everyone," and left.

Courtney craned her neck and looked around the party. "Let's move away from the entrance."

I let her lead and purposefully followed at the back of the group, so I could take my time and see who would be valuable, or at least entertaining, for us to talk to. Sometimes that single act of making direct and intentional eye contact can open the door to conversation. And not just any kind of eye contact; there's a formula to this. Avoiding eye contact can signify disrespect, disinterest or fear; looking someone directly in the eyes can be interpreted as respect or politeness; but a mix of both can indicate attraction. So, if you want someone to know you're interested, look them in the eye, then once you have them on the hook, let your attention trail down to their body before meeting their gaze with a smile again. We'll call this the sexy triangle.

As we walked, I caught and kept the eye of a tall, handsome man with blond hair and cute style. I triangled him until we got very close, then he stopped me. "Those are *not* your real eyes."

I raised my eyebrows to let him know I got his game. That comment was a classic neg, which is an introductory move referenced in pickup artistry. A neg is a comment that is just as much a compliment as it is an insult. For example, *those are not your real eyes* is equal parts *wow, your eyes are out of this world* to *you're a phony and you're not fooling anyone.* Negs are designed to keep you talking by making you feel like you need to win the other person over. But in my case, I kept talking to him because I wanted to bring him over.

"I'll tell you if my eyes are real, if you tell me your real name."

His name was Eric and after I briefly explained I was with a group of single women who needed warming up, he agreed to come meet them. I walked with him in tow until I found the others, who were now standing near a table at the edge of the party. I introduced them all to Eric, then tried to get some light convo going but it didn't really catch. Maya backed up and sat down, Deshawn went on her phone and Courtney continued to scan the room looking for a better destination. Stephanie went back and forth for a bit with him about her experiences on dating apps, but I noticed when she talked to him, she looked around, not at, him. Even though Stephanie was more than likely doing it because she was nervous, the wandering eye gives off the impression that you are looking for someone better to talk to, and no one wants to feel like a placeholder. In truth, most people can't really tell the difference between shyness and rudeness, because both include closed body language, avoidant eyes and incomplete answers.

"Do you plan on joining Crown? It seems pretty interesting," Eric asked Stephanie.

"It's hard to say . . ." She trailed off, effectively killing the conversation.

But perhaps that was her goal and if so, she played it well because within seconds he gave some excuse about needing to find his friends, then left.

A better way to finesse it if you have the attention of someone that isn't your type is to be fun and engaging then teasingly ask where their friends are. Once they respond, offer to go over to meet them too. If you don't like any of their friends or they don't have any, move on to the next group. Meeting new people is a lot like moving through the jungle: it's easier to swing from tree to tree when you have some momentum. Everyone wants to talk to the popular girl.

On our way out, we passed directly by Eric, who didn't even make polite eye contact this time. I looked back over my shoulder and watched him engage happily in a spirited conversation with a group of singles who were ready to mingle. Which evidently Deshawn, Courtney, Stephanie and Maya were not.

Phase One: Know

PART ONE

→ ← ——

Know who you've become by identifying the
core traits of your intimate self.
This includes being fully aware
of your strengths, weaknesses,
blind spots and patterns.

— 3 —

HOW DO YOU LIKE YOUR LOVE?

*W*hen I do keynote speeches, I have an activity where I ask the crowd to turn to the person beside them to describe, in detail, how they like their coffee or tea made. Next, I ask them to explain to that same neighbor how they love and like to be loved. Naturally people excel at the former but despite the level of education in the room, few have the language to effectively explain the latter.

One man once said, "I'm a mirror image of my dog. So, if you want to know what I'm like, spend time with him."

In other words, this man believed that a dog was more capable of expressing his intimate needs than he was. Isn't it crazy that even though we are told communication is the key to healthy relationships, few people know what the hell to say?

Now that the introductions and icebreaking meetups were out of the way, it was time to officially kick off the program by ensuring my group would not fall victim to this mistake. I sent Pricilla, Cherise, Courtney, Deshawn, Stephanie and Maya the "Self-Summary Workbook," which was comprised of quizzes, activities and essay questions to help them gain the language to understand themselves on an advanced level.

The very next day Deshawn sent back an email titled *Done*

that had a three-page document attached. I forwarded her and everyone else my own workbook, which was twenty-six pages, then instructed them that their completed file had to look more, not less, like mine.

That's when things started to go downhill.

It took a full two weeks for everyone to complete their workbooks; two long, painstaking, harassing weeks of follow-ups and encouragement. This was not remotely how I envisioned our kick-off, but in the group's defense this intensive, self-evaluating homework wasn't the how-to-seduce-anyone crash course they'd hoped for. Just like when someone signs up for karate what they're saying yes to is chopping through wood and kicking through walls of brick. No one is there because they're pumped about the weeks of class and mental work that come before you throw a single punch.

But that doesn't make the prep work any less important. As a matter of fact, if you do nothing else that this book says to do, do the workbook alongside us.

ON THE DAY WE MET TO REVIEW THEIR COMPLETED WORKBOOKS, I CLEANED my apartment top to bottom, lit all my candles, and by 7:15 P.M. we were off to a decent start with all six participants seated and ready to rock. Cherise was the last to arrive and since she missed our first group session and our casual outing, I began by giving her the floor to introduce herself to the group.

"Hey, I'm Cherise, I work in business, I'm probably the oldest person here but I'm carefree and fun as fuck." She wore a long black skirt, a black tank top, heavy gold jewelry and a mischievous smile. "I'm pretty close to moving to the countryside to find my husband because the men in big cities are all trash. So I guess I'm trying this out first before I book that plane ticket."

Everyone laughed and then welcomed her. Cherise hadn't finished the workbook yet and of course she'd missed the first two sessions, so I had begun to question whether we needed a sixth participant at all. But her intro gave me hope that she might prove to be the final two shakes of Tabasco sauce that our gumbo of a group would've been lackluster without.

When the laughter and hugs died down, I crossed my arms and lowered my voice to give the group the speech I'd been planning for the past week: "I understand your first assignment wasn't easy nor was it fun but I do want to make it clear that I never want to hound you to respond to messages again. A quote you're going to hear me say thousands of times is, the key to happiness is managing expectations, and my only expectation from you is communication. You don't have to do the assignments, you don't have to show up to every meetup, but to participate, you do have to communicate with me. If you're busy and need more time to finish something, say something. If you can't do that, you shouldn't have said yes to any of this."

Predictably the room was very still but these moments of discomfort were a small price to pay for less overall stress on my end. This is an important lesson on the early stages of forming relationships of any kind: if you notice a trend you don't like, call it out. The sooner you make your standards clear, the easier it gets to do this as new conflicts arise. In short, it's fairly straightforward to adjust new behaviors, but breaking long-term patterns can be back- (or heart-) breaking work. I need you to really understand this if you're going to have a shot at a fulfilling love life: you cannot avoid confrontation. If you don't do it externally you will end up doing it internally. And the absolute last thing that I wanted to do was spend my summer arguing with the participants in my head.

With the tough love out of the way, I uncrossed my arms and lifted my cheeks. "So how did everyone feel about their workbooks?"

Almost every single person admitted the process was time-consuming, emotional but overall extremely powerful.

"This is the first time I'd ever spent this much time getting to know myself," shared Pricilla. "It actually helped put so much in perspective, especially in regard to why my last relationship could have *never* worked."

For the remainder of our meetup, Deshawn, Pricilla, Maya, Courtney and Stephanie read their workbooks aloud. I have included excerpts from what they shared below in addition to a truncated version of the activities they completed.

If you're up for a life-changing challenge, the full workbook is available online for free at TheGameofDesire.com. But included here are six key activities, which will help you answer these critical questions about yourself: what specifically turns you on in an intimate relationship? What is your love language? What is your sexual orientation in reality (and in your fantasies)? What does it take for you to forgive and feel understood by someone? What is your attachment style? And finally, what are the strengths and weaknesses of your character? I promise that learning how to understand your intimate self using this exercise as your foundation will make a massive impact on the quality of relations with others. Because if you don't have the language to describe what you're working with, plus what you need to work on, imagine how difficult it will be to explain what you need to make a relationship work.

TURN-ON TRIGGERS

Turn-on triggers is a method I developed to help people understand what, beyond instinctual biological norms, gets them hot and bothered. I've used this method in my counseling to help some understand why they lack desire in their loving relationships. And I've also used it to help single people assess if they're being manipulated into sexual relationships that don't serve them. Knowing your and your sexual partner's turn-on triggers can lift the veil of fog when it comes to finding and maintaining an intimate mood.

In order to quickly assess what your primary turn-on trigger is imagine that you just got home from a long day and your partner greets you at the door ready to get freaky. What could they say or do to get you in the mood as well?

1. "You look so good and I want you so bad. Go to the bedroom and take your clothes off, I want every square inch of your body."
2. "I ordered dinner for us. Let's chill, talk and connect. I wanna hear everything about your day and tell you everything about mine."
3. "I vacuumed, cleaned the kitchen, laid down some fresh sheets and put on your favorite album. Take your time getting cleaned up, then meet me in the bedroom."
4. "Hey, you're home early. I was going to take a shower and walk around naked for a bit but now that you're here I guess I should change my plans, unless . . ."
5. "I know you've had a long day so if I take care of the house, handle dinner and take your car to get some gas, do you think tonight we could . . ."

Answer Key

1. *Desire:* Skip the filters, you need to be told directly that you're desired.
2. *Mental:* If you're not connected mentally first, physical is hardly an option.
3. *Environmental:* You need the mood to be set before you set it off in the bedroom.
4. *Cat and mouse:* You enjoy the chase as much as the experience.
5. *Transactional:* There needs to be something more than the physical act to entice you.

Now that you know your triggers, try to expand on it in a short paragraph as if you were explaining it to someone else. Here is Deshawn's explanation of her trigger:

Subtle hints and riddles are just too much for me, I love someone who is straightforward. If you want me to know you're into me, here's the trick . . . JUST TELL ME. Desire is absolutely my turn-on trigger because my brain is always going a million miles a minute so if someone plays coy, I'll move on quickly, thinking there wasn't much to the relationship.

Growing up, I was constantly teased and made fun of because of my looks. Let it be how uncool my clothes were, the style of my hair, my glasses I've worn since age five or just my features, like my nose and lips being too full for conventional attraction. It was extremely hurtful to hear those things from my peers, and they manifested into what I thought was my reality.

As an adult, I've definitely grown into myself and have come to accept my beauty. I no longer believe the haunting memories of the kids from school, but I do still hear them from time to time in my head. That is why it's crucial for my lover's voice to be even louder. Let me hear what makes me sexy, irresistible and hot to you. Tell me all the ways I turn you on, and what that makes you wanna do to me. Nothing makes me feel sexier than just being simply told, "Deshawn—damn, you look sexy!"

Love Language

Hopefully you are familiar with Gary Chapman and his internationally renowned book, *The 5 Love Languages.*[1] Love languages are a genius way of understanding the different priorities people have in intimate relationships. Just like if you went to Thailand and spoke in English, you wouldn't expect to be fully understood, if you show others you care by speaking in *your* love language, not theirs, you shouldn't be surprised if your message gets lost in translation.

Here's an easy way of guessing what your love language could be: imagine you are in a healthy relationship and you've had an especially hard day. On your way home you text your partner to let them know your emotional state. How could they help turn your day around?

1. Giving you a long hug and kiss at the door, then carrying you to the couch, where you can touch some more.

2. They reveal that they've already cooked dinner and done the laundry. They press *play* on your favorite album, leaving you with nothing to do but relax.

3. They cancel their previously scheduled engagement so they can stay home with you to spend quality time.

4. They greet you at the door to let you vent about your day; they listen, affirm your perspective, then tell you that you can overcome this problem because you are *X*, *Y* and *Z*.

5. When you get home, you notice a package on the table because your partner bought you something that means a lot to you.

Answer Key

1. *Physical touch:* A little loving goes a long way with you.

2. *Acts of service:* They say actions speak louder than words, and you would say it again and again in case the people in the back didn't hear it.

3. *Quality time:* All those Netflix shows aren't going to watch themselves, and you aren't trying to take on that challenge alone.

4. *Words of affirmation:* When Chris Rock said, "Women need food, water and compliments,"[2] you laughed a little louder than everyone else.

5. *Gifts:* Diamonds are a girl's best friend and an impromptu order at your favorite takeout spot is definitely your homie too.

Here is an example of how Pricilla described her love language:

My love language is words of affirmation. When I was growing up my mother spoke a lot of negative words into my mind and heart. I was yelled at often and it seemed like she took every opportunity possible to tell me what I was doing wrong. It hurt but instead of addressing it or her, I internalized a lot of negativity and carried that with me. This is why hearing kind words about myself really helps to heal me and my inner child. Positive affirmations give me strength to love who I am in the moment and they also help me to combat all those negative agreements that I made about myself in the past.

I am now a mother too and I've noticed that the best way I can love and teach my son is by praising him. Yes, discipline is necessary but being told what he did right versus wrong seems to sink in more. I realized that small children ask their parents so many questions because they think we have the answers. When we tell them things, they believe it because they trust we know best. So, I choose to tell him that he's the most incredible, smart, loving, positive and unstoppable light on the planet.

If you love me and you like something I've said or done, please voice that to me. And even when I'm not at my best, remind me how great I can be.

Kinsey Scale

Sexuality is finally being recognized as a diverse, ever-changing and beautiful part of the human experience. The terms *heterosexual* and *homosexual* do not speak to the vast majority of people who may have had experiences with both. The Kinsey Scale is a rating system, created by Alfred Kinsey, that allows more flexibility when identifying sexual preferences.[3] The letters *XX* represent someone who identifies as asexual, *X* for gray asexual, a 0 for someone who is starkly heterosexual, 6 for those who are completely homosexual and 1 to 5 represent varying degrees of sexual fluidity.

As Maya pointed out to me, the Kinsey Scale does a poor job of representing transgender and nonbinary communities. Sexual orientation and gender identity are distinct, which the Kinsey Scale fails to address. The Gender Unicorn by Trans Student Educational Resources tried to fill this gap so take a look at that if the Kinsey Scale proved unhelpful.[4] To make a quick guess of your Kinsey

Scale number: Imagine you've just returned home from a vacation with a group of people you will never see again. After you've gotten settled you phone your best, nonjudgmental friend to spill the tea about your incredible trip. What do you describe?

xx. I had an amazing time with the group. I feel like I made a lot of good friends and no one pressured me to take our relationship any further, which I loved.

x. There was one person in the group who I really hit it off with. We went on a few romantic nights out, we shared a lot of our secrets and we never felt compelled to get physical, which I loved.

0. I met someone of the opposite sex who I was majorly attracted to and got to physically connect with. I saw a few other people from the opposite sex who were superhot and intriguing too.

1. I met someone of the opposite sex who I was majorly attracted to and got to physically connect with. Also, I flirted with someone of the same sex and we made out, which I loved.

2. I met someone of the opposite sex who I was majorly attracted to and got to physically connect with for the majority of the trip. I also met someone of the same sex who I was majorly attracted to and got to physically connect with for a couple of nights.

3. I met someone of the opposite sex who I was majorly attracted to and got to physically connect with. Then I met someone of the same sex who I was majorly attracted to and got to physically connect with.

4. I met someone of the same sex who I was majorly attracted to and got to physically connect with for the majority of the trip. I also met someone of the opposite sex who I was majorly attracted to and got to physically connect with for a couple of nights.

5. I met someone of the same sex who I was majorly attracted to and got to physically connect with. Also, I flirted with someone of the opposite sex and we made out, which I loved.

6. I met someone of the same sex who I was majorly attracted to and got to physically connect with. Also, I saw a few other people from the same sex who were superhot and intriguing too.

Answer Key

xx. asexual—an aversion or lack of interest in sexual acts with others

x. gray asexual—a desire for romantic connections that aren't physical

0. heterosexual—an attraction to only people born of the opposite sex

1. heterosexual and incidentally homosexual—open to isolated acts of homosexuality

2. heterosexual and more than incidentally homosexual—open to common acts of homosexuality

3. equal parts heterosexual to homosexual—often known as pansexual (an attraction to people regardless of gender or sex they were assigned at birth) or bisexual (attraction to those who identify as male or female)

4. homosexual and more than incidentally heterosexual—open to common acts of heterosexuality

5. homosexual and incidentally heterosexual—open to isolated acts of heterosexuality

6. homosexual—an attraction only to people born of the same sex

---

The best way to do this exercise is to do it twice: once keeping in mind what you would likely do and the other, what you would fantasize about doing.

Now that you've completed this assessment for the first time, write a short paragraph about your results. Here is Maya's answer:

Me: 24, queer, writer, true Taurus. Likes: bad TV, curios, beer, celebrity gossip, people who can skateboard. You: must love dogs, trying new foods, early 2000s teen movies; laugh easily; are curious, spontaneous, and can appreciate a comfy couch and a good movie. As per sex/gender: there are no boundaries to me finding someone that I can have a romantic or physical relationship with. I am pansexual, meaning that I can have feelings toward someone no matter how they identify (cisgender, trans, bisexual, queer, nonbinary, etc. . . . gender and sexuality is a spectrum!). It's very important to me that my partner understands this, especially if they are cisgender/straight.

I got a score of 2 on the Kinsey Test because of my lack of experience, but I am a 4 in fantasy. Although I have yet to have a romantic connection outside of the heterosexual experience, I am predominantly attracted to queer people.

APOLOGY LANGUAGE

After *The 5 Love Languages,* Gary Chapman teamed up with Jennifer Thomas to write *The Five Languages of Apology.* I loved this follow-up, because while we can all acknowledge how important it is to feel loved in a relationship, we often forget, until someone is yelling or crying, how important it is to feel understood. The apology languages address this gap by giving us five ways of acknowledging that we've made a mistake in hurting someone we care for. Chapman and Thomas's five apology languages are: expressing regret, accepting responsibility, making restitution, genuinely repenting and requesting forgiveness.[5] But the only three I don't see overlap in is expressing regret, accepting responsibility and making restitution, so those are the ones I will focus on here.

To quickly estimate your apology language: Imagine you just got in a big blowout with your romantic partner over behavior that you've told them before is unacceptable. After much explaining you are finally able to break through to them. So, to make things right, what would you prefer them to say?

1. I get it now and I'm so insanely sorry. If only I would have listened to you the other times you've explained yourself, we wouldn't be fighting again. I wish it never came to this.

2. This is all on me. I should have been paying more attention to my actions and how they've been affecting you. My behavior is my responsibility and I totally dropped the ball.

3. I made the same error again and this time it could have really damaged our relationship. Please let me do *X* to make this right.

———————— *Answer Key* ————————

1. *Expressing regret:* An apology to you is best when it includes a clear indication that the other party knows their wrongdoings and wishes they'd made a better choice.

2. *Accepting responsibility:* If someone is going to apologize effectively to you, they need to take full ownership of the offense, without passing the buck.

3. *Making restitution:* If someone wants to make things right with you, they should start by offering a make-up, act of service.

———————————————————————————

Once you've got your apology language down, write a short paragraph that personalizes your results so others can truly understand how to make amends with you. Here is Courtney's apology language paragraph:

People know me as happy, confident, filled with self-love, determined and always seeking to grow. But what if I told you not too long ago that I was physically, emotionally and mentally abused by someone I loved who claimed to love me too.

In abusive relationships, the abuser finds a way to demean, dehumanize and discard an individual in such a way to control the individual to not leave. According to the National Domestic Hotline, the abused will return to their abuser seven times before leaving for good. While there are other factors that played into why I gained the courage to leave, one important realization I had to come to was how important true remorse and apologies are to me.

My apology language is "accept responsibility." So many times, apologies by my abuser would be followed up by "but I wouldn't have done it if you didn't . . ." I noticed that he never took responsibility—not even for physically assaulting me.

In all relationships, even healthy ones, I know that being disappointed by others is a natural part of being loved, but to me, if someone really loves me, they will accept responsibility for the pain they've caused. To me that shows maturity as well as humility and it gives the relationship an opportunity for a better future.

ATTACHMENT STYLE

Why are some people clingy and super-jealous? Why are some ghosters? How come certain people want you until they have you? How do some people manage to be pretty chill about the whole attaching thing? And most important, which of those labels would other people describe you as? Attachment theory is an area of psychology first coined by John Bowlby that seeks to explain attachment styles by identifying four different ways people behave in intimate relationships: secure, anxious-preoccupied, dismissive-avoidant and fearful-avoidant.[6] Take the quiz below to get a loose idea of your attachment style in romantic relationships. Try your hardest to answer realistically and not idealistically. Sure, everyone wants to be secure, but in truth anxious people tend to work well together and avoidant types like Steve Jobs can become mega rich and successful *because* they are undistracted by emotional ties. In addition if you're honest and discover something you don't like, that puts you on the path to self-improvement. So, worry less about proving your ex wrong and more about circling what truly sounds right to you in each of the scenarios listed below:

You are having a rough day so you reach out to your romantic interest to get comfort, but you can't get ahold of them. So you:

    a. Move on and try to get ahold of another close ally.

    b. Get more upset that not only are you having a rough day but now you also don't know where/what your interest is doing.

    c. You don't reach out at all. If you're having a rough day that means you need to work extra hard on your own to fix it.

    d. You send a follow-up text to your interest that says, "Hey, never mind my missed call, I figured it out and have a pretty busy day so don't worry about calling back."

You and your romantic interest get into a heated argument and they announce that they are going out for a bit to clear their head. So you:

    a. Get upset that they would leave before things have gotten resolved but you let them go anyway so you can also calm down.

    b. Block the doorway/chase after them/hold them back so they can't leave until you feel like the issue has been resolved.

    c. You're usually the one who leaves the situation.

    d. You let them go but as soon as they're gone, you leave as well because you refuse to be there waiting when they get back.

Your romantic interest tells you the two of you should take a break to reassess the relationship. So you:

    a. Express how you really feel about it, but encourage them to honor their feelings to part ways if that's what they feel is best.

    b. Get angry because you feel like they led you on all this time. You then let them know that deep down you always knew they would leave you as soon as things got tough.

    c. You're usually the one who pumps the brakes on relationships to reassess if they're no longer meeting your expectations.

    d. You tell them there is no point to a break. You won't want them when they come back, so you think it's best to end the relationship immediately.

Your romantic interest tells you that someone they dated five years ago is in town and they're going to meet up with them. So you:

a. Thank them for informing you, ask them to keep you updated, then go about your day.
b. Stress out about why they would be interested in seeing an ex again, then immediately search that person online.
c. Tell them you really couldn't care less because you couldn't.
d. Tell them you don't care, then make a mental note to start keeping your distance since they're clearly keeping their options open.

Your romantic interest has a close friend's wedding to attend, but they didn't invite you to join them. So you:

a. Ask them if they were allowed to bring a plus one and leave it alone from there.
b. Immediately start combing through their social media accounts to see who else they're apparently dating too.
c. You fist pump because now you have a day to yourself uninterrupted.
d. You plan to do something incredibly cool for the entire weekend and make a note not to invite them to any of it.

Answer Key

If you answered mostly *A*'s
your attachment style might be securely attached.

This is the ideal way to attach to others, and the good news is roughly half of the population is securely attached. People with secure attachment freely display interest and affection toward others, but are also comfortable being alone. They make boundaries and they stick to them; they aren't possessive nor are they passive or dismissive. They're capable of accepting rejection and have little trouble trusting people.

As a child a securely attached person probably had attentive parent(s) who were consistent and nurturing but also left a healthy amount of space for them to explore, make mistakes and learn from them.

If you answered mostly *B*'s
your attachment style might be anxious-preoccupied.

Twenty percent of the population are said to be anxious-preoccupied, meaning people who are often nervous and stressed about their relationships.[7] They crave intimacy, but they lack confidence that anyone will truly love them. They worry a lot that someone will lose interest in them and choose someone else. They have a hard time trusting people but also have an even harder time letting go.

People who are anxious-preoccupied need plenty of affirmation from others, so they have trouble being alone, and thus often find themselves in unhealthy relationships long after the red flags start waving.

A major drawback of this attachment style is the obsessive preoccupation with relationships. This can cause an inability to concentrate on anything else.

As a child this person may have had an inconsistent parent or guardian who at times smothered them and encouraged dependency while at other times was too caught up in their own emotions to be emotionally available at all.

If you answered mostly *C*'s
your attachment style might be dismissive-avoidant.

People who avoid attachment are super-independent and often uncomfortable with too much intimacy. They're the kind of people who require a lot of space and a lot of alone time. They're also afraid of commitment but unlike anxious people it isn't because they fear they won't get enough love, but fear they will get more than they can manage. A dismissive-avoidant person may regularly complain about feeling "crowded" or "suffocated" when people try to get close to them. They tend to be hyper-focused on individual achievement and see romantic connections as a distraction.

In childhood, people who are dismissive-avoidant often had some of their needs met while the rest were neglected. For instance, the child may have gotten fed regularly, but was not held enough. Or there was a lot of attention on scholastic achievement but none on emotional security.

If you answered mostly *D*'s
your attachment style might be fearful-avoidant.

This is a combination of dismissive-avoidant and anxious-preoccupied. These are the people who push others away not because they want space, but because they fear once you get too close you will want space from them. They are torn between fearing and craving a level of commitment they don't think anyone can provide. Relationships with fearful-avoidants can best be described as hot and cold with plenty of tests that their partner will likely fail.

   As a child the fearful avoidant may have had a parent or guardian who was manic or possibly had issues with substance abuse, creating a literal day-and-night effect. They were never given the luxury of being completely vulnerable and thus as adults, avoid opportunities to do so.

   This is a very difficult one to self-assess, so after you choose one, try asking someone close to you what they honestly think you are; also refer to the full workbook at TheGameofDesire.com to get a link to a longer quiz. After you find your type, write a short paragraph that describes how your attachment style influences your relationships. Here is Stephanie's paragraph on her attachment style:

Fearfully avoidant

   While I am securely attached across the spectrum of relationships in my life, from my parents to my friends, when it comes to romantic relationships, it turns out I'm fearful-avoidant.

   This breakdown makes a lot of sense, because traditionally, I see the best in people. I'm a lover not a hater, and I prize having deep relationships with people (my mantra for relationships, platonic and romantic, is "If it's not real, I don't want it"). However, in constant competition with my desire to form these real, authentic connections is my hesitance to reveal my true self to people I don't fully trust. And for some reason, when it comes to men, I just find it so hard to trust them completely. I think a lot of it stems from my disbelief that men would want to date me the way I want to be dated (flaunted and shown off). So, I subconsciously relegate myself to a less-than-girlfriend position and (ironically) contribute little openness/intimacy to the relationship to avoid the embarrassment of having them think I cared. I try to keep it really distant/casual and I stay passive so as to not rock the boat/get too hurt when they inevitably want to abandon me for the real thing—it's complete self-sabotage. I think that's why dating my last boyfriend was so good for me—him introducing me to his friends and hearing him show me off (*she went to Cornell, blah blah blah*) was so awesome for me, even though he turned out not to be.

THE BIG FIVE PERSONALITY TRAITS

The Big Five is by far my favorite character assessment method, and the fave of many credible psychologists as well. Big Five theory suggests there are five major traits that all characteristics fall under: agreeableness, extraversion, openness, conscientiousness and neuroticism.[8] It's easy to remember by using the acronym OCEAN. A lot of people's strengths and weaknesses can be boiled down to where they rank high and low on this system. In addition, certain pairings can tell you a lot about someone's tendencies. For example, in Dr. Ty Tashiro's *The Science of Happily Ever After* he notes that people low in conscientiousness and high in openness are more likely to cheat on their significant other![9]

In order to assess where you are on the Big Five scale, answer *A*, *B*, or *C* to the following hypothetical questions.

You are the kind of person who:
- **a.** Loves to try new places/travel, is accepting of different lifestyles and is always open to new ways of looking at the world.
- **b.** Is open to different kinds of people and their needs but has a firm grasp of what works for them and prefers to stick to that.
- **c.** Loves routine, enjoys familiar settings and is skeptical of change/new ideas.

If right now, I walked into the space you spend the most time in, I'd probably think:
- **a.** This person is organized, clean, on the ball and has a good eye for detail.
- **b.** This person isn't dirty, but I wouldn't say they're organized either.
- **c.** This person is either extremely lazy, extremely busy or a mix of both.

If we went out for a night on the town, you'd be the one:
- **a.** Talking to new people and making connections at every turn.
- **b.** Talking to familiar people and making some new connections for the first hour then be inexplicably MIA for the rest of the night.
- **c.** Looking for someone familiar to engage in a private, in-depth conversation with before heading out.

If someone suggests an idea that you're not really keen on, but they seem very excited about you are likely to:
- **a.** Go along with their idea since there's a possibility it could be better than yours; plus, your main objective is to have a good time, not to have your way.
- **b.** Go along with their idea reluctantly and inevitably say "I told you so" at some point in the night.
- **c.** Try to convince them that your idea is better and if that fails, suggest you do things independently.

If you went out to dinner with a romantic partner and they weren't speaking much, you'd probably think to yourself:
- **a.** I guess something happened before they got here. I'll give them more time, then ask if they want to talk about it.

b. If they don't want to talk to me that's fine, I'll just go on my phone and keep myself busy until they notice me.

c. They probably don't like me anymore.

——————————— *Answer Key* ———————————

a: You are open. **b:** You are moderately open. **c:** You are not very open.

a: You are conscientious. **b:** You are moderately conscientious. **c:** You are not very conscientious.

a: You are an extrovert. **b:** You are an ambivert. **c:** You are an introvert.

a: You are agreeable. **b:** You are moderately agreeable. **c:** You are disagreeable.

a: You are emotionally stable. **b:** You are not very emotionally stable. **c:** You are neurotic.

———————————————————————————

Once you have your results write a paragraph briefly explaining how your five personality traits can help others better understand your behavior. Because I believe in the Big Five so much, I'd love to give you a snapshot of the group's results that I put together for them:

Deshawn scored high on extroversion, which was incredibly apparent since she was the personification of a home-cooked meal: warm, funny, vulnerable, intelligent and never judgmental. On the flip side, she was high on neuroticism and low on conscientiousness, which could explain her scattered nature.

Stephanie's results confirmed that she was very open and agreeable. She gave everyone else ample space to be imperfect or unexpected, but ironically, she left little for herself. Hence why she scored high on both neuroticism and introversion.

Pricilla and Stephanie had very similar results, both scoring high on introversion, neuroticism and agreeableness. This came as no surprise as one of the other quizzes we did (included only on the full workbook) was the Myers-Briggs Type Indicator test. There, it was revealed they were both INFP. Their difference was that Pricilla was neither open nor was she very conscientious. This made sense because she didn't seem to want to do much of anything beyond the status quo.

Courtney was the only person who scored high on emotional stability, which was fitting since she had neatly carved her lane as the rock of the group. The Big Five also pinned her as a moderately-conscientious extrovert who was just about as open as Chick-fil-A on Sunday.

Maya scored high in conscientiousness, as she was both honest and organized, as well as neuroticism because she was fearful and anxious. But on everything else, she was just below room temperature. This made sense because I recognized that she was an open-minded person, but with her aggressive nerves at play, she was rarely open to new ideas. She wasn't an extrovert, but she did demonstrate a confidence in social settings that a lot of introverts do not possess. And finally, because of her intensity and rigidity she erred on the disagreeable side, despite her deep desire to get along with others.

Lastly, later I learned that Cherise had scored high on openness, which she absolutely was. As someone who grew up in a tight-shipped religion, she hadn't been very exposed to the world. But once she broke away from the church she was starved for the unconventional! She was conscientious, hence her pristine appearance and strong-to-the-point-of-pushy morals, as well as introverted, which is why she pre-ferred to observe rather than contribute. Her Big Five test also confirmed what I knew from the jump: she was a little neurotic and a lot of disagreeable.

We officially concluded the reading of their workbooks at 11 P.M., two hours later than I had projected. I thought everyone would grab their shit and head for the exit but instead they embraced, clapped and spoke excitedly over one another as if the words just wouldn't stop coming. They seemed to have felt genuinely heard and seen, which is arguably more satisfying than chocolate and sex.

Courtney turned to me and said, "Girl, I'm gonna be honest, I was really questioning all this damn homework because I didn't sign up for school, but I see what you did with this. I get it and I'm glad it's done."

I offered her a high five but kept quiet. Of course, we weren't done. Certainly not with the program and definitely not with phase one, but I also wanted them to have their moment. What they had accomplished was a remarkable start to a lifelong commitment to know themselves intimately.

But there was still a massive chunk of the puzzle unfinished. Everyone's workbook vulnerably, beautifully and bravely addressed their hardships in terms of what others had done to them, but there was no mention of any remorse for pain they may have caused others.

I was proud that the group could now identify their love language, but I still wasn't sure if in the past they made an effort to speak others'. When emotions ran high, were they the type to admit their wrongs and apologize effectively? Was their ego tame enough to accept and adapt to their partner's turn-on triggers? Did their attachment style stand in the way of their ability to empathize with others?

Of course, being that everyone in the group was single, they didn't have an intimate partner to ask these questions. But, with the exception of Maya, everyone did have an ex. And these exes held gems of personal growth that simply could not be overlooked.

Phase One: Know

PART TWO

→ ◄—

*Know what others think of you by
seeking advanced feedback from those
who have known you intimately.*

— 4 —

EX MARKS THE SPOT

"All of my exes have been blocked," Courtney said flatly.

"There is one person I am still very angry with and the thought of inviting that person to interact with me makes me angry," said Cherise.

"So, it's been a minute since I've been in a relationship that I consider a relationship and not a situationship," began Deshawn. "So, um, should I dig up an ex or do I talk to a situationship?"

"I'm just going through this in my head," said Maya, who wore the most exaggeratedly terrified expression I had ever seen. "Do I have to date someone and have them break up with me? How long do we have to do this?"

"It's still very fresh with my ex. I don't know if now's a good time to reach back out," warned Pricilla.

"I'm actually into this," said Stephanie, who, in support of her workbook results, was truly open to anything.

I had explained that their new assignment was to connect with an ex to ask where they had come up short in the relationship. I emphasized that this conversation was not about closure but instead it was designed to give them clarity on which parts of their game needed work. If they had a hard time apologizing, lacked emotional control or veered toward self-absorption, they needed to recognize that about themselves in order to successfully move forward in my five-phase program.

"You don't have to do this but if you don't, you're cheating yourself out of a lot of progress," I reinforced. "Look, I'm not asking you to do anything I wouldn't do. As a matter of fact, I'll do this assignment too."

"Okay," said Deshawn, still working it out in her head, "so what exactly do we do? Call them up and say, hey, I know we haven't talked in a while but just thought I'd ask how I sucked?"

"Kinda," I admitted.

I advised the group to use four principles of influence when crafting their request:

1. Set the tone immediately; make it clear that you come in peace and that you've made peace with your shared past.
2. Make your request as soon as possible and include the word *because* since without justification, people tend to have a hard time assessing why they should care or comply. This is an important influential technique that you should always keep at the top of your mind because it will improve your communication and get you better results (see what I did there?).
3. Root your request in something greater. Tell them you're doing this as a part of a course or personal pilgrimage. People are more likely to comply when they believe they are helping you work toward a bigger goal.
4. Acknowledge that they are your top choice but that you've also asked others, so no stress if they can't. Make it an honor that you chose them but also keep it casual.

In addition, I drafted up a list of questions for the women to ask their exes if they chose to connect with them. The list was designed to help them stay on track of the end goal (learn what they may need to improve for future romantic success) without their emotions or pride hijacking the convo:

Questions to Ask Your Ex

Was I a good listener to you? _____

Did I speak your love language? _____

Did you find me reasonable?_____

Was I too sensitive or emotionally unstable? _____

Was I emotionally unavailable or distant? _____

Did I make an effort to understand and meet your needs?_____

Did I talk too much about myself? _____

Did you find me grim or negative? _____

Did I apologize often and effectively to you if I was in the wrong?_____

Did you consider me an independent person or a needy person? _____

Did I create a good contrast between being your friend and being your sexual partner? _____

Did we have similar values on sex/a similar sex drive? _____

Did I ask for too much too soon? _____

Did I not ask for enough? _____

Do you think I saw you for your highest potential? _____

Where do you think we were incompatible? _____

Do you think that I changed for the worse, at some point in the relationship? _____

It was with a mix of excitement and dread that I read over the question list, knowing I had volunteered myself. It had been years since I dated someone new and the odds that any of my exes had insight that Jared didn't were Snoop Dogg slim. So, I tried to approach things from a different angle and reflected on what open cases would be healthy for me to close.

My previous long-term relationship was an absolute no. It was an awful and unfortunate chapter in my life that preyed on my insecurities and resulted in a plot line fit for VH1, not personal growth. This exercise, although naturally risky since you're putting your pride on the line, should not put you in any form of real danger. The litmus test for selecting the right candidate is this: if during the relationship the ex in question did not consistently want the best for you, they are not the best person to ask. In addition, use your judgment to avoid any exes who may misconstrue this exercise as a ploy to reconnect with them. The ideal choice is someone you still like, who still likes you, but when it comes to the romantic department the lights are off and all parties are well aware that no one is coming home.

With all this in mind, I flipped through my mental Rolodex of names until I landed on one filed under *What happened?* We'll call him Mark.

I included the full story of one of the biggest heartbreaks of my lil life on TheGameOfDesire.com/exmarksthespot. You can head there if you're feeling nosy, but in summary, the story is one we all are familiar with: I wanted Mark to love me as I loved him. And when he didn't, I tried to overcompensate for his lack of interest by offering up my dignity to fill the gap. Spoiler alert: it didn't.

After a couple of hours of Googling, the best thing I came up with was the Instagram of a casual mutual friend. But the only contact he had for Mark was an old email address, Hotmail, to be specific. He might as well have given me his AIM or pager number, but I sent the message anyway:

Hey Mark! I know it's been a while, and I hope you're well. I wanted to say that I do think kindly about you and am appreciative of the connection we had. Despite how things went down, I hope you know I see only the positive and wish you well!

I wanted to ask a favor. Wait, no, I don't need help moving or anything lol. I'd love your input for a project I'm working on that aims to help women better their chances at successful, meaningful relationships because love is a big part of our lives that we receive very little guidance on. And one of the steps of my project includes reaching out to people from the past to hear how I came up short in the connection with them. So, I was wondering if you'd be down to talk for ten minutes about your experience with me? I have a few others in mind, so no stress if you're busy, but you were the first person I thought of because I've always found you insightful.

All the best,

Shan

After I pressed *send,* I waited a few moments for the Mail Delivery Rejection response, but surprisingly, it never came.

Meanwhile, I set up the group's first expert session. Everyone had a week to complete the assignment so I wanted to give them some simultaneous food for thought on the common reasons that relationships fail. To accomplish this, I called on my friend, Dr. Barry Goldstein, a psychologist and couples' therapist who has been in practice for over twenty years. Dr. Barry and I became acquainted on *Make Up or Break Up,* a talk show where I sat with couples on the brink of splitting and assessed their relationship. After I counseled them on-camera, Dr. Barry gave them further assistance off-camera. We were a great team then and I was confident we'd be even better now with this eager-to-grow group.

We connected with Dr. Barry on Google Hangout and immediately he got down to business: "I am here to teach you all how to definitively, one hundred percent fail at every relationship."

Someone in the group snorted sarcastically.

Dr. Barry paused for a second then continued. "Obviously I am talking paradoxically; what I'm really here to talk about are the critical moments and behaviors that knock a relationship off its course. A good relationship isn't easy per se, it just has a hundred little things that line up so it's not hard. Today I wanna summarize all of that by talking about four big things."

Dr. Barry's Four Steps for Failing at Romantic Relationships

1. **The physical.** It takes about four seconds to know if you are attracted to someone. So, if you want to fail at a relationship, try to force yourself to date someone you are not attracted to or force yourself on someone who clearly isn't attracted to you.

2. **The emotional.** Your emotional response is based on your values system. The number-one way to ensure a disastrous relationship is to have different values. Make sure you ask your potential partner these questions early on to see if the connection has a real chance: Who and what do you care about? How do you have fun? What makes you angry? Remember, values are things that we act on—so listen to their answers, but also pay attention to their actions.

3. **The intellectual.** Morals are your opinions on how the world works. They serve as your motivation and the big-picture thinking that inspires you. Most couples with intellectual compatibility share the same morals. Some questions to ask are: What do you think about justice? What do you think about religion? What is your belief on life's purpose? A relationship without intellectual compatibility may survive in the beginning, but if you want to ensure a rocky future, keep surging on with someone whose core beliefs do not reflect your own.

4. **The lifestyle.** Your lifestyle is made up of where you live, who you love, where you worship, where you work and how you like to fill up your free time. Trust takes time and consistency to build, but you can't do that if you're never together because your lifestyles don't mesh. The farther removed you are from someone's day-to-day, the farther you will drift apart.

Dr. Barry finished speaking then opened the floor to questions. At first, everyone was silent but then Courtney chimed in. "If I meet someone who doesn't share my values, I try to help them by telling them where they're coming up short, but if they don't improve, I move on. But then I get accused of being this praying mantis who goes through people, plucking off their head if something is wrong with them. Is that wrong to discard people so quickly?"

"I think you are a romantic, Courtney," said Dr. Barry. "The praying mantis may not be that you're ripping off people's heads and discarding them but that you're putting pressure on someone to open up to you because you're in a rush to find out if they're your forever or not. The dating journey can't be rushed, no matter how bad you want to get to the destination."

"My problem isn't quite the same, but I also tend to attract people who aren't the right fit for me," interjected Cherise. "I tend to attract people who are not very truthful but also do whatever is in their power to not let me go."

"When things start to repeat, it's almost always because we are trying to solve some unfinished puzzle inside. If you've had the same thing happen with different people, you have to look inside— what is the hurt that hasn't been healed?"

"These people are often great deceivers, though," said Cherise. "I don't seek out the bad person because I've already learned that lesson, but they put on a front like they're something different for a long time before their true colors show. So how am I to avoid that?"

Dr. Barry paused for a while. "You have a very tough vibe and that might be misperceived by individuals as you not needing them."

"That's the story of my life." Cherise laughed.

I sat silently on the other end, riveted by this back-and-forth. Dr. Barry had picked up on Cherise's personality challenges within minutes of speaking to her, but I suppose attitudes speak louder than words.

"So even though you value being taken care of and protected you project the morals that you don't need anybody, and nothing affects you. So maybe you have a revulsion toward men who are the giving, sweet and goofy guys trying to give you what you actually need."

"No, I'm not like that," she said flatly.

"Well, good," he continued. "That's a hard cycle to be in. Some people project invulnerability to protect themselves from the bad guys, but that demeanor isn't always attractive to the nice people of this world."

I hoped that Cherise read between the lines of what Dr. Barry was warning her of. She had submitted her workbook to me a couple days before and it was an even mix between anger and anguish. No one could survive on that diet, something had to give. We still had a long way to go in the program so I remained confident that we would find that light switch for Cherise and the others.

I told Dr. Barry about our present assignment to seek counsel from an ex about our intimate flaws. He smiled with approval, then remarked, "That sounds like a great next step. There are people who have an aversion to introspection. They don't want to look at themselves, unless the mirror is positioned in the best light. I think that is a characteristic of someone who is not ready for love."

THE NEXT DAY I GOT A FLOOD OF EMAILS FROM THE WOMEN ABOUT THEIR AS-signments. A couple wanted to update me, one wanted help crafting her request, and Stephanie asked if I would moderate the conversation with her ex, Fred, a 9-to-5 guy who was a part-time comic.

I think asking a friend to have this conversation on your behalf is an extremely good option. This way you can get the concrete information without the risk of the discussion turning into a battle of egos. We decided she would make the introduction, but I would lead and execute the call without her. She immediately sent out an email to me and Fred. He wrote back before the night was up with a calendar invite titled *Stephanie's Roast.*

The next day I called Fred the minute I was scheduled to. We spoke casually for a bit to break the ice, which somehow led to him sharing a quip I will literally never forget: "Seriously I'd rather lose someone's kid than lose my earpods, those things are so expensive!"

When our small talk died down, I went straight for the big question: "In all lovingness, what do you think is holding Stephanie back from being in a healthy relationship?"

"I would definitely say . . . she was just really, I mean she is just very . . ." Fred sighed heavily. "Her biggest issue is that she needs a confidence boost."

"When you say a lack of confidence, do you mean just in your relationship with her or you don't look at her as someone who is confident overall?" I pressed.

"I'd say both, she lacked confidence in both, which to me was crazy because she's pretty badass."

BINGO.

Not that this was an earth-shattering revelation but from what I had witnessed, this was Stephanie's issue to a *T*. She lacked confidence and not in a "no biggie" way, but like a cheeseburger that lacked cheese. When you don't have confidence that you are enough, it's extremely difficult to be confident that you are enough for anyone else. In Stephanie's case she wanted desperately to be loved but she wasn't convinced there was anything lovable about her, hence her dismissive-avoidant attachment. The result was a mix of being closed off and needy.

Sure enough, later in the conversation when I asked Fred if Stephanie was independent or needy he said, "I would say she's more on the needier side. She was obsessed with knowing how I spent my time, even when I was at work."

When I asked if Stephanie spoke too much about herself, he immediately cut me off. "No! Not at all, she's extremely selfless in conversations, and if anything, I'd love if she spoke about herself more."

He also explained that because she didn't talk about herself enough, he had a hard time understanding her emotional reactions. "She's sensitive, she's definitely sensitive. It's hard because on one level she's probably the most logical and emotionally stable person but then, like, one comment she's crying immediately. And not only that but in public—in front of her friends, in front of my friends . . ."

Finally, I asked Fred if he believed she changed for the worse, at some point in the relationship.

"Almost as soon as we became official there would be small things that would happen, things that wouldn't even warrant an argument and she'd jump to questioning the whole relationship. After a while, I'd say that takes a toll on someone."

He also mentioned that Steph was positive, a great listener and supportive—all things that I also admired about her. I ended the conversation with Fred with a deeper appreciation for the value of this exercise because it laid out a few call-to-action areas that Stephanie's workbook had eluded to. Understandably it's uncomfortable to reflect on how our weak areas may have caused harm to the relationships we once cared for, but if done carefully, it can be a catalyst for change.

One of the most important lessons I learned in my counseling practice is that people are the protagonist of their own lives. In other words, everyone thinks they're Mufasa; no one looks in the mirror and sees Scar. But in truth we've all been both and probably at the same time within one relationship. Of course, there are extremes where people have been brainwashed or manipulated, but for the most part we are responsible for our behavior in our adult relationships—people can't make you do something, but they can evoke a behavior you may still need to do something about. Which to me translates into great news: we are always capable of better outputs and thus, better outcomes.

I met up again with the entire group on a Thursday evening with the absolute highest of hopes. Deshawn had spoken with not one but two of her exes, and Courtney teased through text that she had a lot to share.

"Okay, who wants to go first?" I said as I excitedly passed out cookies like it was my first day as a Girl Scouts troop leader.

"I'll go because I don't have anything," said Maya. "I tried messaging my last situationship on Twitter, Instagram and Facebook and I did not get a response. But he fell in love with me and I didn't return his feelings, so he might be still hurt."

I wasn't sure about that reasoning. If an ex who I loved but didn't love me, gave me the opportunity to express my feelings about the relationship, I'd take it. I thanked Maya for her efforts and encouraged her to reach out to an old friend or coworker if she was still interested in gaining feedback. Cherise raised her hand to go next. She had met up with her ex in person, which was great. The downside, however, was because Cherise had been single for so long, it had been a decade since she'd been in a serious relationship with this man.

Back in the 2000s, their relationship was on and off because he was in jail for a significant amount of it. He described himself in retrospect as emotionless and apologized for that as well as the rampant cheating. According to him Cherise was an excellent listener, spoke his love language (even though he didn't know what that was), was emotionally unstable at times, independent, not demanding enough (which he attributed to why he cheated since she let him run wild) and he believed she had changed but only after he got incarcerated.

Although their conversation wasn't timely, it did provide ample insight into why Cherise had become the way she was today. With her parents gone, her religious beliefs abandoned and her heart broken repeatedly, it was understandable why she may have taken on her me-against-the-world persona.

Deshawn raised her hand to go next.

"I contacted two people and they were both very, very nice, but one thing that I did get from them is that I'm a terrible listener.

That's something they were both adamant about." She giggled. "So there was that, but neither of them had a foul taste in their mouth about me and we kind of just parted, not because I did anything wrong."

I prodded for her to elaborate, surely after two calls there was more to say, but she deferred back to her final line: *they couldn't really pinpoint what I'd done wrong.* Okay, how was it possible that so far, none of them was doing anything wrong? Either I had stumbled upon a group of unicorns who were chronically single because they were simply too awesome, or there was a dose of delusion in the air. Courtney apparently saw what was going on and decided to raise that dose to a bona fide heaping.

"My biggest fear in doing this is that I didn't want anyone to think that I was trying to reattach because I reevaluate relationships once a year. So, when I reached out to one ex, I think he thought this was his yearly review time and he just latched on, so I stopped communicating. And when I reached out to someone else, he was very honest and said, 'I don't understand why you're asking me this because you explained everything that was going wrong with us. I was wrong and you were right.'"

"So, were you able to have a conversation with anyone?" I asked.

"Yes, I asked a third person who did participate." She smiled. "The conversation went how I knew it was going to go: 'Courtney, you were fine, you were everything to me!' The only thing he said I could have done better is that I was too quick to react. Then I asked him, 'Is there anything else you want to say to me now, because you're going back in my block box?' and he said nope, that's it. I forgot to put him on block and I woke up to him pouring out his heart all over again in fifteen text messages."

The women erupted into laughter and hoots, eating her story up like candy. And to me, that's exactly what it was: high-fructose corn syrup, artificial coloring and no nutritional content.

I crossed-examined the witness. "So the majority of the relationships you've had, you've ended because of something they did wrong, it's nothing you did?"

"Correct," she replied.

"So, your issue is more partner selection versus partner maintenance?"

"Correct. Wow, that's exactly it! You put that into words so perfectly, that's exactly it!"

"I'll go next," volunteered Stephanie. "I actually didn't speak to my ex directly, Shan did it for me. It's funny because what you just said to Courtney really hit home for me."

I held my breath and tongue to see where this was going.

"Like, I know this is meant for me to be reflective of myself but after listening to the recording of the call I couldn't help but think all of the reasons he gave were kind of him-focused. So, the problem was with him, not really with how I treated him. But at the same time, he said some good things. He said I was a good listener, but I don't really talk about myself and multiple people have told me that. So that's something I need to work on, but I do think on the other hand it has more to do with him."

"Yes, yes," encouraged Courtney.

"Another thing he said is I was too quick to give up on the relationship, which makes sense because I'm such an idealist and if someone does something wrong, I'll be, like, *I don't think my soul mate would do that!* So, I never thought about that, how hard it can be to be with someone who is constantly threatening to end the relationship. But yeah, those are the major takeaways I had."

That was all the confirmation I needed. Although this exercise had broken ground, they still needed to drill harder to get a good look at their foundation. Stephanie's ex Fred had said a wealth of insightful things that I too had noticed in her, but those aren't the things she chose to hear. The criticisms she highlighted could easily be spun into positives: don't talk enough about yourself = selfless martyr. Idealist = high standards of gold. Even in Courtney's and

Deshawn's experiences there actually was constructive criticism, but they were both so adamant on protecting their egos that they glossed over those parts.

Readers, I hope that when you do this activity, you will avoid the temptation to inflate the compliments and downplay the criticism as the group had. Although of course it's better to focus on this positive in life, this exercise is specifically designed to help you understand what you should consider working on in order to have a dramatically better love life in the long run. Because if someone doesn't understand their role in love lost, they will have greater difficulty finding the real thing.

Finally, Pricilla took the floor and at first, she began like everyone else. "The guy I reached out to almost didn't work out because he still wants to be with me. So instead of meeting up, we agreed to email because it would be too painful for him to see me."

But then in a stunning change of direction, she revealed a series of very vulnerable and applicable things she had learned about herself.

"He mentioned that in the beginning I was really optimistic but toward the end I shut down. And as soon as he said that, I realized I do that in other relationships I've been in. Once my sense of security in the relationship has been shaken, I do shut down completely. Then at that point, the relationship becomes all about me and my need for reassurance."

She went on to describe how her anxious-preoccupied behavior got the best of her common sense. She wanted constant validation in private and in public. They'd often argue about how frequently he posted about her on Twitter and she found herself obsessing over how their relationship appeared from the outside.

"And I get a little bit crazy if I feel ignored," continued Pricilla. "I start getting very anxious and I stop thinking straight. He did say that I was a little needy, which I am. I told him once that he reminded me of my mother and that's why he brought that side of me out. But I don't wanna get into that because it's gonna make me emotional."

Too late. Pricilla was dabbing at her eyes and breathing deeply. All our hearts went out to her.

"The main thing I took away is that when your relationship is being tested, that's not the time to shut down and I do that a lot. I realize that I'm never going to make a relationship work if I'm too afraid to put in the work."

"There's so many things I didn't say, now that I'm hearing you talk," said Stephanie.

We all gave Pricilla the comfort she needed for her emotional release. Although the activity had drudged up old pain, I knew that breakthrough was the start of an exciting future.

BY TEN EVERYONE HAD LEFT. I CLEANED UP THEN PICKED UP MY PHONE TO call Jared, who would have just gotten off work, but before I dialed, I was distracted by a new email notification:

Hey Miss B

Of course I'd be willing to add to your project. You can find me here or on my direct line: (416) XXX-XXXX

I've seen your movement online and let me just say that I'm super proud of your dedication and drive to greatness. You've always had it in you.

Positive vibes only:)

Mark

I hate to admit this, but it felt great to hear from Mark again. In some ways loving someone is like riding an old bike, even if you know the bike has two flat tires. So, with the sour taste of dread on my tongue and more excuses for why I shouldn't go through with this than I'd care to admit, I phoned Mark the next day.

He picked up after a few rings. "Hello?"

"Hey Mark, long time. How are you?"

"Oh, Miss B! Hey, how are you? The caller ID said this is a Beverly Hills number, fancy you!"

He sounded like it had been minutes not years since we had last spoken. But most of all, he sounded hella Canadian. I don't know when I became the snooty American who pointed out the long vowels and slow speech of my people, but I do know I hear it like a dog whistle!

We did the small talk, I told him about my project, explained the philosophy, then asked the question, "So in short, where did I come up short when we were together?"

He started to talk about our relationship and blamed our demise on the old, cliché cause: poor communication (clearly he didn't do the workbook or else he would have had a less vague response, like we differed in apology languages or turn-on triggers). I listened for a bit then politely redirected him by explaining that this call wasn't about us or him; it was strictly about my wrongs and what I could learn from them. That's when things got interesting.

"Oh, I mean, I don't know if you're like this now, I'm sure you're not, but you were just a very raw person. Like really raw and very blunt, which I'm not saying is a bad thing, but you seemed to lack a sensitivity. And for me I needed that soft side because I'm a guy who likes to talk about feelings and be in touch with my emotions."

On his end I'm sure he thought my silence was a sign that I was listening intently but in reality, I had to place a Kung-Fu grip on my tongue. *I like to be in touch with my feelings?!* How could the guy I loved who suddenly decided to ignore my texts and screen my calls with no explanation pull the I'm-an-open-book card? But on the other hand, maybe he didn't communicate his feelings with me because I didn't present myself as someone capable of holding that kind of conversation. Damn.

"I don't think we ever even had the dialogue of what we were or how we felt about each other. I mean, I knew you liked me, and you knew I liked you, but did we ever even say that once in those five years? I just felt like I couldn't share my feelings with you, and I could be wrong, but I always got a sense you were talking to other guys. So, it just seemed easy to accept things for what they were.

"And . . ." He hesitated for a second. "Sometimes, you had BO."

I nodded. He was dead ass right on both accounts. First, I did keep other men around in the background as a crutch during our on/off tenure, I guess in case he broke my theoretical love legs along with my heart. But it turns out that through my attempts to protect myself, I had created a self-fulfilling prophecy. Double damn.

Second, I wasn't even going to attempt to dispute his BO claim. It's probably a genetic trait, since hell, sometimes my parents have it (sorry you had to find out this way, Mom and Dad). But DNA aside, it's no secret to people who know me that personal grooming is not my strongest suit. Those who love me have to give space for that. Don't get me wrong, I eventually learned how to play the game: I own a specific wash for practically every part of my body, I keep a bar of deodorant in my car, I've gotten laser hair removal and I've even learned to love doing laundry all in the name of the attraction game. But if I'm honest these are choices I have to consciously make, they certainly do not come natural to me. Thus, my romantic partners have to be aware that while I'm known for being cute and spunky, sometimes I'm gonna be dressed down and a lil funky.

And I suppose that is the asterisk that this exercise needs: *Of course we can learn from our past on how to improve, but sometimes it's our stubborn yet magical imperfections that make us special and different. The trick is to make a clear distinction between the qualities that just need the right beholder and the ones that Jesus himself would've struggled to vibe with.

I ended the call with Mark and we agreed to keep in touch, even though I doubted that would happen. Afterward, I sat on the balcony in the sun for a long stretch of time just thinking, feeling and checking in with myself. Although that call was nothing but ancient history, the fact that I closed the chapter gave me peace of mind. Most wounds do heal over, but we may not realize that for some, the cut underneath is still fresh.

Maybe an hour later, Jared got home from work and joined me. I held on to him and buried my face in his hair. He smelled like me, a beautiful by-product of living with each other and using identical hair products.

"I called Mark," I shared.

"And how did it go?"

"He basically said that I lacked sensitivity, like a soft side, and that I was too raw. Also, that he couldn't emotionally connect with me . . . oh, and that I tended to smell."

Jared smiled and nodded. "You're not surprised by any of that, though, right?"

I shrugged. "Not really but still, that's not exactly what you expect the person who once stomped on *your* heart to say about you."

"Well, maybe that's it, you're the most insensitive when you're hurt, so maybe he had you hurting a lot of the time. It just sounds like you two were in a vicious cycle that brought out both of your flaws. But maybe that's a good thing because it helped you to face them." He slapped a hand on my knee and headed back inside.

It's in these moments that I appreciate Jared the most. He understands my winding complex parts and knows where my potholes are, yet I still feel loved as a whole person by him. I also know this appreciation of being accepted is mutual.

About a year into us living together he pulled me in tight and said, "Thank you. I know I'm not an easy person to love, so thank you."

This comment stunned me. In stark contrast to his belief, Jared has been an insanely simple person to love. But then, I also recognized how hard we both worked on ourselves independently with cooperative guidance, to make our connection run smoothly.

I thought about our relationship and realized we had been having conversations like the one I'd had with Mark for the entire duration. In the beginning when we were friends with benefits, we'd casually discuss over lunch things that the other did that rubbed us the wrong way: He pumped too fast. I bounced too hard. That one tongue trick was cool once in a while but chill. And the licking of the ear thing? Just stop. Since the very nature of fuck buddies is optimal pleasure, we never took it personally, we just applied these critiques to make our experience better each time. When Jared and I began to expand our relationship beyond the bedroom, we kept this trend up, but it stopped being about how to please the other and instead how to become our best selves for each other.

I have probably changed more in the past five years than I did in my first five on this planet. While the majority of that has to do with the decision I made to fully devote my life to the study of intimacy, I'm proud to say that having a partner who communicates my errors without awakening my ego has beyond helped too.

All relationships are filled with criticisms but seldom are these heard and understood. Too often our pride, emotional responses, insecurities, or lack of respect for the other person's opinion get in the way of the message being received. But in order to change, you must give someone else's truth a chance to possibly have some solid (albeit sour) points. While it didn't seem like a majority of the group outright received this message, I felt good about the seed that this exercise had planted and knew we would continue to work until something took root.

The end of this assignment brought Phase One of the program to a close. Now that they had begun to know their intimate selves, we could begin uncovering the lessons in their perceived losses, while setting them on course toward their rightful gains.

Phase Two: Change

PART ONE

———→ ›‹ ←———

*Change the habits and perceptions that are
holding you back. This includes changing
your appearance—and changing your
mind about your limits.*

5

THE POWER OF BANGS

*P*hase One had clearly been emotionally taxing for everyone, so I decided to give the group an extra couple of days off to reflect, while I did the same. At this point, the participants had uncovered more about *who* they were through the self-summary workbooks, next they gained insight on *what* behaviors may have been sabotaging their dating lives. And now, we had to tackle the *why, when* and *how*: *why* had bad habits like clinginess, passiveness and inflexibility turned into traits, *when* did they begin and *how* could I help them to shut that shit down.

Cracking this case reminded me of a plotline in HBO's hit show *Westworld*. During season one, it was revealed that the engineers of the AI robots had embedded a unique tragic incident into each robot's programming, referred to as their cornerstone memory. This manufactured memory was designed to keep the near-limitless AI under the engineer's control through fear and emotional manipulation. But, when a robot realized that memory was BS they subsequently gained the power to override their cornerstone, defy their perceived limits and then, break free.

In order to help the group accomplish that same freedom, I had to pinpoint what each of their cornerstones might be, as well as what traits they'd since fused into. I combed through each of their workbooks a second time, then reflected on what I'd personally observed before identifying the following:

Deshawn believed she wasn't as pretty or interesting as other people. In school she was bullied for her looks, so she thought she was ugly. At home if she spoke about science she was met with blank stares, so she thought she was boring. These beliefs woven together created the perfect material for her self-proclaimed awkwardness to take shape, then eventually take over.

Pricilla believed everything her mother told her. Unfortunately, this included awful statements like, "You are pathetic" and "You can't do anything right!" Even more unfortunate, over time those words morphed into Pricilla's complacent attitude, which stopped her from seizing opportunities to stand out, or up.

Cherise felt the world and those closest to her had turned their back on her. So, she simply returned the favor. With a shaved head and a flattened smile, she was committed to never allowing her kindness to be mistaken for weakness again. She held her shield up so high that it was near impossible to truly see the beauty she possessed behind it.

Courtney was bullied all throughout school, then in her early adulthood she was rejected by her church and found herself in an abusive relationship that almost destroyed her spirit entirely. By age 30, she had come to believe that she had to be blunt, cutthroat and reclusive in order to survive.

Maya described herself as not that pretty and not that smart, and had set low expectations for herself to accommodate that reality. With the help of her anxiety, that began in childhood and worsened in adulthood, she had convinced herself that it was futile to challenge her comfort zone. So, she bought a bunch of books and an awesome lawn chair then resigned herself to a life of watching from the sidelines.

Stephanie stuck out in all the wrong places growing up: she didn't fit with many cultural norms in her community, she disagreed in church and felt ostracized by the beauty standard. Exhausted from years of feeling like an outsider, she clung to anyone that seemed to choose her, all the while counting the days until they rejected her.

Understandably these traumatic experiences had hardened over time until they were no longer just experiences, they were a part of their characters. My job was to chip away at these reactionary personas, so I could uncover the boundless creators underneath. And in brainstorming how I could gently but effectively do so, I thought of my mentee, supermodel Winnie Harlow.

I MET WINNIE IN 2011 WHEN SHE WAS A HIGH SCHOOL DROPOUT LIVING IN Malton, Ontario. She friended me on Facebook, and when I saw her profile picture I thought, *Wow, what an interesting way to do your makeup.* However, when I clicked through her profile, it became evident that it wasn't makeup at all, but a skin condition called vitiligo that resulted in the loss of melanin for 40 percent of her body. But what stuck out to me wasn't her condition, it was how seemingly unaffected she was by it. Winnie had countless adoring selfies and pictures of herself, every shot more flawless and fuck-less than the last. Without hesitation I messaged this beautiful stranger and asked if I could photograph her (my pride would love to note I was the first person to ever do so).

When we met up, she told me between snaps that she wanted to be known by the world either through modeling or hosting. Both ideas seemed fantastic but also far-fetched, given that there was no one else in history who looked like her who had done those things, even on a local level. Eight years later and guess who has amassed over 5 million followers, a place on Victoria's Secret Fashion Show, a spread in *Sports Illustrated*'s Swimsuit Edition, over twenty covers, including international *Harper's Bazaar* and a solid hold on the fashion world's it list.

Winnie was soaking her nails and having her hair done (of

course) when I phoned. I explained what I had been working on, then got her aboard my current train of thought: What cornerstone memory had she broken free from in order to achieve the unimaginable success she enjoys today? As someone who developed a rare skin disease at age four and grew up in a low-income neighborhood where she was bullied to the point of dropping out of school, I expected her to respond along those lines. But, she took the question in a completely different direction.

"I honestly don't have a direct answer to that," said Winnie. "I mean, yes, I've had traumatic things happen, but I don't look at them like defining moments. The thing is that ultimately, we all get to choose what changes us, so why would I choose something negative? I really don't focus on the past or think about my skin the way everyone else does, or thinks that I do."

She was right and furthermore, she wasn't lying. In my years of working with Winnie, I witnessed how far one can go when they aren't anchored by resentment. In 2014, after her season of *America's Next Top Model* had aired, she booked an international campaign with Desigual and had practically every press outlet around the world buzzing about her. So, she took her portfolio around New York looking for representation, but not a single high-end agency took her seriously. Furious by this, I began venting to her about how stupid these people must be, but she stopped me to say, "I'm like a train, I know where I'm going and I know what I have to do to get there. If people want to get onboard, great, but if they don't maybe they'll show up at future stops."

Perhaps she should've said she was a plane because that's precisely what she boarded months later. Winnie moved to London to start building her career overseas before returning to live in America after becoming a bona fide supermodel. She is now signed to the very agency that once closed the door on her. Furthermore, in 2017 she vigorously campaigned for a spot in Victoria's Secret Fashion Show, and when she didn't get it, she was crushed. Thinking that I was being helpful, I asked if she planned on waging a war on social media or marching into their offices with her entourage in tow? She looked at me like I was half-baked then said without a hint of bitterness that her only plan was to get better and hope for a better outcome next year. In 2018, she walked in the show.

"Okay, I get that you don't focus on the no's in life," I retorted. "But most people can't do that, it's like you have a superpower. So what advice would you give to the women in my group who can't fly yet?"

"That's the thing, the way I see myself is not a superpower. It's not at all like flying and that's what I would tell those women: there is nothing that magical or extreme about having confidence in yourself. Confidence is less like a power and more like a skill. Kind of like whistling. It's something that you know you want to do so you start practicing until one day you're a whistling-ass motherfucker."

"All right, how do you whistle?" I asked.

"I wake up and decide how I feel about myself based on who I am, not on what I've been through. That doesn't mean every day I'm showering in self-love; some days I wake up and decide I'm not that cute. That's okay too, that also takes confidence to admit."

"And what do you do on those days?"

"Last week, for example, after I was finished with Fashion Week, I was just feeling so drained, my skin had broken out, my face looked tired—I was just not cute. So, I ordered myself pancakes and sausages, put on my wig even though I had nowhere to go and finished reading *The Alchemist* because it was getting on my nerves how long it was taking me to get through it. You know, I can't always force myself to choose the best feelings but it's always in my power to choose things that make me feel better."

I hung up the phone with that wise young woman who has always been destined to fuck shit up in the most beautiful way.

My goal with Courtney, Deshawn, Maya, Cherise, Stephanie and Pricilla was to get them on Winnie's winning level. To accomplish that, we had to start making some aggressive transformations of the body and mind. Phase Two would end with an intensive one-on-one where I planned to address the emotional baggage of their cornerstones head on. But first, I wanted to tackle the physical insecurities that left a sizable portion of the group feeling like less of a seductress than they were capable of becoming. Plus, nothing whets the appetite for change like seeing what a long way a lil sprucing up can do. Meaning, it was time for some makeovers.

Hold on, before you roll your eyes, I'm not suggesting all of life's disappointments can be cured by switching your hair part. But love it or hate it, when we see ourselves look different, we tend to see ourselves differently. In addition, there is nothing wrong with leaning into your looks to unlock your full seductive potential and given how accessible the beauty community now is, I believe it to be unwise not to. I also think this strategy is most effective when you use cosmetic tools to enhance your strongest features, rather than cosmetic surgery to create new ones. Don't get me wrong, I am all for plastic surgery as a last resort, but I do think we owe it to ourselves to tease out our undiscovered beauty before engaging in drastic alterations.

I had been sharing my own enhancement secrets with the group throughout our process so I suppose it's only fair I reveal them here too: I have water bras in every conceivable color, I'm no stranger to Spanx, if my hair goes past my shoulders, please believe at least half of it goes back on the shelf at night and if my eyes look especially green, don't blame it on my mood—give credit to my tinted contacts by Alden Optical. *Boom.* I've actually never said that publicly before and I can name four dudes who probably have their jaws on the floor reading it. But sadly, no, boo, I'm not mixed with dragon like you thought, I just know how to expertly weave in the real with the fake to create magic.

To help with this process, I made a short list of beauty professionals I've worked with and loved like Laura Jane Schierhorn, the manager for global professional artistry relations at Smashbox

Beauty Cosmetics. I emailed Laura Jane and asked if she could hop on a call to give the group some insiders on makeup that would enhance, not mask. Within minutes she replied and said that not only could she do that, but she was willing to host all of us at a Smashbox store for a full tutorial.

One short week later, I walked into the bright store filled with more colors than I could name and spotted Laura Jane looking like a queen and sitting in a director's chair. Immediately we got wrapped up in a fascinating chat about the origins of the art she had dedicated her life to.

"Makeup began as a form of communication," she shared. "It told people who you were and what your social status was. For example, people used excessive powder to seem fairer because that was the mark of someone who did not have to go outside and work."

I found that perspective incredibly fascinating especially since through my studies, I had also come to view makeup as a form of communication. Except in my books, it was a tool that started a whole *other* kind of conversation. While completing my sexology certification, we learned that the basic principles of makeup were based on making people look both pretty and pretty horny. Eyeliner and mascara give the impression of dilated pupils, which is a telltale sign of attraction. Blush mimics the look of a youthful and flushed face, which makes one appear in heat. Foundation tells suitors that someone is in good health by giving them an even complexion. Bronzer and highlighter create a glow that catches the sun and eyes of onlookers, plus signifies fertility. Slightly darker, glossed lips look larger, which is a sign that blood is rushing and throbbing everywhere. Like, all over someone's hot-and-bothered everywhere.

"No kidding!" exclaimed Laura Jane. "Funny enough that's exactly how I'd describe the perfect date-night makeup: even out your complexion, fill in your brow, dust your cheeks, give yourself a light smoky eye then moisturize your nude lips—done! It has to be a slightly exaggerated, slightly more sultry version of you but you also don't want someone to be scared to touch, hug or kiss you. People need to see you under the makeup—that's where that beautiful glow comes in and no highlighter can replace that."

The entire group arrived on time for once, which I suppose shouldn't have been a surprise since I promised to treat them all. Within minutes after our introductions, Laura Jane pulled Deshawn up into the spotlight and onto her chair.

"We all have some kind of shield, I suppose," she said as she worked moisturizer over Deshawn's bare face. "If someone is using makeup as a shield, I believe it's because they started applying it to hide rather than accentuate themselves. So, I always work on people's faces by starting with self-love. Think about who touches your skin: your lover, your family, or the people who want to heal you, like a doctor. When you touch your own face, approach it with the same loving energy. That being said, Deshawn, tell me what feature you absolutely love."

Deshawn giggled and looked down. "My lips. My lips are full and beautiful."

"I agree." Laura Jane smiled. "We'll make sure to highlight them today."

She then applied full-face makeup to Deshawn using principles that could work for practically anyone. Here are my favorite tips that Laura Jane shared:

SKIN CARE

The more hydrating products you can use on the skin the better! The plumper the skin, the easier the makeup will set. So tone, moisturize and prime—every time.

Under the eye you want a BLT skin-care product: something that brightens, lightens and tightens. This allows you to use less concealer and powder in later steps. A lot of people invest more in makeup than skin care; I recommend the reverse.

Laura Jane's Product Recommendations

Before Makeup

- Mario Badescu Vitamin C serum
- GlamGlow Glowstarter Mega Illuminating Moisturizer
- Smashbox Photo Finish Radiance Primer

Body Bonus!

- Kayo body-firming serum
- Mario Badescu Summer Shine Body Lotion
- Jergens in-shower gradual self-tanner

After Makeup

- Estée Lauder Advanced Night Repair

⟶ FOUNDATION ⟵

Choose your coverage: light, medium or full. Then use one of these application methods for best results:

For light coverage, use a crosshatch motion to get the product in the pores. This will give the skin a natural look.

For medium, use a sweeping motion to apply so it blends but also distributes evenly.

For heavy coverage, use a dabbing motion so the product builds.

Laura Jane's Product Recommendations:

- NARS Pure Radiant Tinted Moisturizer (sheer-to-light coverage)
- Smashbox Studio Skin Foundation (medium-to-full coverage)
- Mario Badescu facial spray with aloe, herbs and rosewater (can be used as prep or a setting spray)

⟶ CONCEALER ⟵

If you need it, start with a color under your eyes to get the skin back to neutral.

If your under eye is purple/blue, peach or orange will neutralize.

If it's red, use a green corrector.

If it's dark brown, use red (some even use red lipstick).

When applying concealer, remember you always want the focus to be on the triangle of the face: top of the brows to the point of your chin. So use your concealer as a guiding light to accomplish that.

Laura Jane's Product Recommendations

- Smashbox BB eye cream
- NARS Radiant Creamy Concealer

⟶ EYES AND BROWS ⟵

Most people have a hard time drawing a clean line above the eye. Practice makes perfect, yes, but there's also another option: a tight line. A tight line is a beautiful and easy way to give the eye some oomph. Lift your lid a touch then shade underneath your eyelashes with a black or brown liner. For eye shadow, use three colors: lid (medium shade), eye crease (darker shade) and inner eye/top of brow (a highlighter). Brows are very personal, but the basic rule of thumb is to keep them groomed right above the tear duct and slightly diagonal of the outer eye.

Laura Jane's Product Recommendations

- Shadow: Natasha Denona, NARS or Melt
- Eyeliner: Smashbox Always On waterproof gel liner
- Brows: Glossier Boy Brow or Smashbox Brow Tech To Go

⟶ MASCARA ⟵

You're going to want to do the top and bottom (think of it like bra and panties).

Also, don't be shy: the average woman does forty-five strokes of mascara, so this is a place you can go BIG.

Laura Jane's Product Recommendations

- Smashbox Photo Finish Lash Primer *Shan's absolute most fave makeup product EVER
- Grande Cosmetics Lash Boosting Mascara
- L'Oréal Voluminous (curved brush)

 BLUSH

Contouring is the thing professionals see most applied incorrectly. Yes, some faces can benefit from contouring, but most don't. So instead of focusing on creating a dramatic face shape, try your best to highlight the one you have. Take your right pointer finger and move it along your cheekbone until you find the crease underneath. Below that line is your no-man's-land: never drop your blush below there.

Laura Jane's Product Recommendations

- Bronzer: Becca or Guerlain
- Blush: NARS
- Highlighter: Becca or NARS

 BRUSHES

Brushes are your best tool to create a truly natural, blended look. Buy the best you can afford! Brushes are an investment that will pay for themselves eventually since you'll need less product to achieve better results.

Laura Jane's Product Recommendations

- Silver kit = Morphe
- Gold kit = Smashbox
- Platinum kit = Hakuhodo

The group left the store with their faces and shopping bags full. As I walked to my car, my phone had a mini gratitude seizure:

Thank you, Shan, for the makeup and the fun day! Appreciate you! sent Stephanie.

Every time Stephanie talks I feel like she's speaking for us both lol. But Yes!!! Thank you Shan!! sent Pricilla.

Yeeeeessss!!! Thank you soooo much! added Courtney.

Ditto! sent Maya.

I really had a great time tonight!!! Thanks! sent Deshawn.

Notably, Cherise said nothing. Not a single word or emoji. Even though she and I had a rough time connecting like I had with the others, I was still very surprised by this given that her Self-Summary Workbook revealed gifts were her love language. This reminded me of what Dr. Barry had proposed: perhaps she was so consumed with protecting herself from people's bad intentions, that she overlooked opportunities to embrace good ones.

Next, I scheduled a meetup on Google Hangout with Talya Macedo, a brand strategist and image consultant from Toronto who was essentially responsible for my signature sex-on-the-beach/in-the-city style. Not everyone needed this extra help. Cherise, for example, had impeccable taste that she was often praised for. Pricilla and Courtney also opted out because they'd both spent ample time finding a look that worked for them.

I sent the invitation for the meeting, then Deshawn, Stephanie and Maya logged on. Our guest, Talya, was the last to join. "This is a really special group, Shan, I can see that now."

After we got the introductions out of the way Stephanie jumped in by laying her enthusiasm out on the table. "I just wanna say that I'm just so excited to be talking to a stylist. This weekend I hung out with my family and they were nonstop roasting me about how I don't know how to dress and how I'm twenty-eight and I need to learn how to dress better. I kept telling them, well, guess what—I'm talking to a stylist this week!"

"Family is the best but also the worst." Talya laughed. "I just wanna preface by saying Shan sent me a few pictures of you guys in different outfits and no one here is a bad dresser, you don't have bad style. Really, all I'm here to do is amplify what you already know about your look and to figure out how the words *desirability, smart* and *confident* can be related to your clothing."

"I'm happy to hear that because my concern was that this was going to be an attempt to get us all to dress a certain way," said Maya. "Whenever I see clothes or tops for women I just don't see them fitting or looking good on me. Also, I never wear a bra. Sure, like, I have two for when I go see family and stuff but it's not my daily wardrobe."

Talya clapped excitedly. "I'm glad you said that. There is really no way to do personal style wrong and if there was, fashion would be stagnant. You go out into the world to be challenged, inspired, sexy, blend in, stand out and make your mark. For all of this, your clothing is your armor, here to protect and enhance you in every encounter."

For the remainder of our discussion Talya took us all through the four separate, but coordinated, ways she wanted everyone to think about their wardrobe:

1. YOUR STYLE HAS TO FIT YOUR LIFESTYLE

Take a moment each morning before you get ready to think about what you want to exude and where you might end up. Whatever you wear should reflect your personality, your mood and your environments. In regard to choosing clothes that reflect who you are, notice that I said to do this daily rather than once every couple of years. As you grow and your lifestyle changes, your wardrobe should be in step with your evolution.

In regard to choosing clothing for your environment, being and appearing comfortable is key because when you're at ease, you radiate confidence. Nothing translates anxiety like constantly adjusting your clothes or attempting to walk in a pair of shoes that you simply can't.

2. HAVE A CLEAR UNDERSTANDING OF YOUR BODY AND YOUR MEASUREMENTS

I'm assuring you that "knowing your body" is NOT about a type or a shape. I never want to hear about a woman being "pear-shaped" or compared to any other fruit/gourd/legume again. So, to me the best way to get to know your body is by learning about its beautiful measurements and ratios. The more you know the better, but there are two measurements in particular that people frequently and unfortunately, get wrong:

- *Waist:* Where does your natural waist TRULY lie? Typically, you should take your measurement two fingers under the bottom of your rib cage, just above your belly button. Knowing your true natural waistline will inform where the top of your most flattering pants, skirt and shorts should snuggly fit.
- *Bras:* If you choose to wear a bra, then it's quite likely that your bra doesn't fit. Your cup size can fluctuate throughout the month so having a few different styles and sizes on hand is key. The wrong bra can actually pull down your shoulders or create unnatural rolls. This is why it is imperative to get measured by a professional ASAP. Most department stores staff someone who can help with this. Trust me, you owe it to yourself (and your back) to see how a well-fitting bra can both flatter and enhance you, in and out of your clothing.

Fill in the chart below

Height: ....

Bust: ....

Bra: ....

Waist: ....

Hips: ....

Inseam: ....

3. KNOW YOUR COLOR STORY

A painter doesn't just throw random colors onto a canvas and call it art. They thoughtfully consider theory and how tones will enhance each other. Get dressed with a guide or color wheel until you can effortlessly throw together a monochromatic or analogous outfit. When you get really good at this, you can even pull off color blocking with complementary tones.

If color overwhelms you, then start simple. Build off a neutral item (black, gray, cream or even denim) and add colored items slowly. Once you've spent some time with a color wheel (see Talya's printable version on TheGameofDesire.com), you'll learn how to see color in relation to other colors. That random but beautiful green top you bought on sale will become even more brand-new with a yellow or fuchsia bottom.

4. CHOOSE YOUR MUSE

In order to take the math out of dressing, choose a person whose style you admire and construct one capsule outfit inspired by them. It's not so much about wanting to embody someone else's style but drawing inspiration from someone who probably has a professional helping them. But remember, you must know your measurements; that will help you determine what trends to hop on and which ones are best to sit out.

"I really love Angelina Jolie," shared Stephanie. "She has this, like, subdued coolness. I think she has an awesome style that isn't trendy but she's not super-boring either."

Talya Says Angelina is known for classical contemporary style and the equation here is approachable: white button-up shirt + well-fitting pants + simple, small jewelry = Angelina's staple look.

"Tracee Ellis Ross," said Deshawn. "She has a very quirky personality and a very outgoing, risky style that complements that. She always looks different;

she's never dressed in the typical way that the event she's at calls for, but it always works. I want to take risks and pull them off like that too."

Talya Says Tracee is one in a million and her style is so coveted because it spells out the kind of person she is through color (bold), cuts (even bolder) and accessorizing. An understanding of color and measurements is important here, as is embracing your sensuality. I get the feeling that Tracee practices a lot of self-love in the mirror so make that your foundation.

"I like FKA Twigs," said Maya, "but I can't necessarily be a floating angel all the time."

Talya Says I think it can be helpful to embrace the qualities and energy she embodies and run with it. Have you ever seen her when she's not performing? She dresses for comfort and daily movement and mixes in bold pieces for flair. What you see onstage or in her videos are amped-up versions of this. Invest in a pair of killer boots and some comfy, stretchy pieces and see how you feel.

For our final glam expert, I phoned Makeba Lindsay, a natural-hair guru and my personal curly-haired savior. Makeba is responsible for my staple halo cut as well as my highly coveted and perfectly blended curly-hair extensions. Again, not everyone in the group was in need of this coaching but three in particular were: Courtney, Maya and Deshawn. Maya's hair lacked personality; it was parted down the middle with zero layers or life to it, Deshawn's blue-pink hair had way too much going on and Courtney's hair lacked luster due to lack of love.

Courtney's ex-boyfriend used to instruct her to put on her "white girl hair," and on a dating app she once got made fun of for the one natural-hair pic she posted. It's not easy for a black woman to love her hair in a world conditioned to hate it, which is why black-hair experts like Makeba are worth their weight in shea butter.

"Tell me about your hair," said Makeba.

"It's fine, I guess. It's kind of dry and hopeless," answered Courtney.

"Hmmm," Makeba remarked as she touched and detangled. "You have to look at your hair as an extension and a product of yourself, it's telling you what's happening inside of your body. I want you to try something different when you do your hair; don't just rush to the result, listen to what it's telling you in the process. If it's dry that's an indicator that you're lacking hydration and good fats. Have a conversation with your tresses as if they were your children because frankly, they need your love, patience and attentiveness, too."

Courtney nodded. "That makes sense. I do just think of my hair as another thing I want to get done. So usually I just braid it down, put a wig on and get on with my day."

"Wigs are great, but if they're something that you're slapping on to mask your hair, you can cause more damage with the glue, the tightness of your braids or by giving more attention to styling the fake hair rather than treating your own. They're supposed to be protective styles so you can change up your look without causing any damage. Wigs should not be used as a way to hide your natural beauty from the world, whether that world understands you yet or not."

Courtney got a crash course on hair care and then departed with a bob that left her neck deliciously exposed, which she revealed was a big deal for her. "Growing up I used to grow hair on my neck, which left a lot of scars from ingrown hairs. I always wore long hair as a way to hide that shame, but I don't have anything to hide anymore."

When it was Deshawn's turn, she looked herself over in the mirror with her yellow top, blue-pink hair and purple polish, then said, "Is there any way we can keep the color?"

No! I thought. I was so far over Deshawn's Halloween hair, I couldn't even see the wall anymore.

"Yes!" exclaimed Makeba. "You wear colored wigs and hairpieces, which is going to be easy to blend with your hair once it's a neutral tone. Going darker is not about limiting your expression, Deshawn, it's giving you the base to experiment so much more."

I gestured to the mermaid ombre wig that transitioned from black, to green, to blue, to pink which I had purposely worn that day for this exact moment. Deshawn flashed a metal grin then gave the thumbs-up. Makeba got to work and when she was done Deshawn had a dark, curly style that had personality and prestige all in one—just like her.

Maya was last to go. Her hair was essentially a national conservation site: she never styled it, seldom washed it and it hadn't been touched by another person in ages. Makeba got to work cutting in a multitude of layers so that Maya's curls no longer fell in a limp triangle. When Makeba put down her scissors, Maya's hair was a stunning cascade of bouncy curls with a rocking side part that made her look effortlessly sexy. I clapped, Makeba fawned but Maya just sat still and stared back at the reflection of her new curlycut with squinted eyes, attempting to hold back her tears.

"You don't love it?" Makeba asked.

"I don't know," she answered.

"Is this look you?"

"I don't know . . ."

"What change do you think would make you fall in love with your hair?" pressed Makeba.

Maya turned her gaze to the ground. "I don't know."

Makeba raised a hand. "Maya, you have to decide who you want to be and own that. I know you know what looks good on you; every reference photo you first showed me had consistencies. I know that we aren't far off, but I think you're second-guessing because you're worried about other people's opinions. But guess what? They don't get to wake up as you, so let's give *you* the haircut you want."

We had a scheduled group meetup at my apartment in thirty minutes, so I had to get back. I asked Maya if it was okay to meet us there when she was done. She nodded at me but kept her eyes fixed on her reflection.

Cherise, Pricilla and Courtney were at my apartment when I

arrived. I smiled at Jared, who was in the kitchen pouring water and putting together snacks. He hugged me, buried his face in my neck and whispered, "Cherise doesn't want anything, she's waiting for you to order food."

I squeezed his arm then handed my phone out for everyone to select a meal from Uber Eats. Just then, the door opened and the new-and-improved Deshawn strode in.

Pricilla stood up and embraced her. "Wow, you look incredible!"

"Thanks, I feel pretty incredible," Deshawn said, touching her hair. "I FaceTimed my mom to show her and she said, 'great, now we can take pictures together at church tomorrow!' And I was like, has my mom been avoiding church pictures with me because of my hair!"

The group laughed, chatted and ordered. With each meetup we felt less like a curated assembly of different archetypes and more like a collective of one: one goal, one mission and one unanimous passion to support each other on this journey.

The food and Maya arrived at the same time, but everyone pushed their appetites to the side to praise the human snack that now stood in front of us. Maya now had full, blunt, bouncy bangs that served as the exclamation point to her layered cut. She looked like a modern-day Farrah Fawcett.

Before anyone could get anything audible out Maya spoke up first: "I love my hair! You know when you see a dog and its owner walking together and they match each other? That's how this cut makes me feel."

I loved that she claimed her feelings before anyone else could share their opinion. I also loved the irony that when I left her, she was on the verge of melting down and now she was practically soaring because of bangs. Literally, just bangs. I wondered if the rest of the group's problems could also (seemingly) be solved with one, decisive snip.

"I could never pull off bangs!" said Pricilla.

"Oh my gosh, me either," added Stephanie.

"Do you see how small this forehead is? A swoop, yes, but bangs—NEVER!" exclaimed Deshawn.

Well damn, so much for that idea. I pulled out a pink-frosted cake with yellow trim from the fridge and set it on the coffee table.

"As you know, today we're taking pictures for your dating app profiles," I announced. "And to give you an edge, we're going to be using the cake as a prop. Can anyone guess why?"

"Because you're a hater who doesn't want us to look good in our crop tops?" said Courtney.

"The actual opposite, girl." I laughed. "This is a psychological trick I learned while reading *Methods of Persuasion* by Nick Kolenda. He used a picture with a birthday cake to get him more sales, but you're going to use it to get more attention on dating apps."[1]

"I still don't get it," Courtney said, speaking on behalf of the group.

I explained the method behind the madness by asking them one simple question: When you see someone with a cake, what immediately comes to mind? If you're like most people, the words *birthday* and *celebrate* are probably kicking around and that's precisely why this technique works. On someone's birthday we are conditioned to give them more attention and more time; thus, if someone is on an app swiping away in a trance-like state and a picture of a person holding a cake pops up, it will likely prompt the brain to get to work by pulling up the birthday schema and the ritualistic behaviors that go with it. In short, including a cake in your profile photo is a way to ensure more people stop what they're doing to give you special attention.

The group let out a collective, "Oh!"

I smiled victoriously then told them they had about thirty minutes to freshen up before I got to snapping. They paired off two by two and scattered around my apartment taking up mirrors and standing by windows to see themselves clearly through their compact cases. I stood to the side and observed the group in quiet awe as they bonded, applied blush and helped one another choose the perfect lip color. Since I was a kid, I've loved watching people playing with makeup together. That day, I realized why: it's self-love and community care in perfect balance.

Maya traditionally did not wear makeup, but since our Smashbox meeting, she had taken a liking to mascara and lip stain. So, naturally she was the first done. This was the best-case scenario since I suspected she would be the hardest to photograph.

I say this only because she did: "I'm horrible at taking photos and most of the time I attempt it, it ends in a panic attack and tears."

So yeah, when people tell me that about themselves, I tend to believe them.

Maya walked in with her hands clasped in front of her and her head down. She wore perfectly oversized bright-green coveralls that needed no alterations and a timid expression that I wanted to change immediately. I instructed her to close the door, so we could work in private.

"All right, Maya, I want you to really stretch into your masculine side here. Embody that androgynous energy you possess that's so seductive."

"I don't even know what that means," she said, getting noticeably worked up.

I handed her a brown crate to sit on and squatted to demonstrate the vibe I wanted her to tap into. "That means you release all *fucks*. You sit how you're comfortable, you look at the camera like it's the one that has to prove something and you let your face do whatever it needs to. Except of course, if what it wants to do is panic."

Maya took the box, set it down, then exhaled. "Okay, let's try."

We shot for as long as we could. I kept the requests for pose changes to a minimum and gave her plenty of time to take breaks to re-center herself.

About ten minutes later she looked at me squarely and said, "Okay, I don't think I can do anymore."

"You don't need to, we got it!" I high-fived her and asked her to send the next person in.

Before she left, she turned back and said, "This is the first time in a long time that I've been able to take pictures without completely crumbling. I know that sounds small, but this is a big deal for me."

The remainder of the group also clearly had issues in front of the camera, with the extreme exception of Cherise. Cherise was born to be photographed. Through the lens of my camera I saw the real her that she often spoke about but rarely exhibited: sexy, fun, flirty, mischievous, open, goofy and confident. I was smitten with her, until I handed her the cake.

"This icing looks like melted plastic, where did you get this? It looks toxic."

Deshawn and Pricilla photographed identically: with one giant question mark over their face for every single frame. While some pictures came out nicely, specifically the ones where they were naturally smiling, whenever their face was at rest you could see that their spirit was not. It's not just your eyes, but your whole face, that provides a window to your soul. How do you hold your mouth? What are your eyebrows doing? Where is your eye line? All of these factors serve as a road map to your truth. Most people foolishly believe they have mastered the poker face, but in reality, if you're thinking it, we can see it!

Courtney and Stephanie had a little more ease, but still a layer of apprehension that made it clear we'd probably be doing reshoots. Which is fine; the beauty of 2019 is that everyone and their grandma's cat has a camera so there's no excuse not to practice taking your photo. Selfies aren't just for the narcissistic, they're also a great tool for the enlightened to truly see their feelings, as others do.

READER, HOW ARE YOU DOING? IT'S BEEN AWHILE SINCE I CHECKED IN WITH you. I hope that this chapter was an inspiration and not a discouragement to anyone who feels left out of the beauty box. Remember what I said in the beginning of this book: attractive is not an adjective used to describe some, it's a verb that can be utilized by anyone. This is why I wholeheartedly believe that working on your physical aesthetic will help to open your romantic options and best of all, the results are twofold. For one, shiny things catch the eye but more importantly, shiny things move with confidence because they *expect* to capture eyes.

As Winnie and the other experts in this section taught us all, your greatness can begin when you feel beautiful in your skin. But, it is also worth noting that satisfaction with physical appearance alone is not a substitute for any of the other work we have done, or are about to do.

As evidence, consider the study done by James McNulty of the University of Tennessee. McNulty recruited eighty-two newlyweds then separated them so that volunteers could rate the attractiveness of each participant. Next, his team interviewed participants and asked about their satisfaction level in their marriage; their answers might surprise you. Researchers found there was no correlation between how good-looking someone was and how satisfied they or their partner was in the relationship.[2]

All this to say, hell no, looks aren't everything. But they sure as heck aren't nothing either. Like everything else in life, this area is subject to balance and I say, if you can tip the scales in your favor by slaying your fit and your brows, why not? Especially if what you got going on underneath your healthy, bomb-ass hairstyle, is even more woman-crush worthy.

Phase Two: Change

PART TWO

———— ➤ ◄ ————

Change how you present yourself.
Play up your seductive qualities and learn
to curb your anti-seductive tendencies.

6

DON'T JUST BE YOURSELF

The six women sat in my living room for what I later learned would be the last time. I handed each of them a packet titled "Seduction and Anti-Seduction" (which could also moonlight as a manual titled, The Do's and Don'ts of Human Interaction). Now that we had gone through the physical transformation, I wanted to prime them for the character alterations I believed they needed to address next. But people have a much easier time swapping hairstyles then dropping traits, so I knew I had to go about this process a little slower and gentler.

I once had a client send me a scathing email after a session because she felt I had crossed a line in suggesting she had qualities she needed to fix. She felt that being yourself is the key to finding the right mate, and that there shouldn't be any tactics or adjustments necessary in the search for companionship.

This of course is far from an unpopular sentiment. As a matter of fact, if someone was struggling in the love department and asked a roomful of people for advice, the most popular response would be, *The key is to just be yourself.* Many therapists may even share some rendition of this in fear that the bold reality, *actually it's not just them, there's a whole lotta you in there too*, would be too off-putting. But,

I'm not a therapist and my goal is big results for some not a pleasant experience for all, hence why you will not hear this advice from me, ever. Partly because I believe that we should all constantly strive while we're alive; I never wanna *just* do anything that matters to me. And mostly because I don't even get the practical application of that message. We have many different versions of ourselves: our work self, home self, after-hours self, hungry self, when-no-one-else-is-watching self and the version of self that may have been formed in reaction to past trauma. So which self are people referring to when they share that sentiment? I believe that the only true self is the one someone consistently chooses to be, and that simply points to the fact that you do have a choice. Thus, if who you're choosing to be isn't working, what's so wrong with choosing to become something else?

To vent about this just a tad longer, name one other instance where that advice would be appropriate for someone who is consistently missing the mark. If a med school student was on the brink of failing and asked what they should do, would you tell them to be themselves—even though their current self is at the back of the class? If someone had tried out for the basketball team two years in a row and failed but was determined to make this year the one, would you advise them to maintain the same course of action as their previous attempts?

Of course not. We would tell those people to study harder, enlist the help of coaches or teachers and to mimic the habits of those who have found success. Why should dating be any different? Yes, there is someone out there for everyone, but this program is about transforming women into someone widely desired—and there is a proven strategy to that. Hence why I wanted to take them through a crash course on seductive and anti-seductive behaviors before our big chat.

The Art of Seduction by Robert Greene is a book that changed my life by illuminating where I had been turning people off and the nine different ways that I could turn my interactions around.[1]

Jared recommended this book to me when we first started dating and now that I think about it, maybe he was dropping hints, because I know for damn sure that's what I was doing with the group!

Below is a hella truncated version of *The Art of Seduction*. I also went ahead and put my own spin on everything to make it easier to understand and remember. Actually, I recommend each of you remix the content in this book as much as possible if you're serious about winning the game of desire. Education experts agree the best way to retain information is to put it in your own words.

Also, keep in mind when reviewing this list that, much like Gary Chapman's love languages, most people have one or two seduction styles they use well. But exceptionally good lovers understand the importance of all the styles—and how to deploy them. Finally, it's wise to think of learning about seduction as if you're learning how to dance. The absolute best dancers know the choreography until it's a part of them, until the moves are an effortless extension of their own.

Here's my adaptation:

How to Be Seductive

1. The jaw/panty dropper. Simply look and act the part of the person whose bathwater we'd all guzzle. Marilyn Monroe and Henry Golding are excellent examples of this seducer.
2. The faucet. Because you're hot and cold, get it? Tease your playmates with your sharp edges and round curves until they don't know which way the exit is. Sarah Michelle Gellar as Kathryn in *Cruel Intentions* was a faucet. I also think Selena Gomez is a great modern-day example since she bounces expertly between sweet as heaven and sexy as hell.
3. The kindness killa. Give tons of compliments and be the kind of person

who moms and waiters adore. Agreeableness is the number-one trait that determines the success of long-term relationships, so remember—it's cool to be kind. Michelle Obama and Tom Hanks are exemplary kindness killas.

4. The keg. When you go out, make an entrance, be the center of the party and leave everyone in your vicinity begging for more when you exit. It's no surprise that these two are friends, but The Rock and Ellen DeGeneres are prime examples of kegs.

5. The zero fucks. Do what makes you feel good and don't ask for permission or wait for others to join. Be a natural, and by that I mean be the kind of person who is untainted by the pressures and expectations of others. Channing Tatum and, of course, the queen Chrissy Teigen play this like a pro.

6. The centerfold. Be gender-neutral without apology or explanation. This can be accomplished through your style or your personality, whichever feels most authentic. Prince and Ruby Rose are sexual icons for a reason—they dare to defy our gender-conforming culture and they look irresistible doing it.

7. The player. Be the kind of person whose reputation gets around almost as much as you do. Those who want to tame or experience a beast will not be able to resist. Drake and Rihanna are classic rakes. Is it any wonder why these two are so drawn to one another?

8. The Oprah. Be supportive of others' highest potential. When they're around you, they should feel like they are the reflection of their truest, highest self. Oprah of course is the pinnacle of this seductive trait, but Leonardo DiCaprio as Jack in *Titanic* is also a good example. He was able to woo Rose away with a gift worth more than diamonds. He looked her in the eyes and told her, "I see you."

9. The It factor. Embody, ooze and emit that special kind of special that people can't put their finger on. These are less well-known names but there are two people who I recently felt, wow, they've got *IT*: Zhavia (a singer known best as a contestant on *The Four*) and Salif Lasource (the Michael Jackson impersonation dancer).

When we finished running through the list, I asked the group to explain one of the seduction styles in their own words, plus identify a fellow member who exemplified that technique.

Stephanie went first. "I'm gonna pick the zero fucks seducer. These people have a child-like essence because they aren't super-self-conscious and they aren't worried what other people are thinking, they're really just enjoying themselves. And I think the person in the group who embodies that is Deshawn."

"I choose the keg," shared Pricilla. "They are the kind of person that lights up every room and is very comfortable being the center of attention. But what makes this person really seductive is they use the attention for good by making others feel appreciated and more comfortable in their presence. I think that is Courtney to a *T*. She's the hype woman for everyone."

Everyone agreed enthusiastically, and Courtney grabbed ahold of her cheeks as though they might explode with joy. "Well thanks, guys! I chose Maya as the centerfold because she really does dance on the line of masculine and feminine so effortlessly in the way that she dresses and holds herself."

"I chose the It Factor, and I understand that to be a person who people are just drawn to even though they can't always explain why," said Deshawn. "I think that person is Cherise because when she comes into the room everyone just looks at her. I feel like she has a secret something that makes people want to know more."

"That's funny," added Maya. "I was going to also pick Cherise for the jaw dropper because that is someone who brings you in with their overall appearance and beautiful call."

"Can I just add to the jaw dropper?" interjected Stephanie. "I think Pricilla is one. I feel like she would kill it at the club. If I had to bring one person to the club who would bring all the boys to the yard, it would definitely be Pricilla!"

Everyone exploded into laughter.

"What's funny is that people see me and expect me to be this vixen type," Pricilla said, blushing. "But when people actually get to know me, they're like, *aww, you're actually supersweet!* A part of me is like, no, I wanna be the seductive vixen!"

"Well, you can be the seductive vixen too," I said, raising my voice above the laughter.

I explained to the group the magical concept of contrasts. When done right, they are undeniable seducers, as outlined by the faucet seduction technique. For example, Pricilla being super-sexy *and* super-humble at the same time was a very effective contrast that made her hotter. I believe we should all have a baseline at rest, but at play, there's nothing wrong with using extremes to keep people guessing—as long as you're careful not to be contradictory (saying one thing and doing the other) because that certainly isn't seductive.

"Does anyone have a contrast of their own that they are aware of?" I asked.

"I think based on how I look people are often shocked that I'm nice," said Cherise. "People have thought that I'm mean for my entire life but I'm completely super nice. I love people and I love making people feel comfortable."

I wanted to tell her that I'd never met an actual nice person who felt the need to defend how nice they were so exhaustively, but I knew my time to have that one-on-one discussion was coming soon.

"But if you know you are a visual contrast," I said instead, "you almost have to counter that first impression right away."

"I usually do," she said.

"Meaning the first thing you would do is walk into a room, smile and say something kind."

"I usually do," she repeated.

Now, I couldn't resist: "I'm gonna be honest, Cherise, I haven't really seen you do much of that."

"Well, we don't go much of anywhere, do we?" The group laughed and she continued. "Anyway, I chose the faucet and that is someone who has mastered the art of not saying yes or no and they keep people intrigued and guessing. I think that . . . oh my God, why am I blanking on your name?"

"Stephanie?" offered Deshawn.

"Stephanie, right." Cherise continued. "Stephanie here is kind of that way because you never know what she's thinking and I think it also comes from a place of trying to remain safe."

For those of you who recall the neg, that comment was a classic example: an observation that is equal parts compliment to insult.

"I don't think the tease does it because she wants to remain safe," I added. "I think she does it because she feels in control and likes to keep people on their toes. For example, Steph, the first time we met, remember I was saying how flirty you were being with me? In my head I kept thinking, *dang does this girl know she's totally seducing me!?*"

NEXT, WE WENT THROUGH THE NINE ANTI-SEDUCTIVE QUALITIES. I TOOK MY time with these as they were things I planned to reference on our upcoming one-on-one calls. Again, these are inspired by Robert Greene's *The Art of Seduction*, and I also added three of my own at the top.

If you've ever been curious why someone that you believed you had a great connection with never called you back, it's likely because you exhibited one of the following:

How to Get Ghosted

1. The cactus. The cactus puts up deterrents to keep people away in the belief that those who are meant for them will fight through their wall of spikes.

Why it doesn't work: I came up with this term in my counseling service, after coming across multiple people who thought potential partners should work to earn their kinder/softer side. But in a global market, there isn't much incentive to put up with someone's unkindness especially when there's no guarantee for a reward down the line. There are many examples of the cactus type triumphing in movies, but remember life is not a movie and our lovers aren't actors paid to stick around for the plot twist!

2. The Peter Pan. This person does not want to, or simply just hasn't, grown up.

   Why it doesn't work: While it is seductive to have a carefree, *almost* child-like essence that reminds us of simpler times, it is not seductive to behave immaturely. The Peter Pan does not inspire others to engage in an adult relationship with them, since they don't appear to be up to the task elsewhere in their lives.

3. The red marker. The red marker lives to correct people, no matter how innocuous their "error" is. If the fashion, grammar and politeness police were real, they'd be sheriff on each force.

   Why it doesn't work: Needless to say, it feels shitty to feel like you gotta mind your Ps and Qs to avoid constant judgment. Mistakes are the mothers of many great inventions; the red marker is the grim reaper of 'em.

4. The bulldozer. They came, they saw . . . and they took charge. The bulldozer wants things to go their way and they have no interest in hiding that.

   Why it doesn't work: The phrase "go with the flow" is not something the bulldozer understands—and they aren't willing to compromise for the people around them. Being around a bulldozer is exhausting because you rarely get a say in what happens.

5. The clinger. Clingers are in love with the idea of being in love and thus are unable to let someone go once they've hitched their hopes onto them. These people are often anxiously attached, thus will have a difficult time forming healthy bonds until they address this void.

   Why it doesn't work: While it may seem like clingers really like someone, in truth they like the idea of being liked and will hold on to this hope even when it doesn't make any logical sense. At first someone may be flattered by the attention but eventually they will get turned off once their true motivation is realized.

6. The shadow. Like the clinger, this type needs your approval and seeks to gain it by parroting your thoughts, beliefs and values.

   Why it doesn't work: Healthy relationships are built off mutuality and reciprocity, but the shadow will forgo their beliefs to validate yours. Not many will be enticed by this one-sided deal, because it's inauthentic to a true partnership. Unless you are partnered with a bulldozer.

7. The pusher. The pusher believes they know best and will not rest until you agree with them.

   Why it doesn't work: It is not practical or tasteful to push your values/goals onto someone else. The pusher thinks you should be vegan, doesn't know why you don't sign up for SoulCyle and buys you things they already own. Although their actions seem kind at first, people eventually recognize that their intentions are narcissistic.

8. Penny-wise and people-foolish. This person is willing to trade in the quality of their interactions to protect their finances.

   Why it doesn't work: They aim to save their money by spending yours and they aren't very good at hiding that. They may be a gold digger or just cheap. Either way they make it clear that money and how to keep most of it for themselves is always top of their mind.

9. The Nervous Nelly. This person is so awkward and self-conscious that it's awkward to be around them.

   Why it doesn't work: Worry is usually contagious: Are you the one making them uncomfortable? Are they going to have a meltdown? Are you safe around this person? These questions initiate someone's fight-or-flight mode, and make it difficult for people to relax around the Nervous Nelly.

10. The long talker. This type would seemingly rather suffocate than take a breath and give someone else a chance to chime in. The long talker rarely asks questions and is noticeably uncomfortable when any other person has the floor.

    Why it doesn't work: No one can listen for that long without getting irritated or bored. In the book *Words Can Change Your Brain*, by Andrew Newberg, M.D. and Mark Robert Waldman, they recommend speaking for thirty seconds or less at a time, because the human brain can only absorb three new pieces of information at once. So if someone speaks for five or ten minutes trying to argue their points, the listener will only remember a small portion.

11. The eggshell. Eggshells have a fragile ego and a shaky self-esteem that can be bruised with the most minor slights.

> *Why it doesn't work:* When you are around these people you get the sense
> that everything you say or do is on the cusp of offending them. They are prone
> to whining, sulking and out-of-the-blue emotional outbursts.

In the same fashion as I had done with the seductive qualities, I asked the group to identify who they felt embodied these anti-seducers. But, since no one wants to get called a clinger in public, I asked if they could write down their answers so that I could share them at a later date. This is a snapshot of what they said:

I think Cherise is the cactus because she gives off a vibe of like, I don't need anything or anyone, so I don't know why I'm here. But as soon as she talks it's clear she has issues and needs to be here. And I really don't like or understand why she makes fun of people for approaching her, but then complains that people find her unapproachable.

—Pricilla

I think Deshawn is the Nervous Nelly. I feel this uncomfortable energy around her to the point that I feel like she's not having fun at all. I also can't imagine her in a romantic setting where she could turn off her awkward, nervous side.

—Stephanie

I think Courtney is the bulldozer. At NASA, I worked in mission control and we planned the astronauts' days during their mission. In addition to making space for their work, we had to add in contingency: days for them to get sick, days for them to not complete something properly, days for equipment to malfunction. Courtney seems like she doesn't add space for things not to go according to her plan. She's lost that trust, but if you get to know her, you can see she actually wants to be vulnerable.

—Deshawn

I think Steph is the shadow because she's just so yielding. She comes across that whatever is better for others she'll just adjust to. It makes it hard to connect to her because you never know if she's saying what she wants or just what she thinks other people want her to say.

—Courtney

I think Maya is the eggshell because she seems too easily offended. She feels like the person you must be so cautious of speaking around. She has this anxious face most of the time, which makes you feel like if you say the wrong thing, this whole other person can come up.

—Cherise

I think Pricilla is kind of like the cactus except she doesn't have spikes, just a hard shell. So, I'd like to submit a new term: the turtle. It's like she just can't or won't open up. Whenever Pricilla talks, I really like listening to her and when she doesn't I want to hear her but I also don't wanna push her out of her comfort zone. So, I would say if she was doing that on dates, just sitting there and not giving a lot, that would be exhausting. And yeah, I am totally seeing the irony of me pointing this out about anyone else.

—Maya

I tried my best to break up the session with activities, but somewhat unavoidably, I took on the character of the long talker. When I finally finished rattling on, the group looked tired. I called it and told everyone I'd be in touch soon with instructions on what we'd work on next, but for now there was no homework. With this, Stephanie and Pricilla headed out to make their evening plans but everyone else just sat there and stared at me.

"Do you guys wanna stay and chat? I think I have some wine."

And that is precisely what we did. Or more accurately, they did. Me, I just sat back in awe listening and affirming their stories while feeling more affirmed than ever in this process. Not only had this project improved these women's odds at finding meaning-ful relationships but also, it brought six unlikely people together to create a special bond of their own. As I watched them share and laugh, it dawned on me that I truly considered these women friends. Which somehow made me feel equally better, and much worse, about what I had to do next.

Phase Two: Change

PART THREE

→ ←

Change your attitude. Have an honest
check-in with someone who sees the best in
you and who recognizes how you may be
blocking your own blessings.

7

GROWTH VS. EGO

*I*n this final step of Phase Two the group must tackle the toughest question to date: what's more important, your growth or your ego? I have been foreshadowing this next part for some time and that's because it is a particularly crucial step in this program. For the conclusion of Phase Two, there would be no workbooks, expert speakers or group work; it would be just me, them and the truth as I had observed it. I planned on having a one-on-one talk with each woman to help answer the "Why do I always get the short end of the love stick?" question with them.

Now, I promised you in the beginning a repeatable format that you could do as well, and that still holds. You really don't need a Shan to do this shit. As you saw in the previous chapter, the women in the group were able to recognize each other's anti-seductive qualities accurately. Bear in mind, these women had no expertise in the relationship space, and they'd only known each other for a couple of months. Thus, there is no doubt there is a Shan in your life who knows what your roadblocks are, but hasn't said anything because you never asked. If you have done the Self-Summary Workbook plus you've asked an ex about your intimate flaws, you've probably already uncovered what habits you need to address. The point of having a third, safe person to work through your findings with is that together you can go a little deeper and create new pathways to avoid your old, ineffective route. Of course, a therapist is the ideal person to do this step with if you have access to one, or if you were looking for a nudge to visit one. This chapter is designed to give you the courage to seek out the best illuminator for you. And when you do, hopefully it will go as well as 5/6 of my discussions had.

The next day after our meetup, I got right back to it. I opened my email and sent out six different messages with a subject line comprised of those infamous four words:

We need to talk.

As mentioned, I never revealed next steps of the program until it was time to execute them. This was especially important for this step, since people are prone to putting on a front if they suspect they're being watched for good behavior. I made it clear in the email that the purpose of this call was constructive criticism, but it would be criticism all the same.

FORTY-EIGHT HOURS AFTER I PRESSED *SEND*, COURTNEY HAD BEEN THE ONLY person to respond, which gave me déjà vu from the days of their Self-Summary Workbooks. But on the other hand, it made sense that the only person who was immediately open to—and excited about—the talk would be a bulldozer, ready to get in there and problem-solve.

The next day, Courtney and I connected. Immediately I was reminded how great of a conversationalist she was. Whether we spoke about rent increases at her building or her family history, I was genuinely engaged.

"Courtney, I admire that you know who you are and what you love. Your certainty is not something I would dare take away," I said. "But what I would like to see you add to your skill set is finesse. Effective communication isn't just about what you want to say, it's also what you want to accomplish. And you do want to be a more effective communicator, right?"

"I do," she said, sounding suspicious.

"What do you want your words and tone to say about you?" I asked.

Courtney didn't hesitate: "That I am a smart, strong and an independent woman. Also that I am very thoughtful, understanding and flexible as long as people don't try to take advantage of that."

"You do realize you don't come across as very gentle and understanding, though, right?"

This time she did hesitate. "But I am, though. That's actually the reason my ex was able to manipulate me into an abusive relationship for so long, because I kept trying to understand things from his side. When it comes to finding my life partner, I just want someone who is kind, understanding and genuinely wants to learn to love me. But again, I also don't want to be taken advantage of."

I thought of how Courtney presented herself when we'd gone out: impeccable clothes, the highest of heels, black lipstick and crossed arms. I asked her the big question, "Is being blunt and appearing intimidating your way of avoiding another abusive relationship?"

She went silent for a while. "I promised myself and everyone who loves me that I'd never go through a relationship like that again."

"But Courtney, did you ever consider that presenting yourself as a bulldozer isn't very appealing to the understanding, flexible and reasonable people you want to attract? What it sounds like you've been attracting with this approach is men who either want to be overcome and are looking for a second mom, or men who want a challenge to overcome, the kind who find joy in conquering not collaborating."

We concluded the call by agreeing that it was time for Courtney to let go, of both the reins and of the past. She was not the same person that she was years ago when she was manipulated by her ex, so there was no need to move through the world leading with that fear. Understandably letting down her guard would take some time. Courtney had been bullied at every stage in her life and it wasn't until she took on an extreme persona in the opposite direction that the pain seemed to stop, but unfortunately the loneliness had not. What she needed to find was a happy balance and I was happy to help her discover just that.

After we hung up, I noticed that the others had still not emailed back. So I had to make like a substitute teacher and handpick volunteers. The next morning, I sent Pricilla a text to ask if she had received my email and if she was able to hop on a call. She informed me she was spending time with her son before he started up school, so she had been busy (hence no reply). Of course, that was understandable. I then hit up Stephanie, and she confirmed to connect that night at seven.

Stephanie answered on the first ring, then we had a fascinating conversation about her job, since admittedly I wasn't sure what she actually did. Through our chat Steph also reiterated how unfulfilled and out of place she felt there. In fact, she attributed a lot of her dissatisfaction with her life to not being in her true calling and overall, not being certain of her purpose.

However, after listening to her describe her situation, it didn't sound as hopeless as she made it seem—just like everything else in her life. I agreed that her current job didn't sound like the exact right fit, but she loved what she went to grad school for, which in my eyes put her in the perfect position to discover her true calling. However, what good were my eyes to her? And that was the running theme with Stephanie; it didn't matter how others looked at her, because she refused to adjust how she saw herself.

"On that note, Steph, can I be honest with you? I was a little shocked when I heard what you took away from my call with Fred."

"I know. As soon as I finished talking, I thought, I didn't even mention the biggest thing."

"Which is?"

"He said I lack confidence."

"You do," I confirmed.

"I do," she echoed.

I explained that her lack of sureness about herself seemed to have made her highly susceptible to anyone who demonstrated high levels of confidence. Hence why she found herself in the arms of alpha bulldozers that made her question herself even more. It was a vicious cycle that could only end with her decisively pressing *STOP*.

"You kept saying that your problem is mate selection and you're half right, but you also have a responsibility to address your behaviors, provoked or not. You need to find your zone, Steph—that space where there is no uncertainty for you."

I told her about a childhood game that I still like to play with myself when I think about something or someone that's bothering me, called Which One of These Things Doesn't Belong. For example, as a contracted intimacy expert, I am constantly being added to new teams, productions, professional boards, etc. Often when I begin a new project, I come across one person that rubs me the wrong way. When this happens, I start asking myself questions: do I see them exhibit the same problematic nature with others, or just me? Do they seem like a happy person? Have I noted that they often make decisions they feel good about, or are they constantly highly critical? If in the end I see a pattern with their behavior, I depersonalize my experience with them, then try my best going forward to let slights go because I'm not out to fix things that aren't in my garage. But if I notice that there is no pattern and their relationship with me is the anomaly, I change. I troubleshoot the way I've interacted with them and try to switch my approach. I asked Stephanie if we played this game with her life, what would be more out of place: her dissatisfaction with one particular thing, or her satisfaction with anything?

We agreed that she was missing the courage within herself to say *hell yes, Stephanie!* I also emphasized that it was time for her to stop waiting for a man, a self-help book or a job to do that for her.

"What kind of man do you think you'd find happiness with, Steph? Who brings out the best in you?"

She paused for a bit. "Well, for starters, I need to be with someone who views the relationship as a very high priority because of my attachment style."

That kind of powerful self-insight is precisely why the Self-Summary Workbook is crucial. I was very proud to hear her say that.

"We also have to be sexually compatible, have the same politics and he needs to be a strong leader. I don't want to be with someone who can't make a decision."

All right, that statement I was not thrilled with, especially in light of what we had just discussed. How could a bulldozer be her ideal when all this time that type had been her nightmare? It was clear she believed she needed a yang to balance her yin. But I believed she needed to find someone in the center of the Venn diagram just like I knew she was. "Do you consider yourself a follower, a leader or someone who is comfortable in either position?"

"Actually, I am really comfortable in either position," she said, notably confident. "At work, for example, I'm the extrovert and the socializer. If I sense people need a leader, I have no issues stepping up. But if someone else wants to take that role on, or if an extrovert enters the room, I'm okay with letting them take over. I know that can be hard to believe."

It actually wasn't. Stephanie was an outlier who didn't follow the crowd. She studied industrial and labor relations at school because she was passionate about working on policies that were made in the interest of people, not profit. When I asked her to define what political differences she could not tolerate in a potential mate she said plainly, "Anyone who thinks that people who are poor are lazy, are not my kind of people." Underneath the giant question mark she put on everything she did and said was a woman who understood what really mattered to her. That's the woman I needed to bring to the forefront.

We decided that on Stephanie's list of qualities that she wanted in a man, "strong leadership skills" could stay, but "able to take instructions" also needed to be added. I noted that she and Maya had a very similar issue in relation to their aversion to leadership even though it played out in very different ways: while Maya was afraid to speak up for fear of making herself uncomfortable, Stephanie was afraid to own her ground, for fear that she'd be stepping on someone else's.

While I understood where both were coming from, neither of them had a thing to be afraid of: they were intelligent, striking, funny, insightful, compassionate, worldly and fiery. Their greatest mistake was believing that these parts of themselves should be kept a secret.

The next day, when Maya and I connected, she launched into her usual bit: "I really don't know what to expect from this call and that makes me very nervous."

"Really? I've been looking forward to chatting because aside from knowing that you hate capitalism, love teen movies and consider yourself very nervous all the time—I have a lot of blanks to fill in."

She laughed. "Yeah, okay, what else do you wanna know?"

"Everything!"

Maya was an only child of parents who owned a tattoo shop together. Her dad had a full bodysuit of tats and both of her parents were responsible for the eighteen that spanned from Maya's shoulders to her knees. She had a great childhood and attended an arts-focused school in her early years but recalls her anxiety really stepping in when her parents began to put a lot of pressure on her to perform academically. She was only allowed one sleepover a month and remembered being grounded for most of her high school years because she didn't get the right grades or disappointed them in some other area. When she turned eighteen her parents let up on her, but the foundation was set. In college she became extremely reclusive and developed insomnia. After that, her anxiety became so pervasive she was unable to go about basic daily routines. She spent hours on end alone in her dorm and although she had a lot of crushes, she had no romantic connections during that time.

It seemed that Maya's anxiety was formed in response to an immense pressure to perform exceptionally, at all times. This pressure was so severe that it seemed as though she truly believed it was safer not to try something at all, then to try and fail (e.g. with dating). Then again, anxiety doesn't always have an obvious cause, but it does have very clear ramifications. Our nervous system has two distinct operating "platforms"—sympathetic and parasympathetic—and like Mac and PC computers, they can't run at the same time. The sympathetic is responsible for our fight-flight-or-freeze response and our parasympathetic for the calm-and-connect response. In fight-flight-or-freeze, your brain prepares you to respond to crisis by dumping adrenaline into your system, increasing your heart rate, inducing mild hyperventilation, and tensing your muscles, which makes it near impossible to focus on—or connect with—others. In calm-and-connect you're relaxed, your heart rate is normal, and you should be able to focus all your energy on one person or thing.

"Which mode do you think you spend most of your time in?"

"It depends. Around my friends I'm extremely outgoing, funny and relaxed. But if I'm in an unfamiliar or stressful environment I can go into panic mode easy and just close up all together. I've just come to accept it as a part of my life, which sucks."

As odd as this advice may sound, I suggested she stopped loathing her anxiety and instead, started appreciating it for what it was. Our fight-flight-or-freeze response is our bodies' natural way of protecting us from harm. But just like some mamas, some bodies can super overdo it. The trick is in medication for some, exercise for others but I've also heard that talking to your anxiety as if it were a separate person, can work wonders: *hey body, I get that you're scared because you love me and you think I'm in danger—good looking out. But take a good look around, there's nothing to be afraid of and furthermore this fear is making it hard for me to find and love myself. So. I'm going to take a second to let you get comfortable, but then we need to get back in there and be great, together.*

On the flip side, the communication that I observed that was *not* working for Maya, was the kind she did externally. Every meetup we had thus far, she verbally acknowledged and introduced her anxiety as if it was the annoying kid sister she couldn't leave the house without.

"You gotta stop speaking your nerves into existence," I said. "I know in your mind it's the elephant in the room because it weighs so heavy on you, but as you've heard people in the group say many times, they wouldn't know you were nervous if you didn't feel the need to call it out. Your intelligence, confidence in your opinions and wit are what people see when they interact with you, remind yourself of that often."

As you'll recall, the biggest downfall of the Nervous Nelly is that their energy is contagious and thus, repulsive. So, Maya and I came up with a proposed solution: if she felt herself starting to get worked up, instead of announcing it, she needed to give herself a break. She could take a sip of water, ask someone else a question to take the heat off her—hell, she could break out into a dance—literally do anything except call her nerves by name.

Now that we'd spoken about her fearful persona, I wanted to address some of the other impacts of it that I didn't think she was aware of. "I haven't done this with anyone else, but I'd like to read you word for word something I wrote about you based on what I noticed from your Self-Summary Workbook. Is that okay?"

"Yeah, that would be fine."

> When I assessed Maya's Big Five personality reading, I was
> genuinely intrigued, but in hindsight also not surprised. Maya scored
> high in conscientiousness, as she was both honest and organized,
> as well as neuroticism because she was fearful and anxious. But on
> everything else, she was just below room temperature. This made
> sense because I recognized that she was an open-minded person,
> but with her aggressive nerves at play, she was rarely open to new
> ideas. She wasn't an extrovert, but she did demonstrate a confidence
> in social settings that a lot of introverts do not possess. And finally,
> because of her intensity and rigidity she erred on the disagreeable
> side, despite her deep desire to get along with others.

"I think I can see where all of that is coming from," Maya said slowly.

"How do you want to be perceived by others?"

She went quiet for a bit then confidently declared, "Intelligent, passionate and funny."

I nodded. I saw all those things in her because we had developed a rapport, but I rarely saw all of those magical traits at work in the group setting. The other day Maya and I were alone waiting for her Uber when a man who looked like a spoken word performer walked by. Maya said, "Just a note, dating a poet is a hard no for me. Believe me, I went to school for creative writing and have heard enough people complain about their boring lives with creative line breaks and grammar to know I can never date one. I couldn't care less about how eating croissants reminds someone of their ex."

I laughed and thought to myself, *I wish the whole group could hear and see her now.*

"Speaking of others, you know, I've been really disappointed with myself that I haven't been able to connect with one person in the group," said Maya.

This was one cross I would not let her bear alone. No one in the group had developed an outside relationship with another member, but that's why it was important to remember what had brought this group together to begin with: everyone struggled to make intimate connections. And that's why I instructed Maya to start approaching my experiment as her own experiment. "Use our meetups as the testing ground for intelligent, passionate and funny Maya! Practice the version of yourself that you want to be perceived as."

"Okay," she said. "Okay."

We ended our call on a much lighter note than it had begun and that was a victory in my books. One Nervous Nelly down, and one to go.

A couple of days later, I connected with Deshawn. As expected, out the gate she sounded hella apprehensive, so I put down the big guns and began with gratitude.

"Deshawn, I just wanna say thank you for your warmth and openness; you are the personification of a home-cooked meal. You have really been a bright spot throughout this whole process, and I know everyone is really rooting for you. But how have things been from your perspective?"

"It's been . . ." Deshawn exhaled and shuffled around, ". . . tough."

"Tough?"

"Yeah, I hope that's okay for me to say but there was definitely a time where I seriously felt like quitting. I've never had to look at myself this way before and it's been uncomfortable and brought up a lot of things I didn't realize were there. I even ended up getting in a big fight with my grandma about it because she called me out on a few things. It's just been a lot. But I slept on it and when I woke up, I felt like, 'okay, at least I am now recognizing what's going wrong and that's a start.'"

I revealed to Deshawn what I had learned from my previous

phone calls: everyone else at one time considered quitting the group. I didn't take it personally since this program included a lot of tough critiquing in a short amount of time.

"Sure, pressure makes diamonds," I continued. "But it also causes meltdowns, so it's totally understandable what you've gone through and I promise going forward it gets much easier and more fun. But, that being said, right now are you up for some more uncomfortable honesty?"

"Oh Lord," she laughed. "No, but I mean, sure, why not. Let's do it."

I revealed to Deshawn what I had observed about her from day one: she was a smart and fascinating woman who tended to present herself like a quirky teen who was still trying to find her homeroom. I knew for a fact that she had so much knowledge to offer and so much value to bring to every room, but I hadn't seen her leave that mark any of the times we had shared together.

"Okay, so what am I supposed to do to change that?"

"I want to see you step into your expertise more. I know you think your job is boring to people but maybe you just have to find the angle where it's interesting. Heck, everyone drinks water, it shouldn't be that hard! Find those spaces that you can showcase the intelligent, secure and adult Deshawn. I'm not saying to get rid of your youthful glow, I love that about you. But right now, you are somewhere between a zero fucks seducer and a Peter Pan anti-seducer that still lives with her mom; I just wanna see you lean more into the former. You can be playful without being childish."

"Yes," she said slowly. "It makes a lot of sense. As I told you in the past, I tend to get friend-zoned a lot. I'll get close to someone only for them to stop seeing me in that kind of way, so yeah, I can understand that. It's been a long time since I've had sex and I'd like to do that with someone—and do it well—soon. So, getting a little sexier is something I can get on board with."

That last line stunned me just a bit. Deshawn was the church girl in the group and even though I knew she wasn't a virgin, I didn't know she wasn't abstinent by choice. I thought back on her workbook and her horngry description of her Turn-On Trigger. It dawned on me that part of what was holding her back from presenting like a sexual woman was that she wasn't finding opportunities to explode into her sexual side. I made a note to add that to the list of things that had to change.

"Speaking of men from your past, I wanna get into what your exes said about you not listening. Do you know what they meant?"

"Not really."

I did. After observing her during the informal parts of our group meetings, I could see where they were coming from. So, I pointed out to her that talking a little less and listening a lot more, was actually just an extension of what we'd already been discussing, maturity. As children, we aren't expected to be interested in others, instead, it's other people's job to engage with us. But eventually that *has* to flip if we want to participate in a mutually satisfying, adult connection. This problem is so rampant in our me-me culture, that I'd bet my last dollar you can think of at least one full-grown person who never got that memo.

But in Deshawn's defense, she wasn't a long talker. Instead, she failed to give people the opportunity to elaborate. As soon as someone told a personal story, instead of asking them a follow-up question, she'd immediately launch into a parallel experience of her own. And while yes, it's great to relate, if we don't ask follow-up questions once in a while, it gives off the impression that we're competing or that we were only listening for a break in conversation so we could talk about ourselves again.

I didn't think that was Deshawn's motivation, but I did think this bad habit formed with good intentions in reaction to her past. Deshawn grew up in a family that couldn't relate to her, so I believe she became overly focused on jumping on every opportunity to immediately point out what she had in common with others.

"So, try this in conversation instead: when someone shares

something that you can connect to, ask them at least one follow-up question before adding on to the discussion. Sound doable?"

"Okay, so be more comfortable stepping into my expertise, show my sensual side more and ask more questions about another's experiences before going on about my own?"

"Exactly. I call this the two to one ratio: for every one question that someone asks you, be mindful to ask them two in return. Trust me it works wonders. If I could offer one piece of advice for how to make a first date go well, that would be it."

Pricilla and I connected a couple of days later around noon. For the first time, we spoke at length about her son, and after over a month of knowing her, I finally learned his name.

In light of this, I told Pricilla that I appreciated that she didn't define herself as only a mom, since being a mother should be a wonderful part of someone's identity, not a substitution for it. But I also pointed out that she tended to shy away from talking about it altogether. I explained that being the only mother in the group gave her a unique kind of power and knowledge that she should be proud of. And speaking of pride, she had exceptional self-insight, exemplified by the personal workbook and exes' feedback activity, but again, in both instances she had waited to share last, as if she didn't have much to add to the conversation.

Everything about Pricilla since we began the program begged the question, "Why are you so afraid to call attention to yourself?"

"I guess if I think about it, being the center of attention as a child was never a positive experience for me. If you brought too much attention to yourself it was a problem, and if you were receiving a lot of attention it was because you did something bad. So I just prefer to stay out of the spotlight."

"Do you not step up because you think you have nothing to offer or because you are afraid people will think you have nothing to offer?"

"A bit of both, I guess. I'm just scared people will judge me or that I'll say something stupid or wrong. For example, a lot of times in the group I'll have something I want to say, but it takes me so long to decide to do it, that by the time I'm ready to talk, the subject has changed. How do you stop second-guessing yourself?"

"You don't," I said.

This is something I made peace with a while ago: the human condition is designed for us to be progressive, not content. The same reason why there's a new smartphone, new tallest building and new cure every other day is the exact same reason why there's always going to be something about ourselves we don't like. Think about it: when other mammals like cats and dogs have all their needs met—they're safe from predators, they have shelter, they have food and water—what do they do? They find a patch of sun to nap in, chill out and wait for their owner to play with them. If humans were pets, they'd be trying to find ways to transform their beds into cannons. We are by nature constantly asking the question, *how can this be better?* The bright side is that this question challenges us to improve our lives. For example, if it weren't for the person who thought, "I can't take this shit!" we wouldn't enjoy the luxury of toilet paper today. The downside of asking this question is that we're rarely satisfied with our own reflection. Your critical voice and your innovative voice are the exact same thing—it's what makes us dreamers, creators and yes, sometimes miserable as all hell.

"You've just got to learn when that voice is helpful and when it's a hindrance. For me, I mute my critical voice when I'm actively doing something and then I turn the volume back up as soon as I'm done and alone again. That being said, I don't think the issue is just *your* voice, Pricilla. I think you're keeping your mom's trapped up there too."

"Yeah, maybe," she replied.

"And don't get me wrong, it can be good to take on the critical eye of others if it helps us improve, as we did with the ex's exercise. But, if that person's critical voice never shuts up, you need to find the *mute* button for the sake of your growth and sanity. In general, I'll hear anyone out, but when it comes to making decisions, I only take heed to what happy people have to say. You have to ask yourself, if your mom or anyone else who has put this doubt in you, is happy with themselves."

Pricilla sighed. "I know you hate it when people just agree because that's the mark of the shadow type, but I don't know what else to say because I do agree. So just know that I hear you."

"Okay, good."

I had to accept that being heard by Pricilla may be the best I was going to get. Like Maya had pointed out, she always left me wanting to hear more from her, but I was grateful for the honesty and vulnerability she had shared. Plus, even though change is the only constant in the world, that doesn't mean transformations should be instant. When it comes to changing your character it's more realistic to expect that process will happen at the same speed that rocks turn to sand. Of course, I hoped the program would speed up that erosion, but hope is all you can do when it comes to someone else's personal journey.

For the remainder of our conversation Pricilla remained adamant that she was better off in the background as a support system, not as a leader. In a romantic partnership she wanted someone who was looking for a cheerleader and possibly a coach, not a starting player.

I asked her the question I posed to Stephanie. "When are you at your happiest? When you are leading or when you are being led?"

She said, "When I'm being supportive."

"Okay," I said, getting the message. "I do think you could step up your role as a supporter. People naturally look to you for approval, so try to be mindful of that."

"I can do that," she replied.

You could probably do anything if you let yourself try, I thought.

LAST BUT NOT LEAST, CHERISE AND I WERE FINALLY ABLE TO MAKE TIME TO connect. Given that our relationship had been the least fluid in the group this was the conversation that I was most nervous about.

But taking my own advice to Maya, I didn't mention that. Instead I tackled that elephant from a different direction by explaining that our choppy relationship was actually a good thing because it allowed me to get a clearer picture of what's been holding her back in the dating space.

"I just want you to note that while I'm talking about our personal experience, I've taken none of this personally. My purpose in your life is to help you. I appreciate that you show up and that you've been willing to at least try everything, but I don't know if you've liked or found value in any of it. You have never said a kind thing to me. You seem closed off to showing gratitude, but I've noticed your comfort in issuing criticism."

Cherise cleared her throat. "I mean, I used to be nice and open with everyone, but I've gotten burned so many times. I've been in abusive relationships and I've had friends backstab me. I also grew up watching my mother be so kind to my father and he'd just turn around and abuse her and then verbally abuse all of us."

That response threw me for a bit of a loop, but I rolled with it. I affirmed the importance of protecting herself from disturbed and manipulative people. But I asked if it was possible that using that same approach for everyone was hurtful to those trying to do good in her life. As I was.

"I mean, maybe but in regard to me not saying thank you to you, I just figured you were doing things for the project, and they are things you outlined from the beginning you'd be doing. It never really felt personal. Like, I don't think, *Wow, look what she's done for me.*"

I explained to her something that I had already said a few times to the group: good habits are worth way more than perfect incidents. Meaning, if someone does something for you that's kind of what you like, it's more to your benefit to applaud them than to red-marker them. Otherwise you run the risk that person may stop altogether, in fear that you aren't pleased with anything that they do. If you asked me what Cherise did not like, I could tell you, but what she did? I had zero clue, so I asked again.

"It's hard to say. Look, everything also happens so fast and it's like we're always on to the next thing without getting time to absorb it," she continued. "Like, how are we supposed to put any of these things into practice if we barely have time to understand it?"

I explained that with any program, the pace is going to work great for some and not so great for others. In our group, I felt there were two people who had really kept up and excelled, two who were somewhere in the middle and one other person who also felt a little overwhelmed.

"We can always go back or slow down, depending on your needs. I'm available in between group meetups too. We can even work on that now, what are some of the things you're still struggling with?"

"How to talk to people, I guess. But then again, sometimes I don't want to be talked to. There isn't a perfect way to say this but as a beautiful woman, people come and talk to me all the time. It's hard for me because people always notice me and then they feel compelled to start a conversation even when there's nothing to say. I just wanna be in the cut sometimes, just observing. I don't always want so much attention."

Again, I pointed out that she was placing the focus on the negative. I noted that even through her Self-Summary Workbook, which was the most vulnerable I'd seen her, what was often missing from her recounts was an upside or actionable solution. It's great to know what you don't want, but you can also express that by sharing what you do. This is the yum vs. yuck approach. For example, if someone is not a killer kisser you can say, *Yuck, can you stop opening your mouth so wide because you're dripping saliva everywhere.* Or you can say, *Yum, I love it when you kiss me with your lips slightly parted because it gives me just enough of you, while leaving me wanting more.*

"I don't know how to be anything else but honest and it's taken me a while to get that way. If people do some fuck shit, I let them know right away. I used to let things slide but now I let someone know as soon as they step out of line."

"Trust me," I affirmed. "I am not one of those positive-thoughts-only people. I'm not telling you to ignore your feelings or to manipulate your truth, I'm just saying there's a lot of good out there and just like you had to make a conscious effort to start discussing what bothers you, you may have to start making that same effort to be more positive."

In a stunning turn of events, she didn't rush to defend this time. Instead she just said, "All right, I can appreciate that. I can receive that."

We spoke for some time longer: I asked her about her opinion on the other women in the group, her friendships, and we talked a bit about her career. At the two-hour mark I gave her an out to end the call and reiterated she could call me anytime if she needed more guidance.

She took the out but before she left, she offered an olive branch: "I just wanna say thank you and I do appreciate your time, I know we've been talking for a couple hours. And you know, I am grateful to be a part of this and I'm glad I said fuck it and signed up for this. I really am."

"Thank you for saying that. That really does mean a lot coming from you. And I'm grateful you are a part of this too; I think you bring something very unique to the group."

And that time, I also genuinely meant every word.

That night, Cherise sent over a couple of assignments she hadn't completed and responded to a slew of emails I figured she had been too busy to read. With that phone call completed, Phase Two was now officially over. But, as Cherise had pointed out, this program's schedule didn't leave a lot of time for tarrying. The next step was all about learning and that included bringing together a series of dating experts from a variety of fields, to ensure they had the best information, in order to bring their best to the table. In short, my butt needed to get back to my desk and back to work!

As I refocused my mind on how far we still had to go, I got an insanely beautiful reminder that for at least one person, we had come a hell of a long way:

Ok, so go ahead and put me on a payment plan for your services because with our call you gave me a confidence that I wouldn't have been able to build on my own. I legit feel marketable and datable now. You lifted this huge-ass weight and gloomy cloud I was walking around with. Ok let me go, 'cause I'm like seriously crying and having a huge emotional release right now. You are so refreshing and inspiring and say the simplest things that create positive massive waves of great change. You're literally a caffeinated iced tea! Thank you!! Thank you so much, Shannon.

—Courtney

And while it would be grand to end the chapter with that, there's more to this story. Two days after my call with Cherise an email with the subject line *This isn't for me* came in. She cited her departure due to several things but mostly focused on one: she felt the program was filled with too much criticism that she didn't like or need.

I sent a response to request that we talk it out. I encouraged her to stick with the process because she had come so far, and even if things didn't make sense now, in the end they would. Unfortunately, she never responded. Although it hurt to lose her on this journey, I was also able to see the beautiful irony in the timing of her email: everyone else had gotten their harsh review, why shouldn't I have also gotten mine? Cherise's perspective that no one should have to change, again, was a popular one and who knows, maybe even the correct one for her. Neither of us had a glimpse into the future, and I truly hoped that she eventually would find the right fit for her, on terms she felt good about.

When I shared the news with the rest of the group, Deshawn, who seemed to be maturing before my eyes, put the perfect button on it. "This whole time you've been encouraging us to find our power and step into our expertise. It's unfortunate that as soon as Cherise found hers, she quit."

Phase Three: Learn

PART ONE

———→ ›‹ ‹———

Learn how to target, find and connect
with your ideal playmate(s).

— → *8* ←—

FIANCÉ, F*CK BUDDY OR FINANCIAL SPONSOR?

The five original, and now remaining, women gathered at my place a couple days later so we could begin Phase Three. I announced that we would be doing a 180 in our approach, then led them back to my office where I'd prepared something that I was really excited about.

"Now that you've gotten to know yourself, I think it's a good time to start getting to know your future boo. So, this is what we're working on today." I gestured to my large dry erase board, which was covered with the following:

Job title(s): Who are you looking for? A long-term partner? Fuck buddy? Financial sponsor? List all titles here and complete one job listing for each.

Job location/term: How close do candidates need to live to you? Are you looking for someone contract, part-time or full-time?

Preferred experience level/age:

Frozen Five requirements: a candidate cannot be considered for employment if they fail to meet these.

Skills of interest: Anything that didn't make your top five which is still important to you, place here.

Areas of flexibility: What are some attributes/habits of potential candidates that you can work with, even though others may view these as a deal breaker?

Do-not-applies: What are the attributes/morals/values that you know don't bring out the best in you? List your deal breakers.

Job perks: What makes this position incredible? List all the things that you have to offer that make this role a once-in-a-lifetime opportunity.

Job description: Using your answers above, summarize the role you are offering and the ideal candidate who you hope will occupy it.

I handed out paper and pens while Stephanie eyed me and the board suspiciously. "Wait, we're working on work?" she asked.

"Oooooh no, I think I know what this is." Courtney clapped excitedly. She dug in her purse and pulled out her soft case of gel pens and markers. "Does anyone want to write with one of these instead?"

I continued. "This activity is going to serve as the basis of everything we will be doing moving forward and it's what we'll be using to attract your dream mate. It should be fun!"

"By putting an ad in the classifieds?" questioned Deshawn.

"Wait," said Pricilla, as though she'd just clued in. "We're not, like, putting this out there, are we?"

The job listing method is something I invented in early 2015, during my prime of online dating. Sorting through mass amounts of profiles proved to be arduous and uninspiring, especially since I wasn't 100 percent sure what I was looking for. So I sat down one night and developed a simple list of my criteria: loves, likes and dislikes. Then I added a few other things, like how far I was willing to travel to see someone and what age range I was comfortable with. When I was finished, I looked over what I had done and thought, *Well, damn, it looks like I'm looking for an employee.* And that's when the lightbulb went off: *That is precisely what dating is.*

Think of yourself as a multibillion-dollar corporation. You, of course, are the CEO. Sure, you might have some family and friends on your board of trustees but ultimately this is your company. You have worked your ass off building this thing from the ground up into the successful, highly respected and above all, precious entity that it is. So, are you going to consider hiring any random schmo for your executive suite just because they took a selfie with a tiger?

Creating the job listing makes it clear who qualifies, who doesn't and who seems like a decent fit to work in maintenance or perhaps even as an intern. At any given time, you could be looking for people to fill several different positions and if so, make a unique listing for each. Maybe you're looking for a friend with benefits, a workout buddy, a mentor, a financial sponsor and/or a life partner. The clearer you can be about what qualities make up the right candidates, the fewer opportunities the wrong ones will have to waste your time. I firmly believe you can have a relationship with anyone, but I also believe you need to be realistic about what kind of relationship that person is capable of successfully having with you. In the romantic department most people are simply searching for a long-term partner and if you're new to this, that's where you should start. Don't get lured into opening more complex positions like friends with benefits unless you are disciplined enough to see beyond any biologically induced passion that isn't based on your logical needs. Relationships built on proximity, availability or mutual loneliness are not the goal of this book, and, as a matter of fact, they are the nemesis.

Sadly, I've worked with so many people who made the mistake of promoting their plumber to their executive suite simply because that person knew how to lay the pipe. So if you feel yourself making this mistake, review your listing for a long-term lover and remind yourself that your loyalty needs to be reserved for the success of your company, not for the company you keep.

"No, you're not going to post this anywhere," I said, answering Pricilla's question. "This is for internal use only and it's going to massively help us, especially during our final assignment, where you'll be required to date someone of high interest. A high-interest playmate has to pass your Frozen Five test."

"This is going to be a short assignment for me," said Pricilla. "I'm just going to describe Matt Barnes."

This wasn't the first time Pricilla had brought up Matt Barnes, an ex-NBA-champion-turned-philanthropist-and-businessman. In our very first in-person meeting she identified him as her ideal type and when I asked her why, she explained that he embodied everything on her wish list: handsome, tall, successful, charitable, tattooed and, above all else, he was a loving parent. I hadn't thought of this until that moment, but I had actually met Matt briefly a few years prior when we were both guests on Keke Palmer's daytime show, *Just Keke*. I wondered if he still remembered me and figured it was worth a shot to find out . . .

"But wait, how are we supposed to know how to fill this in?" asked Stephanie. "Just like your standard tall-dark-handsome stuff?"

"Excellent question." I beamed then pointed to another dry erase board that had a list of twenty-six crucial traits that make up a romantic bond. This was my absolute favorite activity I had developed after reading *The Science of Happily Ever After*, by Dr. Ty Tashira. I instructed the group to look over this list and rank each trait in order from most to least important. "Your top five will serve as your Frozen Five and how you order the rest can help inform the remainder of your job post."

For everyone reading this book I highly suggest you participate in this activity as well. So go ahead and shuffle this list around until it is arranged from what's most to least important to you in a romantic partnership:

Agreeable (easy to get along with)

Emotionally stable

Securely attached

High novelty seeking (likes to do new things)

Supportive/happy for my good news

Intelligent

Physically attractive

Takes responsibility for self

Unlikely to withdraw (not avoidantly attached)

Has similar interests

Has similar values

Speaks my love language

Good life skills (cooking, cleaning, budgeting, building, etc. . . .)

Wants children

Sexually compatible

Financially well off

Charming/humorous

Trustworthy

Faithful

Strong leadership skills

Follows directions/allows others to take the lead

Highly ambitious

Independent thinker

Compatible with my friends and family

Excellent conflict-resolution skills

Has good relationships with others

Speaks my apology language

Once you have finished ranking, take a second to analyze your Frozen Five. Then look at your bottom five. Do you see any patterns that jump out? Also, try comparing your previous romantic partners against this ranking—would they qualify, if you knew then what you do now? If you need an example of what the finished product of the job listing exercises should look like, Deshawn agreed to share hers with you.

Job title: *A long-term partner/relationship*

Job location/term: *Full-time, L.A. County, 50 miles or closer*

Preferred experience level/age: *25–35, has had at least one long-term relationship*

Basic requirements (the Frozen Five)

1. Intelligent. *They need to have expertise in something that they do.*
2. Has good relationships with others. *They must know and be committed to a deep, family/family-like bond.*

3. Sexually compatible. *I love when someone makes me feel sexy. Seeing and feeling when someone wants me is important. I want to feel seen and be felt.*

4. Shared politics/outlook on life. *It's important that people treat people different from them with dignity. I have compassion for others and that is my outlook on life.*

5. Financially independent. *You must be able to pay your rent and bills then also have a disposable income.*

Skills of interest *Speaks my apology language, securely attached, physically attractive, speaks my love language, similar interests, wants children, trustworthy, faithful, partnership oriented, takes leadership, knows how to take instructions, high novelty seeking, knowledgeable about black culture/ race relations specifically in the U.S.*

Areas of flexibility *Fashion sense, drinking, smoking, living with parents, personal grooming, sexual experience, religion, race.*

Do-not-applies *Trump supporters, narcissists, misogynists, people who are selectively respectful, people who are gym obsessed or diet obsessed, pessimists, people who pressure me to "keep up appearances."*

Job perks *When you work with Deshawn, you get: an honest person, very loving (I cater to people's specific love language), faith oriented (non-denominational Christian), ambitious, compassionate, intelligent, excellent scrambled eggs with cheese, great blow jobs, skilled gift giver, high novelty seeker, witty, excellent kisser, flexible, easy-going, charismatic.*

Job description *An independent, adventure-loving, intelligent lady in the streets/freak in the sheets is seeking a full-time boyfriend. Successful candidate must be intelligent, family oriented and be well-versed in current affairs. This role has flexible hours, lots of making out, hikes and will encourage you to use Uber Eats far more than you probably already do—unless you're in the mood for eggs. Oh, must love dogs and must not be a dog.*

If, like Deshawn, you completed this exercise thoroughly, you should start to get a clearer picture of what occupation this person is likely to be in and where they might hang out in their free time.

Here's what we were able to determine after examining the group's completed job listings:

Deshawn was looking to date herself: an intelligent, community-focused, family oriented, sexually apt person who cared more about adventure than aesthetics.

Pricilla was in fact looking for someone who was loosely like Matt Barnes.

Stephanie was looking for someone dedicated to the betterment of others—like a teacher or a personal trainer.

Courtney wanted someone brave and strong, with exceptional life skills and a steady paycheck. A firefighter would be the perfect fit.

Maya also wanted to date herself, except she wanted the version that she hadn't quite stepped into yet: outgoing, funny and brave in their pursuit of who and what they loved.

While I think everyone should complete this activity (and I've made it easy for you by giving you a blank template on TheGameofDesire.com/joblisting) I'm going to underline and put a star beside it for anyone who lives in a big city and/or those planning on looking for love online. The women in my group ticked off both of those boxes. So, to make sure they were extra prepared, I called on two professionals whom I admired: Chief Marketing Officer of OkCupid Melissa Hobley, and Meredith Davis, head of communications for the exclusive dating app The League.

Meredith connected with us via Google Hangouts from The League's birthplace and headquarters in San Francisco. She was the second employee to join the company and cited that she knew it was the job for her when she learned their tagline, "Date intelligently."

"So how do we do that?" I asked after the introductions. "How do we online date and come up with more than just ridiculous stories to tell our friends?"

"The League earned a reputation for being an elitist Tinder, but in actuality we just saw a market for a dating service that didn't allow anyone with a phone access. So this is not a plug but honestly, the best thing you can do is use dating apps that have some form of quality control. After you've done that, there's a bunch of other really interesting things you can do with your

How to Make Your Best Dating Profile
by Meredith Davis

Photos

Wardrobe: Wear white or solid bright colors.

Expression: Smile, leave the duckface for Instagram.

Communication: Make sure your pictures aren't just about looking good. They need to tell your story.

Picture 1: a great head shot with eye contact (think of magazine covers)

Picture 2: travel/you doing something out of the ordinary (full body if possible)

Picture 3: you doing something normal that you love (eating, hanging with friends, painting, reading, etc. . . .)

Picture 4: a group shot, because it communicates a lot about who you are, including your height.

Picture 5: your choice (you with an animal, you at a wedding, a professional pic of you, etc.)

Picture 6: Your weed-out photo. If there is something that is an intrinsic part of you that is going to be a make-or-break for others, put it here to save yourself time. (Do you smoke? Are you heavy into politics?)

After you have selected your six photos ask yourself: Can someone come up with three questions per photo? If so, move on to your "about me."

About me

This is a place to give someone a taste of you. This is *not* your biography, so keep it short (fewer than two hundred words) but not too short because that shows low investment.

profile to get the most out of your experience. Should I just list them?"

"Hell yeah!"

Your "about me" should be regarded as a conversation starter. Here are some rules of thumb:

Do

- Make statements that invite people to start a discussion with you (*I was born in Cali and know where to get the absolute best carnitas*).
- Invite people to ask a question (*Ask me about my second photo . . .*).
- Show your favorite thing about your personality.

Do not

- List your criteria (*must be tall, university educated and love animals*).
- List your weed-out criteria (*Looking for a hookup? Don't waste my time!*). First, sleazy people don't *read* on dating apps so you're wasting your time and second, when we tell people what we don't want, we indicate what we've already had and we tend to come across as bitter.
- Just put a link to your Instagram. If you're too lazy to write something, what makes you think people won't be too lazy to open an entirely different app to get to know you?

Crafting the First Message

Make it meaningful

Look at a profile and comment on something specific that you like or have a question about. Saying "hey" in a first message is almost equivalent to saying nothing—in fact, the vast majority of "hey" messages never get a response at all.

Make your first message brief, but not short

Messages with the best chance of a reply are between 40 and 100 characters long (again, saying "hey" twenty times isn't going to cut it). Something like, "I see you went to Paris, what was your favorite café?" should suffice.

Next, we connected with CMO Melissa Hobley to discuss how to make your dating apps work for you and not the other way around.

"First and foremost, people can't be afraid to put the work in," said Melissa from OkCupid's headquarters in New York. "At OkCupid we actually just came up with the term *storking*. Storking is when someone deeply desires a serious, romantic relationship but doesn't put in any effort." Instead, they just hope their dream lover turns up on their doorstep.

As I've said several times, you don't get great results at practically anything without putting the work in, BUT, there's a difference between working hard and working smart. Melissa gave us six pro tips on how to do the latter:

How to Make Your Profile Work for You by Melissa Hobley

1. Invest energy in the setup. Spend more time setting up your profile and you'll spend less time turning the creeps away and ultimately more time on meaningful dates. OkCupid has over one thousand iconic questions. You don't have to answer them all, but in order to activate your profile you must answer at minimum fifteen. My advice is to answer as many questions as you can, fill in every field, even if it isn't required and add at least four pictures. The more you do, the more accurate your matches will be and the more you'll stand out from the crowd.

2. Update your profile often. General rule of thumb for how to get the most out of dating apps? Write well, edit often. Just because you made a résumé once doesn't mean that you don't continuously tweak it until you land the job you're looking for, right? So get into a routine of adding a new photo at least once a week and answering new questions or tweaking your profile every five days.

3. Manipulate the algorithm. The more you use the product and update your dating apps, the more the algorithm will show you to different peo-

ple. It makes sense that dating apps would prioritize members who are active since their goal is to connect people. If you stop participating on the app, you're telling it to stop prioritizing you. You've probably heard of an Elo score, a way that dating apps rank their users internally. Most people think that's solely based on how many likes they get—not true. Most dating apps also consider how many rejections versus likes you make and how responsive you are once matched with someone.

4. Message first. Women who message first are two and a half times more likely to get a response. OkCupid's studies show that when women message first, the chances of a longer-term interaction are much higher.

5. Avoid hypnosis. Most people who experience online-dater burnout do so because they feel disconnected, which is odd since, again, the goal is to connect with people. You can keep up the search and keep your sanity by limiting the time you spend mindlessly swiping. If you swipe for too long, you go into a trance-like state similar to hypnosis. So if you get one or two matches, that's great; switch to the message section then give the app a rest.

6. Be open to those outside of your usual physical type. There is an unprecedented rise in interracial marriages and that is directly correlated to when Tinder launched. Dating apps help you think outside the box on who you would typically date, so don't just go for your type—and see where it lands you. Remember, practice makes perfect. Not everyone has to be the one; you just need to connect with great people who help you get closer to figuring out what you want.

Melissa's advice, especially that last nugget, is exactly why I loved my online dating experience so much. I met a number of incredible people of all origins and ethnicities who greatly improved my quality of life in L.A. and my impression of dating as a whole. I met lawyers, artists, actors, motivational speakers—all sorts of people who gave me more clarity about what I really wanted! I know it's typical for people to rag on digital dating and that's precisely why you shouldn't. If you've read this far, you are no longer a typical person and you definitely don't have a typical approach, so why not expect atypical success?

"Dating is neutral," I said to the group after our sessions with Meredith and Melissa. "It is neither good nor bad, it is simply what you assign it to be because—remember—you are in control of your reality."

"I get that, but dating is also not all in your control since there's still a whole other variable involved that's separate from you," countered Maya.

I took this as an opportunity to remind them of what they wrote on their initial applications: Deshawn said dating is awkward, Pricilla described it as stressful, Courtney referred to it as an opportunity to see through people's BS and Maya wrote that she was still trying to convince herself that she was worthy of it.

"If you met women who saw dating as a negative and then they told you they were disappointed with their romantic lives, would you be remotely surprised?"

"No," responded Courtney. "And you know what, I think it's about time we all started surprising ourselves."

I smiled, beyond grateful that someone else said it because I was growing tired of slicing through everyone's skepticism like Fruit Ninja. I could continue to offer up tools and solutions but eventually they had to change their own minds, and at this point they were running out of excuses not to. Before we went our separate ways, I encouraged the group to start building their online dating profiles using the pictures we had taken a couple of meetups earlier. As an update, I'm glad to say that we got one shot of Maya that she absolutely loved and had already begun to use "everywhere."

The important thing to note in this chapter about dating online is that you can't be passive about it. Literally, you can either go hard or *don't* go home (perhaps go to the Apple Store because in my opinion, that's a great place to meet singles in real life because it's well lit, attracts a wide range of people and provides an atmosphere that's easy to start an organic conversation in). There are apps, like The League, that promise to do some of the heavy lifting for you through their extensive vetting process and their promise to remove anyone who has been reported as problematic, but not everyone can afford or get into exclusive platforms. Thus, it's best to get into the habit of doing this yourself by being clear about what you're looking for, choosing an app where that archetype is likely to be, being thoughtful about your profile and developing an efficient system to maximize your safety and optimize your experience.

Here is the online dating system that I created and refer to all my friends and clients:

---

1. If you match, be the first to message and ask a question based on their profile that gives them the opportunity to reveal their personality.

2. If they respond favorably, continue the chat by asking questions, in a subtle way, to see if they qualify under your Frozen Five standards.

3. Once you've established they meet at least two of your standards, set up a phone call with them so you can hear each other's voice. Don't worry, you don't have to give out your number, Google Voice is your friend!

4. If the call doesn't go well, unmatch with them and continue your search. If the call does go well, set up a time to meet at a place that is within five miles of your work or home. This is partly for safety but mostly because you're trying to save yourself from burning out.

5. Ahead of the date, create a time expectation for your encounter: *I am so hype to meet you at 7 tonight. I have plans after so I'll definitely try to get there on time, if not a lil earlier.*

   In my books, setting a time limit for the first date is a must. First, if you want to screen for people who just want to hook up, this will be a deterrent. Second, no matter how much vetting you do before you meet someone, in truth it is nearly impossible to assess if you'll click until you get some actual face time. It's best to look at online dating like

making ramen: you make sure you have all the right ingredients before-
hand, but you won't know if there will be any broth, aka chemistry, until
you're face-to-face. Again, if you do the vetting well, even if there is no
broth, you won't be at a loss; you'll still have stir-fry, thus a decent time
with a decent person. But if there's broth and you both have the right
ingredients—soup's on, baby!

6. Phone a friend. Let someone know where you're going, who you're going
   with, and what time they should call to check in. Safety first, plus if you
   want an out, a well-timed call from a friend can be clutch!

You might be wondering, then what? How do you flirt once
you recognize there's chemistry? How do you secure a second date?
What if you don't wanna date online at all, how do you get to the
ramen-making phase? These are all excellent questions. I knew I
had to dig deeper than Google to deliver answers that would truly
help women, of all walks of life, become masters of dating. And as
we all know, the fastest way to become the best, is to learn from
the best.

So, with that in mind, I have a riddle for you: What do an
androgynous lesbian, a male pickup artist, a phone sex operator,
a stripper and a three-time black belt champion have in common?

Phase Three:
Learn

PART TWO

>———➤◄———•

*Learn from a series of experts how to
become a master at flirting, attracting,
approaching and influencing.*

9

THE 6-FIGURE FLIRT

A tiny miracle about the group of women I chose for this program is that they all had steady jobs and predictable hours. Depending on where you live that may not sound like much, but in L.A. people's schedules are usually as compatible as orange juice and toothpaste. So, I asked everyone if they could block out an entire weekend for me and like magic, there we all were (with the exception of Pricilla who had mama duties) that same Saturday morning. Stephanie, Deshawn, Court and Maya sat shoulder-to-shoulder on the couch while they stared, awestruck at our flirting expert, Ari Fitz.

Ari is not just a close friend of mine, she's also simply put the most flirtatious and seductive person I've ever met. She is a model, digital content creator and filmmaker who fully embraces her identity as a black, queer, androgynous woman by sharing unique stories about gender and identity through fashion and vulnerability. Knowing that the group would love her just as much as me, I asked her to come by to teach us all her flirty ways.

"First of all, I'm really honored to be in this space with such an incredible group of women." Ari sat down, leaned in and pressed her hands together. "Okay, so before I tell you what I think, I'm curious—what do you all think of flirting?"

Everyone stiffened then let out a unanimous nervous laugh.

"Okay, I can pick someone. Stephanie, you look like you're deep in thought."

"No, I'm not. I have, like, no idea but, um, I guess it's what you do to let another person know that you are sexually or romantically interested?"

"I have no clue what flirting is," added Deshawn. "I guess I can recognize when other people are doing it but this has been a lifelong struggle for me so I can't really define it for myself."

"None of those answers are wrong but you guys are making it too complicated," said Ari. "To me, flirting is just communication plus sparks."

There was a chorus of approval. Courtney dug in her bag for her trusty marker collection and notepad then jotted those words down.

"The first thing I wanna teach you about flirting is that intent is everything. It's very easy to get caught up in how amazing or good-looking someone is, but then your intent ends up being to get this perceived, great person to like you. If you approach someone like that, with your needs laid bare, you've automatically put yourself at a huge disadvantage because flirting needs two things to thrive: confidence and mystery."

Ari said that in order to get good at flirting she first had to recognize that she herself was a dope-ass person who people, no matter how hot or cool, were fortunate to be around. No longer was it, *Will this person like me?* but instead, *Is this person interesting enough for me to hold an enjoyable conversation with?*

"Once I flipped it and removed the need to be liked, the whole game changed for me. Now, I don't flirt with expectation, I do it constantly because it makes me and others feel good," said Ari. "I flirt when I get into an Uber because it makes the ride more interesting, I flirt at the bar because just sitting there is boring, I flirt in meetings because it loosens people up to new ideas, I flirt while waiting in line for the bathroom because doing the I-gotta-pee dance is just not sexy."

"Okay so you do it a lot, but what exactly do you do?" asked Courtney with her neon gel pen pressed to the page, ready to rock.

Ari prefaced her explanation by stating that the first rule of flirting is to never make your actions seem disingenuous—and nothing screams phony more than a step-by-step guide. But, this being a very special circumstance and all, she was willing to put that rule to the side.

How to Flirt by Ari Fitz

1. Body position. You can get different reactions from people based on how you position your body. If you're on a date with someone, be conscious of where your gaze is falling. Are you looking up, down or straight across at the person? Those all communicate very different things in flirting. As a queer woman comfortable in my masculinity, if I want to create a sexual connection with someone I tend to straighten up—that's me being daddy, aka the dominant. If I want to be relatable and easy to connect to, I meet the other person on their level. If I want to appear innocent and coy, I look up at them.

   Shan says: Height is important, as is shape. A straight body communicates power and dominance, a hunched body can communicate a lack of confidence and an S-shaped body demonstrates sensuality. Sitting in an S means that you take advantage of contrasting curves, so perhaps your head is tilted to the left and your hips are pushed out to the right, or you lean your chest to the left and cross your legs to the right. Since curves are subconsciously very seductive, create your own whenever possible.

2. Touch. Once you've established that there are sparks in your communication, physicality is essential. Begin by touching neutral spots like the wrist, the shoulder, the back of the arm and if they're engaging and touching back, then graduate to the torso area or thighs. A touch from

someone that you're attracted to never fails to raise the stakes and heighten the vibe.

3. Mirroring. When they say that imitation is the highest form of flattery, they aren't lying. When someone copies you, that is a sure-shot way to tell that you've got them on your hook. So now that you know this, if you want to hint that you're feeling someone, mirror their movements and tone.

4. Be bold. The whole playing-hard-to-get game is cute, I guess, but it's also played out. It's far more interesting to be the person who says how they feel and follows that up with action. Of course, there is such a thing as being overly enthusiastic and giving someone else all the power, which takes away the two things we discussed earlier: confidence and mystery. You must check in to gauge if the flirting is reciprocal. So, once you've given a bit, hang back to see if they give back, before giving more.

5. Slow down. Slow down your speech and your movements. Fast talking and fast, erratic motion makes it clear that you're nervous. And while that can be endearing, it isn't seductive. Pauses are your friend when it comes to flirting; you don't have to be in a rush to answer questions. There's a lot of power in looking into someone's eyes and holding their gaze in silence while you think.

"Let me just show you how this works. Okay, Deshawn, ask me a question!" Ari said, turning her entire body toward her.

Deshawn made a series of fast movements then threw up her hands. "Uh, what's your favorite food?"

Ari smiled, gave her the eye triangle, then held Deshawn's gaze in silence for what felt like a minute. "I guess if you're making me choose on the spot," she said slowly without breaking her stare, "I'd have to say . . ."

Deshawn burst into laughter and hid her face. "But I don't know if I can talk that slow!"

"Really?" asked Ari. "There's a lot of power in being able to set your pace and—oh, sweetheart, you look so stressed out."

Deshawn's nervous laughter suddenly turned into tears of frustration. "Sorry," she said as she held her eyes shut.

"No, it's okay, I'm really curious about this reaction. What about this interaction is inducing anxiety?"

"I have no clue why this is happening. I just know as soon as you started talking to me, I just kept thinking: *I can't do this, this is not helping, I'm so confused!*"

Ari, in expert form, slid her chair over and put a hand on Deshawn's knee then kept it there. "Don't be confused or anxious, okay? Know that I have no hidden intent or expectation from you, so whatever pressure you've put on this interaction, take it off. Look, we're all just out here trying to find love, create a purpose, make some friends and have some orgasms. And right now we're just two people having a conversation, there's really nothing more to it."

After Ari left, I found myself feeling a little stuck. We had done all this great, groundbreaking work and yet the group still seemed to choose their bad habits over the new ones. Granted, it had taken them all twenty-plus years to become the person they were; they were allowed to take a few weeks to own who they were meant to be. But still, I would have hoped to see a little bit more progress.

OUR NEXT SESSION WE HAD THE FULL GROUP TOGETHER, WHICH I WAS VERY grateful for as this was an important one. Pickup artistry (PUA) is something that I talk about a lot because in many ways, I am a student of it. Before I did my show *Shan Boody Is Your Perfect Date,* I read every book possible on the topic, including its core recommended texts. I combed through online forums and watched way too many YouTube videos to count. I wanted to give the group that same opportunity to learn from the PUA community, so I reached out to JT Tran, "the Asian Playboy," and the creator of the ABCs of Attraction boot camp, to assist us.

While asking a male dating coach to help a group of women may seem odd, I felt like there was one striking similarity between the men JT coached and the women I was working with. The women in my group felt like they weren't given the same shot at love as everyone else and according to a 2014 study by OkCupid called "Race and Attraction,"[1] Asian men are considered the least desirable ethnic/gender group. Yes, it would be great if everyone's path to meaningful intimacy was paved, but the truth is for some, the climb tends to be steeper and that's why programs like mine, as well as classes like JT's, need to exist.

As JT explained, "There's a big difference in how a straight white male, who has privilege and conditioned preference in the dating world, would approach someone than a minority would. There are different obstacles, different cultural norms to address, different strengths to try to highlight—all in all, it's just different."

But despite the obstacles, JT made it clear we had to feel more, not less, embattled, and worthy of success. "This is your life. You can be in the passenger seat hoping something will happen. Or you can actively drive your fate. Whether that means directly going after what you want or putting yourself in position to attract what you want. Either way you can't just wait and hope for the best, if you could, you wouldn't be here."

JT taught a workshop that was centered around how to make yourself approachable and how to approach someone. One thing he made very clear is that approaching people is a learned skill, and despite what your grandma thinks, it can be acquired equally by women.

"If someone approaches you it's because they've gotten confident at that skill; it's like riding a bicycle. But just because someone can ride a bike, that doesn't mean they'll be a great boyfriend. So if you're out and the person you're attracted to doesn't approach you, that may not be because they aren't interested, it's probably because they're terrified of rejection, just like you."

The solution? Women need to start making it easier for strangers they desire to connect with them—regardless of what gender your target is.

How to Be Approachable by JT Tran

1. Put yourself in a low-traffic area.
2. Position your body toward your target, despite the distance between you; try to stand pelvis to pelvis.
3. Make eye contact, hold it and repeat. People will make eye contact with someone they find attractive three separate times for three seconds each.
4. Keep your body language open. This means smile, uncross your arms, lean in, tilt your head and if you have a purse keep it down so it doesn't appear like you're on your way out.
5. When in groups always position yourself on the outside or at the back to make yourself easy to talk to. If you're in a group that includes a male or dominant person, make sure they aren't appearing protective of you.

Pro tip: Have fun and be playful because people are drawn to happy people!

How to Approach People by JT Tran

1. Ask an opinion-based question. People love to give their opinions, so use this to your advantage. Treat them as an authority on a particular topic. If you're at the bar ask them what drink is the best, if you're at the gym ask them what machine to use to work out a tight hamstring. Opinion questions can also get more complex and interesting. There are a ton of different directions you can go by starting with this line: "You seem sensible. Can you settle a debate me and my friend were having?"
2. Do a cold read. A cold read is a statement you make about a person that makes it seem like you know them more than you do. Because people crave to be understood, a successful cold read can get someone to warm up to you instantly. If they stand out among the crowd try, "You don't seem like you're from L.A.; you're too real." If they're too much to themselves try, "I can tell, you're the strong silent type. I like that."

> 3. Compliment. A kind word is worth a thousand more! Whatever it is that drew you to the person, what's the harm in walking over and saying that? The worst that can happen is that they say thank you, and if they take it upon themselves to be rude, consider that you've done yourself a giant favor because you may have wasted a perfectly good night lusting over the wrong person.

"Does anyone want to practice? Dan here will role-play with you," said JT, then stepped to the side.

JT's copilot, "Captain" Dan Hyun Kim, stepped forward and smiled warmly. He wore a blue blazer, a pink button-up shirt and cream pants. If the term "Asian sensation" was meant for anyone, it's Captain Dan!

Pricilla joined him at the front, smiled then said, "Do you know if this place usually picks up later?"

Dan pushed his hands into his pockets and smiled back. "Well, it depends. What kind of music do you like?"

"Dancehall," said Pricilla. "I don't really know how to dance to it, but I love to watch."

"Do you know what's crazy? I don't really know how to dance either, but I took a salsa lesson yesterday."

"Oh, wow, that's so brave of you," she said, then touched his shoulder. "I don't know if I could do something like that."

"Well, here's an idea then," said Dan, squaring up to Pricilla. "I'm a beginner, you're a beginner, so why don't we go take a dance class together sometime?"

"So . . ." Pricilla said coyly as she positioned her body in his direction too. "We take this class and you laugh at me and I laugh at you? That sounds like a deal."

"That's perfect," interrupted JT. "And just the right amount of self-deprecation but still confident. You teased, you touched, you were inviting and you kept the conversation going, which allowed him to find a natural way to take things further. You're a real professional at this!"

Pricilla paused and looked like she was about to do her usual routine: deny the compliment, then pledge her allegiance to introversion, but instead she flashed a mischievous smile and said, "Maybe I am."

I loved the class with JT and appreciated how it gave Pricilla an opportunity to see how far she had come, but I knew something was still missing. We had learned a lot of hard skills but there was an IT element still not in play. Something that would make their techniques seamless, effortless and . . . well, sexier.

Odd, isn't it? I talk about sex for a living and yet in a book about harnessing desire, there's little mention of it. In truth, this is just logistics; you don't need to know how to make someone change religions with your tongue in order to manifest a limitless love life. Maybe in a not-so-distant book we can graduate to that, but the kind of sex that I realized we needed to learn about at this stage had nothing to do with the hands, genitals, mouth, feet, butt cheeks, thighs, perineum, G-spot, A-spot, C-spot, U-spot or armpits—yes, armpits, but like I said . . . different book. What the group needed to master next was the subtle art of mind-fucking.

To help us learn this, I wanted to find someone who combined sex and conversation for a living, so I reached out to Nicole Thompson, a phone sex operator (known in the industry as a phone actress), to snag some quick tips. Nicole walked me through her onboarding process, which included a rundown on fetishes, a workshop on storytelling and, of course, an intensive on how to tune your voice.

"When you want to introduce sex with your voice, not your words, you have to learn how to lower, slow down and soften your tone," said Nicole while also demonstrating. "If you have a rasp, use it; if you sound like the girl next door, then play that up because some of my clients go absolutely apeshit for that."

I have been to several speech therapists in order to work on my ability to present with authority, but I had not considered enlisting the help of a coach to speak with sexuality! Nicole had me hooked, but what happened next, sunk me.

"But most importantly you must feel sexy in order to talk sexy. Sure, I can multitask, but it's hard for me to really get into it and say, *oh yeah, baby, I love it when you suck on my toes* . . . if I'm folding laundry with a bonnet on. So, if you're talking to your crush on the phone, why not sit in candlelight and run your finger along the rim of your wineglass as you chat? As a phone actress, my job is to pretend I'm filled with lust, but if you already like someone, all you gotta do is give your natural instincts a boost."

Nicole said the biggest mistake people make when it comes to their voice is that they don't pay attention to it, so they sound angry rather than playful or afraid instead of cool and inviting. I then asked Nicole what the best way was to subtly infuse sex into a conversation that felt too platonic. The response she gave may have been a little out of touch with the real world. Or perhaps it was right on the ball(s).

"When I'm not working and I want to make a conversation that's gone dry wet, I simply ask, *so . . . when was the last time you had sex?* You'd be surprised how often that one works."

The others couldn't make this call because Nicole's schedule was inverted to theirs: home during the day, working evening to night. So instead, I took notes and recorded it for them. Then, because it was pretty freaking awesome, I sent the clip of Nicole acting out the toe-sucking comment via our group chat.

Minutes later Deshawn texted, *When you play the audio while tutoring in a quiet library* ☺

Oops.

Next, I wanted to take things a step further by showing the group how to subtly ooze sex in person. I put out a call on my social media looking for anyone who worked in adult entertainment. But I ended up finding someone even better: a stripper named

Nina Ross who taught other strippers how to take their craft to the next level by making more money and garnering more repeat business with their personality. Bingo. I booked Nina then rallied my troops.

NINA, WHO ALSO GOES BY "THE 6-FIGURE STRIPPER," STRODE INTO MY APARTment looking every bit of her moniker. She wore a black shirt, black tutu and hot pink platform heels that looked higher than Wiz Khalifa. The girls in the group stared at her wide-eyed, which of course she played into. She took a seat in the best lighting my living room had to offer, then played with her ponytail and leaned forward so her two most prominent features, her eyes and her breasts, were center stage. Maya looked fascinated, Stephanie looked curious, Pricilla seemed impressed, Deshawn kept an unreadable expression and Courtney looked confused. Best of all, Nina didn't take anyone's judgment on; she seemed to delight in her own company, which made her a pure delight to watch.

"A stripper's primary objective when she's at work is to capture, hook and keep a client on the line for as long as possible. In my opinion this mind-set is not just useful at the club; every woman should know how to create connections that she's in control of," said Nina.

"How do you take control of connections off the top?" I asked.

"Easy. You make the first move, pick the topic and control where it goes. If someone says something stupid, but you can tell they meant no harm, don't get offended. Instead, regain control by addressing their comment then redirecting the conversation where you want it to go. Address and redirect. That's the formula of all great conversationalists."

"What if you're not naturally accustomed to leading conversations?" asked Stephanie.

"You start practicing," replied Nina, plain as day.

Nina left and everyone stayed back for a while to digest.

A Stripper's Guide to Killin 'Em with Conversation by Nina Ross

Take their temperature. You should never be surprised by, or a victim, of someone else's bad mood. Always observe them first before making your move. Are they in a rush/do they seem frustrated? Or are they relaxed and being friendly with others?

Invade their space. If you want to get in someone's head you need to enter their bubble. Position yourself close to them, walk by and make yourself noticeable.

Nonverbal acknowledgments. There are three things you should do before making your approach and each step needs reciprocation: 1) eye contact 2) smile 3) a gesture. Your gesture can be a wave, you can point, stick out your tongue, or coyly hide your face. What matters is that you've established a relationship before you've even said a word.

The approach. If you did the first steps you will not be walking over unannounced, so pay attention to how they respond as you approach. Consider that if you're at a restaurant and you see your food coming, you're gonna sit up straighter and make space; it's a subconscious action we can't help. So, do you notice them making space for you?

Start by asking them a question. When you approach, ask a question; if they don't ask one back, politely take your leave. This shows that they are selfish or insecure; either way you'll find yourself doing more work than it's worth to get something meaningful from the exchange. If they do ask you a question in return, ask for consent to talk or join them. When you respect someone, they respect you. (e.g. You: are you here waiting for happy hour to start like me? Them: No, life's too short to wait, what are you drinking? You: a mojito, do you mind if I join you?)

Never be typical. Once you've joined them, steer clear of small talk. People want someone to take control and lead conversations into entertaining experiences. So, be that leader. Try asking them a survey question about a topic that interests you because people love to give their opinions. As a bonus, make someone feel special by qualifying why you chose to ask them: "You seem cute; can I ask you a question that I'm only asking other cuties?"

Know the stripper topics. Talk about life's temptations: food, sex, fantasies, alcohol, bold humor or financial splurges. Strippers aren't afraid to talk about the things that bring out someone's edgier side because it gives the other person an opportunity to relax and have fun. If you want to be memorable, make sure you weave in topics that are weird or sexy. (e.g. You: I'm thinking of ordering something. Ever had anything on a bar menu that compared to an orgasm? Them: Not sure, I've never compared my orgasm to a slider now that I think about it. You: Well, maybe you haven't had the right slider or you're doing something extra wild in the bedroom. Anyway, you didn't answer my question, what's the best bar food you've ever had?). The trick is to be playful, witty and light. You don't have to overdo the sex talk, but also remember that talking about something is not a verbal agreement—if it was, we'd all be millionaires.

Cross the physical barrier. Wherever, whenever, however—make it your duty to get in there. But make sure you lead with consent. It makes things a lot sexier when you look someone in the eyes and say, "Do you mind if I touch your shirt, it looks really soft?" Strippers aim to touch the neck because it's a very sensitive, neutral area, and you should too.

Whether people loved her or hated her (correction: no one hated her, they just hated the way she drank from her water bottle), it was clear none of us would ever forget The 6-Figure Stripper. I silently prayed they wouldn't forget her lessons either. Nina was an experienced seductress who didn't just use her moves in the club, like Ari had said with flirting, these were techniques she kept in her back pocket at all times.

Nina was a great example of someone who understood the power of her presence and used it, but with great power comes great responsibility. A massive part of honoring and respecting the wonder of your physicality is knowing how to protect it.

THE NEXT CLASS WAS ONE I WAS BOTH EXTREMELY EXCITED AND EXTREMELY sad about. The five of us walked as a group—a group whose sole intention was to find meaningful connections with good people—into Foxy and Fierce for a self-defense class because unfortunately, it's crucial to know how to protect more than just your heart in today's dating landscape.

The heartbreaking #MeToo movement made it clear that as a society, we are working with two very different definitions of consent. Most of us understand that consent is nothing short of an enthusiastic yes! But, there are far too many who believe that being present and being down are the same thing. With this reality in mind, I couldn't send these women out there if they weren't aware and somewhat prepared for the worst.

According to RAINN, the nation's largest anti-sexual violence organization, every ninety-eight seconds someone in America is sexually assaulted.[2] And a study conducted by StopStreetHarass ment.org cited that 81 percent of women surveyed had been victims of sexual assault.[3] I need you to read those sentences again and this time don't look at the numbers, look at the faces of the people they are referencing: your sisters, best friends, caretakers, doctors and heroes. Taking a self-defense class, especially for those under the age of thirty-four, who are the highest targeted group, is not simply a good idea. In the face of those statistics, it should be a requirement. Of course, taking one class, or simply reading about maneuvers, isn't an effective deterrent to being assaulted but it can be something to draw on in an emergency.

There are few people who understand this better than Crystal Greene, owner and creator of the Foxy and Fierce "Simple Self-Defense" classes. Crystal holds the rank of third-degree black belt in the World Seido Karate Organization. She is a certified kickboxing instructor and has a background in Muay Thai boxing and Krav Maga.

After we had signed waivers and taken our place on the floor, Crystal and her husband greeted us then got down to business.

"This one class is not going to make you a master in self-defense, but it might give you confidence that will save your life," she began with her arms in Superwoman pose. "Predators prey on people that they believe won't be able to fight back and after today's class, that will no longer be you."

One by one Crystal taught us moves ranging from the hammer to the eye gouge (my personal favorite and the best self-defense move an inexperienced fighter can utilize against a much larger attacker). Then she and her husband went down the line with pads and had each of us practice the move until it had some power behind it. Courtney had no qualms whaling away, knocking Crystal's husband back a couple of times, but the rest of the group seemed tentative.

"You have to commit to the move," urged Crystal. "Remember, in real life this happens in a matter of seconds. One second you're talking and in the very next your date could have you pinned. You won't have time to think, just do. So in practice, *really* DO IT!"

Her husband made a *come-on* motion to Maya. "Let's go! Put your hand in a hammer position over your head and use your legs to bring that fist down with everything you've got!"

Maya stepped forward decisively and struck so hard that I felt it in my eardrums. After that, it was as though everyone else had permission to let it all out. We kicked, escaped, hammered, and round-housed until the hour-long class melted along with our damsel complexes.

The following self-defense techniques are potentially dangerous and are provided for informational purposes only. This information should never be used as a substitute for actual instruction with qualified professionals like Crystal. Nor is there any guarantee that the use of these techniques will be successful in preventing injury to yourself in a given situation. Also keep in mind that the infliction of bodily harm on another person is generally a crime unless there is a legal justification, which varies by jurisdiction.

Counterstriking with Vulnerable Targets

Vulnerable areas of the body should be your immediate focus in case of an attack. Counterattacks that are focused on these points will stun or debilitate your aggressor, giving you time to get away. While the groin area is a popular target, it is also one that most attackers predict you will attempt to strike. So try these instead:

Note: The eyes, nose, throat and groin are the most vulnerable targets.
Note: To create a fist, curl your fingers in tightly, thumb on the outside (not the inside) of fingers near the first knuckle.

1. The eyes: There are three techniques that are highly effective: a light finger whip, a thrusting/poking attack, or gouging your thumb into the tear duct because this can crush an eyeball or dislodge it.
   When to use this. If someone has your body pinned to the ground with their hands around your neck, our instinct is to try and remove their fingers. Instead, grab their face with both hands and dig your thumbs into their tear ducts, pushing the attacker's face away from you in an upward

direction while moving your thumbs in a downward motion until you stun them long enough to get away.

2. Temples: This is the area just above the cheekbones and under the hairline. A hammer strike here can stun your attacker. To hammer strike, put your hand into a punching fist, then strike your target laterally with the inside of the fist.

   When to use this. If someone grabs you from the front, strike them in the temple. If they don't let go, bend your knees and bring your weight toward the ground then hammer their kidneys. Continue striking to stun them and get away.

3. Base of skull: Right where the back of the neck and head connect is a vulnerable area because the brainstem is located here. If an attacker is directly on top of you, hammer fist to this area. To hammer fist, put your hand into a punching fist, raise your hand above your head then bring your fist down directly on your target using all of your body weight.

   When to use this. If someone tries to lift you or body slam you, make a hammer fist with your loose hand then drive your full force to the base of their skull. This can also be used as a secondary move. For example, if you're able to wind someone or attack their groin and they hunch over, hit the back of the skull to ensure you have more time to get away.

4. The nose: The nose is an extremely fragile body part. Because the nose is so vulnerable, it can be attacked with punches, hammer fist, ridge hand (the side of your hand where your pinky is), palm heel (the inside of your wrist), elbows and head butts.

   When to use this. If someone grabs you from the front, flex your wrist back, open your hand and curl your fingers, exposing your palm heel. Drive the palm heel up under the attacker's nose, causing extreme pain, swelling and the eyes to tear up. Continue to strike to the nose and groin to get away.

5. The ears: Strikes to the ears, especially with an open palm, can stun the attacker by throwing off the ears' inner equilibrium. This move is best used when followed up with a secondary attack to ensure you have ample time to flee.

   When to use this. If someone grabs you around the wrist, open your free hand and slap it over their ear. Or make a fist with your loose hand and strike the ear, followed with multiple strikes to the temple, face and groin to get away.

6. The chin and jaw: In boxing there's a reason opponents tuck in their chins: a strike to this area may result in an immediate knockout by rattling the brain against the skull. Punching someone square in the chin is often referred to as hitting their "off button" but be careful to avoid the mouth because hitting sharp teeth can damage your fists.

   When to use this. If someone grabs you from behind, bend your knees and turn your body toward them. At the same time, swing your elbow under their chin, using all the power from your legs. Continue to throw elbow strikes and hammer fist strikes to the jaw, neck and face to get away.

7. The sides and back of the neck: To choke someone, the obvious move is to attack the windpipe by grabbing and squeezing, but this takes a fair amount of strength. Another form of strangulation can occur with the compression of the carotid arteries (on the sides of the neck) that supply oxygen to the brain. Grab the sides of their neck and push inward until your attacker loses consciousness.

   When to use this. You can attack the carotid arteries if you can pin your attacker. But, if someone grabs your neck from behind, raise your left arm, turning sharply toward them and driving your elbow down on their arm to break their hold. Next, make a fist and punch the side of the neck; add a knee strike to the groin to get away.

8. Hair: When you have ahold of someone's hair you have control of their head, so grab it, then follow up with a secondary strike to debilitate them.

   When to use this. If someone grabs you from the front with their arms around your waist and their face close to your chest, reach your hand up the back of their neck to the top of their hairline. Fingers spread wide open, clench the hair into a fist, pulling downward and exposing their neck. Create a fist with your loose hand, drive the fist upward into their nose or throat to get away.

9. *Clavicle:* The clavicle or collarbone is a long bone between the shoulders and neck. It sticks out kind of like a handlebar, which you can use to your advantage in an attack by digging your nails into it and pulling down.

> *When to use this.* If someone is holding you up against them chest to chest, insert your fingers into the hollow between their neck and clavicle then use your entire body weight to yank down forcefully.

Even though we covered a lot, Crystal assured us there was much more to learn. She handed us information on a series of classes she taught at Foxy and Fierce all designed to get women apt at fighting back. As we left her studio, we air-practiced our favorite moves and walked toward the parking lot, until we noticed Maya was no longer with us. We turned and saw her just outside the front door with one hand covering her mouth and the other pressed firmly against her chest. In unison, we walked back to see what was wrong.

"Do you guys not know who came in right after us?" she asked.

We all exchanged blank stares. Sure, it had become apparent that Crystal was ready to wrap the class when a woman with short blond hair entered, but I didn't recognize her, so I didn't think much of it.

"Are you kidding me?" Maya said and rotated her hand to her forehead. "*Twilight, American Ultra, Snow White?*"

"Oh, shit, that was Kristen Stewart?" blurted out Stephanie.

Maya fanned herself, as she usually did when she got flustered, and nodded fiercely. "You know when Ari asked us who our crushes are? Well, she is my ultimate crush. I can't even deal right now!"

"Go say hello to her, Maya, she's in there alone," I nudged.

"No. I can't."

"Why not? Just pretend you're getting one of their business cards and then casually say what's up; you don't have to say or do anything else."

"I can't," she repeated.

The group had joined in peer-pressuring her. She looked at me for an out, but I refused to let her disagreeableness or anxiety win this battle. "Fine, well, would you mind going in there and grabbing me a class list please? I forgot one and I definitely wanna come back."

Maya exhaled sharply. She stared at me, I stared back. Then, she spun around, marched back to the door and disappeared inside. After that, I never did see the fragile, mouse-like version of Maya again.

We went back to my place for one final workshop, led by moi. As I mentioned earlier, through my research into pickup artistry, the absolute best thing I did was read the recommended texts. Reading these books gave me insight into how to improve my game, as well as the power to spot when ill-intentioned people were attempting to game me. Of the bunch, my two favs were, *Methods of Persuasion* by Nick Kolenda and *Influence: Science and Practice* by Robert Cialdini. The art of communication is often thought of as abstract, but these works taught me that it's a lot more like a sculpture. You need to have a vision of what you want to make, but also, you need quality material and lots of patience to help you get there.

If you use the power of influence in dating to encourage a genuine connection with someone genuinely awesome, they can be an extremely helpful catalyst. On the flip side, if your goal is to manipulate people into entertaining your bullshit, it can also work too. So, before we dive into my favorite techniques, that I can honestly say landed me my dream husband, I'd like to leave a word of caution. Influence is a lot like a knife: it can be used to create something wonderful or destroy something vulnerable. For this reason, you need to always check in with your intentions before utilizing anything included below. I've also included warnings on how these same techniques could be used, irresponsibly. With this, you'll now be able to spot fools, and see their slithering ass coming from miles away.

How to Win People Over and Keep 'Em Coming Back

Demonstrate value. As soon as you interact with someone new, immediately look for opportunities to exemplify why they should keep you around.

How to use this in dating: When you approach potential playmates (which I highly recommend that you do), demonstrating value justifies the introduction because it makes it clear that you are there to enhance their experience. You can accomplish this by teaching them something new, performing an act of service, giving a gift, boosting their confidence or by making them laugh.

How corny people use this technique: Guilting. *Can I buy you a drink, sweetheart?* is now synonymous with, *Can I awkwardly hang around you for thirty more minutes?* When demonstrating value is done well, it is less obvious and does not have built-in expectations. The means must justify the end for all parties involved.

Demonstrate vulnerability. While we are told to hide our weaknesses, there's a lot to be said about the power of revealing them in a constructive way. 1) It gives people a clear lane to demonstrate how to add value to you. 2) People highly value authenticity and nothing demonstrates that better than vulnerability.

How to use this in dating: In relevant conversation, reveal something that you are genuinely struggling with and ask your playmate for their advice. People love to give their opinion and they love to feel needed so indulge them and possibly get some worthwhile tips while you're at it! The question "Hey, can I ask you about something that I'm having trouble with?" can be a great intimacy builder.

How corny people use this technique: Sympathy mongering. Exaggerating, falsifying or playing into people's sympathetic side in order to get them to feel bad enough to appease you will only result in brief, inauthentic connections. If someone needs a lot of emotional support but doesn't make an attempt to reciprocate, they may be a sympathy mongerer.

Favors. It may seem logical that doing someone a favor is a way to get them on your side, but psychologists find that having someone do *you* a favor is also an effective way to get someone to like you.

How to use this in dating: Use this technique to strike up a conversation with a playmate by asking them to do something innocuous (hold your coat while you go to the bathroom, pass you a napkin, solve a riddle for you, etc.). Once they complete the task, look for a reciprocal way to repay the debt in order to solidify the connection.

How corny people use this technique: Conning. People like to be viewed as consistent so once you get someone to say yes, it's likely they will say yes again. Someone who is out to con will ask for a small favor, return the small favor then ask for the big favor they had in mind the whole time.

Rapport building. In order to build rapport with someone you need shared history but how on earth do you do that with someone you just met? You find something you have in common as soon as possible and relate your experiences with theirs. Another effective tool of rapport building is to share a secret or an inside joke.

How to use this in dating: As soon as you meet a playmate, try to find out what the two of you have in common then expand on that topic. Discovering similarities is an easy way to strike up banter, stamp out awkwardness and begin to make a genuine connection. I encourage people to create a nickname or inside joke as naturally but as quickly as possible because it creates unique, shared history.

How corny people use this technique: Manipulating. Building rapport with someone is also a tool used to get people's defenses down for an attack. Beware of people who try to point out similarities with you in forced or clearly inauthentic ways.

Scarcity. There's a reason why online stores will often tell you that there's only *X* amount of a product left because the less available something is, the more we value it and the faster we will attempt to secure it.

How to use this in dating: It's not that you should play hard to get, it's that as a thriving single person, you *should* be hard to get: you've got family, friends, hobbies, a career and passion projects. So honor your schedule. Don't break plans with friends, cancel your spin class or skip a trip to visit your family to make a date. Make it clear that you aren't available 24/7 because realistically, you're not. Don't worry, they won't meet their soul mate and cancel you out because you couldn't make lunch, and if they did? Good on them!

How corny people use this technique: Love flooding. Love flooding is when someone showers you with attention and praise then suddenly takes it away. This can work because if you want someone to be addicted to you, nothing does the trick like inconsistent rewards. But it creates a toxic dynamic. In reality, if you want someone to see value in you, simply show up when they need you and be honest about what you need. The love flooder fails to understand this.

The power of no. When I first graduated from college, like most, I said yes to everything. That's why you saw me as an extra in the beginning of *Mean Girls* and why I moonlighted as a music critic even though I had zero business doing so. This is because I was desperate, and desperate people don't think they can afford to say no, which is why if you can, you should. Saying no communicates that you have standards and most important, other options.

How to use this in dating: Simply, if someone asks you to do something that you are not comfortable with—don't. This applies tenfold to sex. There is nothing wrong with using sex as a way to feel good, but as a bargaining chip it's fool's gold. When it comes to the early stages of dating, you don't need anything from that person so there's no need to make major sacrifices to keep them around. Remind yourself of that. Often.

How corny people use this technique: Bluffing. This is when someone says no to something they want, in hopes that you will fold and offer them more. In these circumstances, this power can be yielded by someone turning down a compromise in order to get you to consent to an uneven trade.

Challenging. Of course, we all love compliments and positive affirmations, but that doesn't mean the counterpart, challenging, doesn't have power too. By nature, humans want to improve stuff (you can glance at your high-tech phone, that will be outdated by the time you finish reading this sentence, if you need proof); this also includes themselves.

How to use this in dating: In order to influence someone to change a behavior you don't like, you have to find a way not to awaken their defenses. This is why I subscribe to the kindness/compliment sandwich. Start with something positive, follow it up with criticism, then end with an affirmation. This makes the point and keeps things interesting without being offensive or negative.

How corny people use this technique: Gaslighting. This is a malicious strategy designed to manipulate people by aggressively challenging their perceptions or behaviors, then following that up with positive affirmations to confuse them.

Step into Your Expertise.

This is a sentence I repeated over and over to the group, Deshawn especially. Stepping into your expertise means looking for spaces to demonstrate value by talking about and acting on what you know best.

How to use this in dating: People respect authority so if there is a place to naturally make yourself an authoritative source, own it! Becoming the go-to person is an extremely strong tool that holds a lot of value because it helps people clearly identify what you bring to the table.

How corny people use this technique: Belittling. When someone argues with you not by attacking the merit of your opinion but your credentials, age or upbringing, they are trying to belittle you. True experts are always open to learn new things from unexpected sources. So don't let this kind of cornball get to you.

The group left my apartment and lovingly tidied up before doing so. Courtney even took out my large bag of trash. In addition, they had recently taken to sending me funny memes or appreciative texts throughout the day.

Had these women begun to turn their game on me?

I started out with six shy, matte girls and now I knew a quintet of glossy women who were locked, loaded and ready to officially get their mingle on. Or at least I hoped they were because that—and a lil something extra—is precisely what I had planned for them next.

Phase Four: Practice

PART ONE

>――――→ ←――――

*Practice what you've learned thus far
in low-risk environments with a group
of friends. In addition, test out new
hypotheses so you can add to your toolbox
for making connections at will.*

10

SCRAMBLED EGGS AND BLOW JOBS

I remember the 1995 cult classic *Dangerous Minds* as if I watched it yesterday (if you aren't currently singing "Gangster's Paradise" in your head, I'm not sure if we could be friends). A part that always stood out to me was the day Michelle Pfeiffer's character took the class to a theme park to learn physics from riding roller coasters rather than reading textbooks. That is essentially what Phase Four is: learning in the real world without the stress of real-life risks.

The field trips we were about to embark on were all about practicing what we'd learned thus far, plus, I decided to add an extra twist. We would also be testing out four psychological theories related to seduction. The purpose of this extra tactic was twofold: first, it made way for us to potentially learn some new hacks and second, it turned a high-pressure activity, like approaching playmates, into a low-risk game. I considered this low risk because the group didn't really have anything to lose; if, for example, they tried a seduction technique and it didn't work, they weren't the one being rejected, the theory was! Having a covert mission that calls you to do a bit of acting is a sure shot way to numb the nerves because all of a sudden, an activity that is traditionally all about ego now has almost nothing to do with you.

After I had written out my hypotheses, I wrote the group and explained the four different experiments we would be testing out together:

Truth or Stare.
Do women need to start making the first move?

Love Potion Number Vagine.
Can your own vaginal fluids serve as bait, to draw in playmates?

Don(u)t You Want My Bacon?
Which perfume or naturally occurring scent is best at enticing strangers?

Hotcakes or Sweet Pie?
Do you get better results looking hot and behaving introvertedly
or looking dressed down and behaving extrovertedly?

I then made it clear that they did not have to do all four, but I did want them to sign up for at least one. Deshawn had a pre-planned trip to London for Nottingham Carnival and Maya also had travel plans, so they warned me of their dodgy attendance. Stephanie and Pricilla also shared possible conflicts and admitted that some of these experiments were too much so they'd rather sit a couple out. Courtney, who was proving to be more open by the day, emphatically volunteered to attend them all.

EXPERIMENT ONE

Truth or Stare

QUESTION
Do women need to make the first move?

HYPOTHESIS

If a group of women go out and make themselves approachable for half the night and actually approach for the other half, then we can assess which method is more effective.

RESEARCH

According to OkCupid, women are two and a half times more likely to get a response than men if they initiate contact.[1] One out of every three straight League couples started with a woman messaging first.[2] However, most women do not send the first message.

APPARATUS

Five women, in two distinct locations, choose four targets each: two people they will approach and two people they will make themselves approachable to. They will then compare which technique was more successful.

HOW TO DRAW A CONCLUSION

Assess the quality of our connections when we approach vs. when we appear approachable.

This experiment, although the tamest, was the one that made me feel most conflicted. I have long upheld the women-should-not-make-the-first-move rule. But recently, I began to seriously question how much I *actually* abided by it. Sure, I've never outright asked for someone's number, but I've done my share of sliding into people's comment sections and I've never been a stranger to striking up a "casual" chat with someone hot.

By 8:40 P.M. Courtney, Stephanie, Pricilla, Deshawn and I were piled into a booth at a local Mexican restaurant ready to find some answers. Maya was away and after we ordered drinks, I learned that the rest of the women wished they were with her instead.

"I am really terrified of this," said Stephanie as she looked down.

"Yeah, this is pretty much my worst nightmare," echoed Pricilla, who wore tight jeans that showed her ample assets in a way that she hadn't flaunted, or I hadn't noticed before.

"You would both think that," said Courtney, "being personality twins and all."

This was something we had discovered during the Self-Summary Workbooks. Stephanie and Pricilla were both INFPs on the Myers-Briggs Type Indicator. Although in the beginning it was hard to see any parallels, as they both rarely volunteered any information about themselves, as time had gone on it was impossible not to notice.

"Well, I'm not an INFP but I'm also scared shitless," said Deshawn.

"Today is going to be easy. The sooner you get over your fears and go for it, the easier it will get," I said. "The goal is to answer the question, do women need to start doing the approaching or is making ourselves approachable just as effective? This isn't about you, it's about the experiment."

"What do you mean by 'approachable' again?" asked Pricilla.

"Making eye contact three times and pointing your pelvis toward someone," answered Stephanie.

"Smiling, walking by them slowly, staying on the outside of a group—oh, and thinking sexy thoughts," added Courtney.

I raised my eyebrows and nodded, surprised and proud that they had retained that information.

"And approaching? What are we supposed to say?" said Deshawn, still unconvinced.

I paused, hoping for more volunteers, but this time there was none, so I took it: "Remember Nina's advice, keep it weird or sexy but because this is our first time practicing, just ask anything that comes to mind. We're going to a record store first so there's tons of natural topics there. Don't overthink it, the worst thing that can happen is that they brush you off."

Everyone's eyebrows bolted upward.

"Okay," I continued. "Like Ari said, the easiest way to get over your fear of approaching people is to be confident that you have something incredible to offer. So tell me two of your perks from our job-listing exercise that you can repeat in your mind as you walk up to someone."

Pricilla and Stephanie shifted back in their chairs. Deshawn reflexively looked down. Even Courtney had suddenly become fascinated with the menu again.

"Nobody remembers theirs?" I asked.

"I somewhat do," began Deshawn.

"Great, I can help you out," I interjected. "You make great, what?"

She remained silent.

"Eggs, right? Scrambled eggs, to be specific."

She laughed. "With cheese."

"And you give great head," I added.

"Blow jobs," she corrected.

"Now repeat that back."

"Uh, I make great eggs with cheese and I give great blow jobs?"

"Exactly! I want you to repeat that in your brain any time you're feeling intimidated or unsure of yourself. You're also intelligent, adventurous and faith oriented—use any two of those. Courtney, what about you?"

"Let's see, which one of my job perks stood out to you?" she volleyed back.

I peeped her game, but in support of the attempt I played along. "That you know people's friends and family will love you. Your turn, what's a sexy perk you can add on to that?"

"I'm also incredible at giving massages. I know how to make people melt in my hands."

For Stephanie we came up with: *I'm a great listener and I sound like a phone sex operator.* And for Pricilla we chose: *I am highly empathetic, and my boobs are real.*

When we got to the record store everyone split up. For the first few minutes all we did was walk around the aisles and awkwardly wave at one another. Sensing they needed time to find their groove, I moved to the back section where I spotted a cute-enough guy wearing a graphic tee and khakis sifting through records. Like in the movies I positioned myself directly in front of him and began riffling through the titles. He glanced up: one. I moved diagonal to him and hummed a tune. He cocked his head for a nanosecond: two. I moved into the same aisle as him and turned my feet in his direction. He looked up at me and then stood there smiling for a while before he waved with his chin then walked the other way. Approachable: 0.

I walked back to where the rest of the group were circulating and convened with Deshawn, Stephanie and Pricilla in an aisle between funk and house.

"Everyone is either focused on buying something or on their phone. Being approachable is useless!" exclaimed Pricilla.

"There was this hot guy upstairs listening to music and we were all circling him like hawks; he never even looked up once," added Stephanie.

"And what about approaching?" I asked.

"I did approach a guy and asked him about horror movies," said Stephanie. "But it turned out he works here so then I had to follow him to the section and fake like I was going to buy something." She held up a couple of DVDs as evidence.

Just then two attractive guys walked past us. I asked the obvious. "Who's getting that?"

Stephanie looked at Pricilla and threw her hands up. "I already approached someone!"

"You just admitted that he worked here!" said Pricilla.

"I'll go," offered Deshawn.

It didn't even occur to me to ask her. We all stopped and watched in amazement as she made one small step for flirting and one giant leap for herself.

A few minutes later Courtney joined us. "Y'all, I just got rejected from this big ol' man wearing a small-ass T-shirt. Some people are so rude."

"Deshawn is over there holding a full conversation with these two hot guys," shared Pricilla.

True to Pricilla's word, the woman who once said that she was terrified of flirting now had the attention of two high-interest play-mates. Deshawn laughed, smiled and gestured—I even saw her touch one of their shirts! The rest of us stood back and basked in her flirtatious glow.

The second location we went to was a bar up the street and by the time we got there, the wait time to get to the rooftop was indefinite. We decided to make use of the fact that a ton of other people were also hanging about on the lower level.

"See that guy at the bar?" I asked, pointing once his head was turned. "I've caught him looking at me twice already. I'm going to walk by him slowly and lock eyes. If he doesn't take that as a hint to come over, I'm officially giving up on approachable!"

I walked by him, we held each other's gaze, then . . . nothing. I decided to make lemonade and found a vacant corner table, then waved the group over.

"He didn't say anything, huh?" confirmed Courtney. "All right, let me go talk to him."

She walked over to the all-stare-no-action guy and struck up a conversation. Two greasy onlookers took note that the remainder of us were now cornered and swooped in. The first introduced him-self then proceeded to pull up a chair at our table without asking for consent; the second stood back and stared down Pricilla.

"What are you drinking?" he asked her, licking his lips and mas-saging his hands like tonight was the first time he ever saw boobs.

"I'm okay, thanks," said Pricilla as she looked away.

While buddy ogled Pricilla's goods, we chatted with his friend, who wasn't half bad or perhaps just not half as bad. A few minutes later, Courtney rejoined us and said polite hellos.

"Nice guy, but a long talker," she whispered to me. "I guess guys really do get excited when they are approached. Anyway, who are they?"

A waitress came over and dropped off five drinks. We all looked around confused but found clarity as we noted the creepy guy was now creepily smiling.

"We're ready to go, right?" I asked.

"Yes!" said Pricilla the loudest.

Once we got outside Stephanie closed off the night with the perfect anecdote. "Approaching people is scary, but if those are the only kinds of men that approach, I can definitely face my fears. It's kind of nice to be in control of who you get to interact with."

When I got home, Jared was already in bed. "How did it go?" he asked as he threw a heavy arm over me.

"It was fun but I'm not sure about the conclusion. No one made any real connections so it's hard to say if approaching is any more effective in the long run."

"You already did this experiment. We wouldn't be here if you didn't approach me."

I knocked his arm off. "What? You made the first move when you DM'ed me!"

"Right, but only after you followed me, liked my pictures for weeks then left me that long-ass birthday comment."

Maybe he had a point . . .

The next day I woke up to a text Pricilla sent in our group chat:

Ladies I just wanted to share something. Last night I ended up initiating contact with this guy I've liked for a while. Typically, my nerves would get the best of me and I'd get in my own head and not be my complete normal self . . . But you've given me such sweet words since we met, and I literally repeated them to myself before walking into his house. I even repeated that I'm empathetic and my boobs are real several times. Lol. To my surprise my nerves calmed down tremendously, and I was able to engage more in conversation and be my normal kinda funny self and feel comfortable in my own skin.

Conclusion

It's time for women to start making the first move. If women would like to have a say in who they interact with, they need to speak up. If you date people in the queer community, there are no hard rules on this issue, which is an even better excuse to create ones that benefit you. OkCupid's Melissa Hobley, The League's Meredith Davis, our flirt-expert Ari Fitz, Nina "The 6-Figure Stripper," and dating coach JT Tran all gave this advice—and now, in light of this experiment, I would too.

EXPERIMENT TWO

Love Potion Number Vagine

QUESTION

If you make the scent of your vaginal fluids prominent by applying it to your pressure points, will it make you more attractive to those in your immediate vicinity?

HYPOTHESIS

If copulins are used as perfume, then it will attract anyone traditionally attracted to women with vulvas.

RESEARCH

The term "pheromone" is derived from the Greek words *pherein,* meaning "to transfer," and *hormon,* meaning "to excite."[3] Thus pheromones transfer excitement. Pheromones are chemical molecules released to trigger hormonal changes and elicit behavioral responses from others. These signaling molecules are contained in body fluids such as genital secretions.

APPARATUS

Four women will attend a crowded bar wearing no perfume or scented products. For the first half of the night, the women will strike up casual conversations. Then, after successfully connecting with two strangers, the group will head to the bathroom to apply their vaginal fluids to their necks, chests and wrists. They will then circulate the bar a second time and spark new conversations while noting if there is any visible difference between their interactions.

HOW TO DRAW A CONCLUSION
Assess if the application of vaginal fluids made people subconsciously move closer.

Soho House West Hollywood is a private club that overlooks all of Los Angeles. It is a *Zoolander*-esque spectacle every weekend, and that Saturday was no exception. Stephanie, Deshawn, Courtney and I stood at the top of the stairs and stared at the herds of people who spoke too loudly and dressed even louder. Maya was still away, and Pricilla, who was weirded out by the idea, respectfully chose to sit out.

"So now what?" said Stephanie as she tugged at the shoulders of her shirt.

"We're testing if our vaginal fluid draws people in. So in order to do that, we have to talk to people without, then with it, to compare."

"Okay, what do we say to people?" asked Stephanie, who was hypnotized by the busy bar.

"Remember Nina's tip? It's a bar so talk about the temptations." I took a step forward so that I was in the line of traffic, then tapped a handsome guy on the shoulder. "Excuse me, can I see your watch? That's so crazy! I just saw this at the store and was thinking of buying it for my dad. Was it a gift or did you spoil yourself?"

We chatted for a beat, then he kept it moving. I turned back to the group and gestured, *your turn*. The three of them dispersed into the crowd and I went in the opposite direction to keep out of their hair. Luckily, I saw a couple of friends at the bar then went and joined them. Ten minutes later I excused myself to check on the group and almost immediately ran into Stephanie.

"Are you done?"

"No," she said. "I don't know why but I can't do this."

"Stephanie, yes, you can. I'm not asking you to get someone's credit card information, I am asking you to talk to someone. See that guy standing by himself on his phone? Ask him what drink is good at the bar? Ask him what's so fascinating on his phone—"

"Okay, okay," she said, then walked in his direction.

I headed toward the smokers' area and spotted Courtney. "Are you done?"

"Girl, I'm more than done, I talked to, like, three men." She gave me a thumbs-up then pointed behind me at Deshawn, who was once again flanked by two handsome dudes. I smiled until I noticed she was wearing flat sandals that looked like they were made for the beach, not the bar.

Heels just make a person stand different, straighter and firmer, so I like to think of them as a part of the uniform for playmate hunting. But hell—maybe they weren't as important as I thought! Deshawn had apparently strutted over and captivated two strangers while standing on two glorified pieces of cardboard.

Stephanie joined us then and we all stood in Deshawn's line of sight until she was done. When she walked over, we greeted her with a slow clap.

"Are we ready for round two?" I asked.

No one said anything, which I attributed to the fact that the bar had suddenly gotten louder. I motioned for them to follow me back downstairs and I suppose Deshawn's flat shoes gave her extra horsepower because she nearly ran face-first into an unsuspecting passerby. Her hands flew up in embarrassment, she apologized, then sped past me and led the rest of the way down.

The four of us sat shoulder to shoulder on a bench that was really meant for two, at the foot of the white-marble staircase that the club was infamous for. The elevator doors to the left of us opened and a sea of good-looking and exquisitely dressed Hollywood types spilled out in our direction.

"Everyone looks so nice," said Stephanie in a way that sounded like a comparison, not a compliment.

"That was Kofi Siriboe upstairs that I almost ran over," said Deshawn with sad eyes and slumped shoulders.

"Who?" asked Stephanie as she continued to stare at the elevator.

"*Queen Sugar,* the movie *Girls Trip*?" quizzed Deshawn.

Stephanie looked at her with a blank expression.

"Right, right, I know of him," said Courtney as she adjusted her glasses, which suddenly would not sit still on her face.

"Shan?" said Deshawn in a way that made it very clear what she was about to ask. "Is it okay if I don't do this part?"

"We're already here, we're already halfway done, so we're all doing this. Besides, you're doing so well, Deshawn: you were holding a long conversation with two dudes at once and you almost made out with Kofi."

"I almost head-butted him," she corrected.

I smiled and winked. "This is going to be fun. Don't look at it like you have to do something but think of it like you've got something cool to give?"

"My vagina juice?" Deshawn asked.

"Yes but no. The fluid is your secret weapon. I'm talking about the experience of getting to know you. That's what you're giving. That's your gift." I clapped. "All right, let's go through our job perks—run 'em off! What do you have to offer?"

Stephanie and Deshawn instantly looked at Courtney with the letters *SOS* on their faces. Courtney accepted, sat up straighter and adjusted her glasses one more time. "Okay, everyone including parents absolutely love me, I can make you melt in my hands, I know how to make people feel incredibly special in my presence and what was my last one?"

"People are gonna wanna know what your lips taste like, right?" answered Stephanie.

"Yes!" Courtney exclaimed with a smile.

"Okay, so," said Stephanie, sensing she had to go next. "I am an excellent listener, I sound like a phone sex operator, I'm a great cook, I have a great body and I fight for causes I believe in."

Courtney and I high-fived Stephanie, then fixed our gaze on Deshawn.

"You make good eggs, remember?" said Courtney.

"Yes, right," began Deshawn. "So I make excellent scrambled eggs with cheese, I have a strong faith in God, I am really good at giving gifts, um, I am charismatic and I, uh, I give good blow jobs or at least I used to before my braces."

She smiled with a full mouth of joy-filled metal and we all laughed until the bench shook. The elevator doors opened again and a fresh batch of twenty- and thirtysomethings entered the club.

"All right, we ready to do this?" I said as I wiggled free.

When we got to the bathroom Courtney put her hand on my shoulder and forced me to face her straight on. "Okay, wait, how are we supposed to do this?"

I instructed them to wash their hands, get in a stall and then move their finger around their vaginal opening. The goal was to get a new sample from the Bartholin's glands, which are the size of a pea but play a large role in vaginal lubrication. Once they got a good amount of wetness, they could rub it on the neck, collarbone and wrists.

"Why wrists?" asked Courtney.

I waved my hands around as though I were talking then moved in to hug her with my arms outstretched. She nodded then disappeared into a stall. I stood there smiling encouragingly until the other two followed her lead. I took up the last stall then took my pants down. *One for all and all for one.*

We left the bathroom silently and headed back toward the stairs. Just before we embarked on our experiment, I turned toward the three of them. "How do we feel?"

"Sticky," said Deshawn.

I stared at her, unamused. "You're supposed to say intriguing and confident."

"Okay, I'm confident I'm sticky," she volleyed back.

I turned and led the way up the stairs. I paused again when we got to the top so I could issue one final pep talk but Deshawn, Courtney and Stephanie walked right past me and disappeared into the crowded room with their backs arched and arms swinging. I went back to the bar to see if my friends were still there—and they were, just drunker.

"We need to hang out more," said one, leaning in to my neck. At first, I thought this was for support but, then she lingered and I wondered if it were something more. "I was just thinking about my friends who are always supportive of me and it's you. You and Jared, I fucking love him too . . ."

She buried her face in my neck then continued to confess her gratitude in the long-winded way that only a drunk person would.

After a lengthy while, I recognized this conversation was not going to end by itself, so I pushed back to make some space between us. "Let me catch up later, I gotta go look for my girls."

She moved closer, nudged my face with her chin and resumed her place at the nook of my neck. "They're right there."

I turned to see Deshawn, Stephanie and Courtney staring at us with their mouths open. Ten minutes later we stood at the valet desk and waited for my car to pull up.

Courtney turned toward me with the biggest smile. "If I didn't see that girl basically sucking on your neck for, like, five minutes, I would not have believed this thing worked."

"How did it work for you guys?" I asked.

Courtney said they walked onto the balcony and within minutes they all got swept up in conversation. She noted that people seemed to be leaning extra close but it was a little noisy, so it could have been because of that. I also explained that my friend's extra-closeness could have been attributed to alcohol, but regardless of if we got a conclusive answer or not, I was insanely proud of them for completing this challenge.

The car pulled up and we all piled in. As we exited the parking lot and picked up speed, Stephanie let down her window and pressed her face into the night. She hadn't said much all evening.

I glanced over my shoulder to check up on Deshawn who had been vocal about her hang-ups with this experiment. "There's wipes in my bag if you wanna clean yourself off."

Deshawn was staring at the billboards lining Sunset Boulevard. She shook her head and replied, "I'm all right actually."

"Anyone else?" I asked.

"Not me," said Courtney. "I'm about to go see about a boy."

"And what boy is this?"

"I don't know yet, that's what I'm about to go see. And why not have an extra lil boost?" She tapped her pelvic area and I laughed until the wind took my breath away.

The next day I texted Stephanie to see how she was doing after last night. I really wanted to help all the women in any way possible, but I was unsure how effective any of the teachings had been for her in particular. Courtney had been going on ample dates, Maya had come out of her shell tremendously, Pricilla was already dating a high-interest playmate and Deshawn had been a rock star during the experiments—all of them had breakout moments of success, except Steph. But as outlined earlier, Stephanie was one of those people who read countless self-help books about greatness, but still hadn't stepped up and embraced her own.

> I'm good. I'm at an event and I'm like feeling so awkward. I'm like should I make a quick trip for some vaginal juice Lol.

I sent back the water drop symbol.

She replied, Lol we'll see.

Conclusion

Vaginal fluids, especially around ovulation, but really any time you want to feel an extra boost of confidence, can serve as a love potion. Here's why: I'm often asked to confirm or deny the myth that eating an excessive amount of pine-apples will make someone taste better during oral sex. My response is, if you think it makes you taste better then it absolutely works. Similarly, regardless of if vaginal pheromones truly make a person irresistible or not, the fact that you think it does, will cause you to act in a bolder, more confident manner. There are no health risks for others and unless you suspect you may have bacterial vaginosis, it will not make you smell bad. I've used this technique countless times in the past ten years and have had mixed results: sometimes people are flocking to me, sometimes I don't notice a difference. So while I'm not sure how effective this experiment is, I am certain that every single time I employ it, it makes me feel like an enchanted goddess with a delicious secret.

⟶ EXPERIMENT THREE ⟵

Don(u)t you want my bacon?

QUESTION

Is there one perfume that is more seductive than its competitors?

HYPOTHESIS

If I test out four different scents that claim to be the most powerful seducers, then I can determine which milkshake actually brings all the boys (or girls) to the yard.

RESEARCH

The smell of donuts and licorice increased arousal in more than 30 percent of men studied by the Smell & Taste Treatment and Research Foundation.[4]

Bupa revealed a list of the things that make people feel good. The smell of bacon was more popular than exercise or receiving a massage.[5]

Dr. Alan Hirsch of the Smell & Taste Treatment and Research Foundation conducted studies that showed fresh-smelling clothes may have a positive af-fect on how others perceive them. "This may be due to olfactory-evoked nos-talgia, which makes people feel safe and secure, and may even work on a more primal, subliminal level, since these odors harken primal memories," he said.[6]

APPARATUS

Four women will attend a couple of social events, each wearing a different signature scent: a high-end perfume, laundry spray, jelly-donut mist and bacon oil. They will randomly select participants to smell them all and in the end, they will tally up the results to determine which scent was the victor.

HOW TO DRAW A CONCLUSION

Tally which scent was preferred by those surveyed.

Have a random-ass shopping list? Amazon is your best friend. I ordered my personal favorite perfume, Untold by Elizabeth Arden, then found three separate companies that claimed to have captured laundry, donuts and bacon in a bottle. Add to cart.

That weekend I planned to execute the smell experiment but only Maya and Courtney were available; Deshawn was away in London, Stephanie had her sister in town and Pricilla had her son. That left us with one smell on the chopping block, and I couldn't have that. I decided to go back and comb through my original list of applicants for a fantastic fourth so we could get this experiment cracking Destiny's-Child–style (circa '98. Not 2006.).

It didn't take me long to land on Alana, a thirty-one-year-old producer and lesbian who had confessed during our interviews that she had a problem talking to women she was interested in. I thought today could be excellent practice for her, but also for Maya, who identified as queer but had never dated or flirted with a woman. So, I planned for us to go to a women's networking event in downtown Los Angeles called Girl Boss, then to the DTLA Proud Festival.

We all met at my apartment at 5 P.M., unperfumed and uncreamed so that the smell of our products wouldn't tamper with the results. I introduced everyone to Alana then dove in with the million-dollar question: "Who volunteers to smell like bacon?"

Courtney reluctantly raised her hand, which was kind of her since Maya was vegan and Alana was the new girl. I handed her the bacon ointment and unscented cream, since scents stick better to moisturized skin. She then slathered it on her pulse points because the warmth of the body helps project the scent more: inside her wrist, elbow, under the neck and behind the neck. She also applied some to her shoulders, clothes and hair to create a smell dome. When she was done, despite my best intentions to remain neutral, I had to admit that she smelled like roasted garbage. Correction: she smelled like a smoky roasted garbage can that happened to be filled with bacon. Alana chose jelly donut, Maya asked for fresh laundry, which left me with my favorite perfume.

We piled into my car, then immediately I had to take the top down because our clashing scents were insufferable.

As soon as we could breathe again Maya yelled over the wind. "So I went on my first, like, real date yesterday."

Courtney and I burst into hoots, claps and small dance moves. Alana sat still in confusion.

"I met him on OkCupid, he was a skater and really cute," she began.

"How cute?" asked Courtney.

She showed us his photo and even Alana nodded in approval.

"It honestly went surprisingly decent. I was pretty relaxed, and I made a lot of jokes that he laughed at. In the end he asked to see me again, but I don't know if I'm really interested or ready for that."

It wasn't remotely surprising to me that the date had gone well. Of late, Maya had been on fire: she cracked jokes, flexed her intellectual guns and even though she still had the same hipster style, gone were the days of lizard clips.

We pulled up to our first location, reapplied our scents, then headed up to the rooftop mixer. Within minutes of our arrival, a woman who recognized me from YouTube beckoned for me to join her group. The next thing I knew, I was surrounded and engaged in a full-on business proposition from her and her friends. I entertained their conversation for a few minutes until a wave of panic washed over me: *Where were the others?!* The last time Maya attended a party with me was the disastrous Crown app launch; I flashed back to her uneasy expressions from that night, then excused myself with urgency. I searched for my team in the usual reclusive hangouts: the corners, the couches and the bathroom. I was about to text them but then I spotted Courtney by the pool holding a conversation and then Maya a few feet from her with an entirely different group. I exhaled and walked over to them. Maya looked over her shoulder, smiled then introduced me to her two new companions. I stood in awe and watched nervous Maya hold a confident conversation with two beautiful women. A beat later I remembered why we were all there, so I seized the opportunity to kick off the experiment.

"Hey, do you guys mind if I ask you something? We went to a perfume store just before this and tried on all these different brands. Can you smell us and let us know which one you like best?"

And that was the line we used all night long. We took turns delivering it and although Maya was initially reluctant when she had to do the approach, she quickly got in the groove. We spoke to over fifty people that night and not one person turned our proposition down because just like Nina and JT said, people love to give their opinion—never forget that.

After we circulated the rooftop, we decided to head to the next location. We stood by the elevators and discussed how shocked we were by the results; somehow my perfume was in last and Courtney's bacon was tied for second! Another foursome of women walked up and waited with us.

Maya leaned in close to me. "I love that woman's blue suit."

It looked like something out of *Boogie Nights,* exactly the kind of outfit Maya would love. "So why don't you tell her?"

She widened her eyes. We all got on the elevator together then started our descent. I stared down Maya and gave her the classic *girl-get-in-there* look until she relented and shifted in blue lightning's direction.

"I absolutely love your suit," Maya said slowly while she triangled the woman.

The woman looked up and beamed. "Well, thank you, I love your outfit too."

"Hey," Courtney interjected. "Would y'all mind smelling us?"

When we got to the DTLA Proud Festival, I immediately cringed at my own ignorance: the festival was pretty much 80 percent gay men. I hadn't been to many of these events before and thought there would be a larger lesbian crowd. Alana assured me that this was an almost unavoidable mistake since gay men dominated the LGBQT+ scene. There were no lesbian bars, just lesbian nights, and even Pride Parades tended to be a sausage fest.

Nonetheless we made the most of the night and asked everyone within tapping distance for their take. Also, finding women didn't prove to be that difficult but finding a way out of the conversations with them did, which considering Alana's statement made perfect sense.

"I love your hair and your face and your clothes," said a drunk woman in adorable glasses who kept hitting on Maya despite her attempts to slide away. Unsurprisingly, that same woman chose "laundry" as her favorite scent.

Conclusion

The scent of fresh laundry was indisputably the victor: most people loved it and if they didn't select it, they still liked it. Jelly donut and perfume tied for second, but the difference was those who chose the donut were obsessed. And finally, although bacon did come in last, there were still six people who were madly drawn to it. We noted that the more stereotypically masculine the man (security guard, muscleman and construction worker) the more likely they were to favor bacon. Maya took fresh laundry home, which she more than deserved, so I immediately headed back to Amazon and ordered one for myself. If you're interested it's called CLEAN, Fresh Laundry. In light of my tendency not to naturally smell the freshest, I think CLEAN balances me out nicely. Bonus, it's gotten me compliments from Steve Harvey and soap opera royalty, Don Diamont.

EXPERIMENT FOUR

Hotcakes or sweet pie?

QUESTION

Which is more effective in attracting playmates, a sexy look or a good attitude?

HYPOTHESIS

If a group of women dress seductively but act standoffish for the first half of the night, then dress down but are friendly and outgoing the second half—we can assess which tactic is more attractive.

RESEARCH

Sometimes stereotypes are bad but for attractive people there is one stereotype known as the "what is beautiful is good" effect[7] that works in their favor. Essentially attractive people frequently get the benefit of others assuming they have certain positive qualities (e.g. they are kind, intelligent, honest, competent, happy) just because of how they look. So perhaps just looking good will emit a warm energy.

However, according to researcher James McNulty, physical attractiveness has no effect on the probability of a relationship being more satisfactory in the long run.[8] And according to Ty Tashiro's *The Science of Happily Ever After*, qualities that do ensure long-term relationship happiness include agreeableness, openness and conscientiousness—all traits that have nothing to do with looks.[9]

APPARATUS

For the first half of the night the group will be dressed to the nines: skin showing, makeup on and hair out *but* we will not initiate conversation with anyone. Then the second half of the night we will take off all our makeup and put on more modest clothes, but we will spark up conversations with potential playmates. We will then compare which approach is more effective when playmate hunting.

HOW TO DRAW A CONCLUSION

Assess the quality of our connections when the emphasis was placed on our looks and not our personalities. Then, vice versa.

Getting dressed for this experiment was a nice change of pace. For the rest of our outings, I ensured that my look was downplayed by wearing clothes that erred on the sensible side. But today, in the name of science, I got to ho it up! I put on my favorite bustier top, a pleated skirt, my green-tinted lenses, my Chanel belt, peek-a-boo heels and every last track of hair extensions I could find. When I looked in the mirror, I wanted to hit on myself and that's how I knew I was ready to head out.

Pricilla, Deshawn, Courtney and I all arrived in different cars, which made our individual reveals even more dramatic. As per usual Pricilla's makeup, hair and outfit were delectable. She wore a spaghetti-strap tank top with no bra that for some reason made her boobs look even bigger. Courtney looked dramatically divine in a black one-shoulder lace shirt and a hip-hugging black skirt. But the award for most dramatic transformation hands down went to Deshawn. I heard her before I saw her: she had on a pair of nude, strappy heels, a red crop top, red lipstick and perfectly sized jeans. Most notably, her hair was in jet-black, waist-length faux locks.

"Wow," we all said in unison as she approached us.

"Thanks, just a little look I threw together," she said.

We walked inside Angel City Brewery, looking like a moving mass of boobs, butts and beauty. The music bumped, our hips rocked, the wind worked in our favor and yet, no one put down their beer to greet us. Undeterred, we agreed to find a table and wait to see if they would bite once we were stationary. We chose a table at the front, so we would still be in plain sight, then sat down. I noticed each one of us had to adjust our pants or skirts in order to breathe. I smiled at that.

Deshawn clapped her hands together to get our attention then said, "So, I met someone in London!"

If we couldn't catch people's attention before, our collective cry of glee probably did the trick. The first night in London, Deshawn went out and met a guy we'll call Alex. Alex approached Deshawn and immediately they got wrapped up in easy yet intense conversation that spanned from religion to sex to crude jokes and all the other things we're told not to discuss. As per Nina's advice, she kept it weird and sexy. She spoke slower, intentionally sat curvier, demonstrated value, played the faucet, built rapport with him, challenged his opinions and by the end of the night they were intensely making-out. Even though she didn't get the chance to see him again before she left, they had been talking every day since.

Pricilla also had news to share about the dude she had been seeing. We learned that he was famous, which was exciting in one aspect, but also very difficult for her since he only seemed to be in town for less than twenty-four hours at a time. Courtney, who had been using the dating apps almost obsessively, hadn't come up with much luck at all. She had gone out a lot and swiped until dawn, but nothing was sticking. I could sense her disappointment but that didn't stop her from being fully supportive of the others' success.

For the next forty-five minutes we sat, chatted and enjoyed each other's sexy company without interruption. When enough time had passed, I suggested we walk around. We got a lot of glances, some stares, but no real takers.

We were about to leave to see if we'd have better luck at another location, but one onlooker intercepted us: "Hey, why are you sexy ladies leaving so soon?"

He was the kind of backward-hat-to-hide-my-bald-spot dude that I dreaded being stopped by, but this was what we were hoping for, I suppose. I thanked him and smiled. "We are gonna come back, we're just checking out this other spot."

As we walked a few people honked at us and yelled inaudible things. We also had an especially ridiculous encounter with a jersey-wearing dude that I thankfully caught on camera.

"Ladies, you look hot! Can I join you? I'm pretty hot too!" he yelled from ten feet away.

But instead of shooing this creeper off, I motioned for him to come over, so I could interview him.

"Wow, you all are so sexy, how is that possible? And you're all sexy in your own—"

I interjected, "Just out of curiosity, how many women do you approach a day?"

The man smiled and thought about this. His group of friends were back at a stoplight but a few of them had begun to trickle over, sensing this shot might land. "I dunno, maybe twenty, we went to a Raiders game before this."

We all looked at each other in amazement. I continued. "And of these twenty women, what's your ratio of success?"

"About eighty, uh, seventy-five percent," he replied.

There were four of us, so with those odds at least one of us should have been even remotely interested. Delusion is one hell of a drug, my friends, but no one said drugs don't make some people happy; so good for him. We then went into a spot called Barcade, which was exactly that: a bar that was also an arcade. I took out a five, fed it into the coin machine then divvied up the tokens.

"Let's split up, maybe we'll have more luck alone."

We didn't. Ten minutes later we all reconvened, ready for phase two of the experiment. We walked toward our cars and Courtney remarked again how incredible Deshawn looked, especially her new hairstyle.

"Thank you, you know what's really funny?" asked Deshawn. "When I was at the hairdresser this other girl was in there on the verge of a meltdown, talking about how much she liked this guy but how she had no idea how to flirt with him. She was sweet but all over the place and I thought, *oh my God, that used to be me!*"

We changed in our cars and emerged as different but much more familiar people. Courtney and I had our glasses on, Pricilla wore her hair up and Deshawn's red lips were back to pink. We wore comfy sweaters and flat shoes that made the walk back to the brewery a breeze. When we got there, I instructed everyone that they had to approach someone.

I looked ahead at a loud group of bros and said jokingly, "You can start there if you want."

I'm not sure if Courtney knew I was teasing or if she took my words as a challenge, but she walked right up to them and within seconds, they opened up their membrane and made Courtney the new nucleus. Five minutes later she sauntered back over to us and said cheekily, "Done."

Pricilla and Deshawn split up; once again I went in the opposite direction and looked for some game of my own to kill time. I saw a cute guy playing Jenga with a couple and took that as my in. "You guys look like the coolest people in here. Mind if I join?"

Of course, they didn't. I sat beside the cutie and played until the rest of the group made their way over to me, all flashing a thumbs-up. We left that spot and headed back to Barcade since we still had coins to play. This time no one honked or catcalled but we did note that because we were making the effort to talk to people, all of us were having a better time. Back inside, I had to yell over the sounds of the pinball machines to inform them that again, they had to find one person to talk to. Courtney and Deshawn peeled off and Pricilla hung back with me.

"No one here is remotely my type," she remarked.

Pricilla had a taste for high-profile men, which I applauded her for. At one point Chanel had to decide it was a luxury brand, and I respected Pricilla for making that decision about herself. And if you, reader, also want to pursue more high-profile candidates, don't let anyone guilt you into thinking that's shallow. In its early days, the main objective of marriage was to arrange alliances so that families could become more powerful and pool resources (this is a pleasant way of describing what went down, but we don't need to get into female slavery and patriarchal misogyny at this point). In contrast, modern coupledom is now largely based on emotions vs. assets, but that doesn't mean that the historic purpose isn't still a primary goal for some. There is only one word to describe the bond that people share when they are devoted to one another, *love*. And love has a thousand different connotations and billions of valid forms. Don't catch yourself looking down on anyone else's interpretation if it makes the parties involved healthy, happy and connected.

"I know this isn't your scene, Pricilla, that's why you should look at it like practice." I pointed out a cute guy in a fedora.

She walked off then I watched in amusement as she trailed behind him for a few minutes before making her approach. I went and sat down, then a short while later Pricilla joined me again and shrugged. I high-fived her for trying. A heavyset guy in an all-red outfit walked by. I asked him a question to strike up a convo and thrilled with the attention, he immediately pulled up a chair. He talked and talked and talked; dude was a run-on sentence that never seemed to bend into a question mark. I was about to politely suggest that we leave to find our friends, but in that moment our friend found us. Deshawn and a handsome guy also wearing a red matchy-matchy outfit approached us.

We learned our long-talking friend had come to Barcade with Deshawn's new handsome playmate, named Sean.

"But Sean, how do you know their friend?" long-talker said referring to Deshawn.

"Well, I couldn't help but notice that she was trailing me and then she got the courage to say what's up." He laughed and said he was joking. But, in light of our experiment, obviously that's exactly what happened.

Courtney danced over, sometime later, popping and locking as she joined our circle. "This DJ is the bomb!"

"You know how to pop?" said long-talking guy in amazement.

Courtney gave him a little something then he stood up and joined her. They made space at the bar to groove separately, then as one. Other patrons noticed and created a small circle around them; it was something out of the middle of a rom-com. Deshawn and Sean took a few steps back to talk in private and exchange numbers. Meanwhile, Pricilla and I sat still and happily watched both women, who we had come to love, truly living their best lives.

Conclusion

Looking good was not a sufficient replacement for having a good and welcoming personality. While looking sexy got us attention that we didn't have to work for, it was also attention from the kind of people we would've paid to avoid. Being dressed down got us no volunteers, but we got better results from the people we got to choose. I'd say a healthy mix of both would be an absolute winning formula: look your best then go ahead and charm the pants off the best person of your choosing.

That marked the end of our group experiments. I reflected briefly on the results of each, then more thoroughly on each member of the group's progress to this point. What a fucking difference! Maya on a date? Pricilla talking to a *Billboard* artist? Deshawn flirting and making out with a stranger in London? Courtney opening up, without trying to take control? I was amazed and determined to help them turn these budding wins into bouquets of victory. Which meant I needed to start pushing harder at their soft spots. I went to my desk and wrote down the weak areas I knew each still possessed: Deshawn still needed to be pushed to initiate conversations, Pricilla was still afraid to show her less-than-kind side, Stephanie was still too afraid overall, Courtney had proven to be personable but she lacked a sexual undertone and Maya had yet to overcome her fear of romantically pursuing someone in the queer community. For the next assignment, I originally planned to let them select their experiments, but it seemed like their roadblocks had chosen their path for them.

Phase Four: Practice

PART TWO

→ ←

Practice what you've learned thus
far on dates with low-medium interest
playmates. In addition, test out
new hypotheses so you can continue
to add to your toolbox for making
connections at will.

— 11 —

FIGHT-FLIGHT OR FRUIT TESTICLES

Coming out of the group experiments, I felt most of the five women had a firm grasp on what we'd learned throughout the program thus far. This made me excited about sending them out on an experimental first date. But I quickly learned I was alone in that feeling.

"I'm a little stressed about this," said Pricilla. "How are we supposed to remember to practice our seduction skills and do this experiment at the same time while on a date?"

I explained to her and the group that at this point practicing should not be reserved just for dates; they should be flirting, seducing and connecting constantly. Just like Ari said, "I flirt when I get into an Uber, I flirt at the bar, I flirt in meetings, I flirt while waiting in line for the bathroom."

Thus, the experiment should simply be adding one more layer, because they were assigned to go on a date with the kind of person they'd find at any of those random locations. As a single person, if you want to test out new game, it's best to begin with people you see as people, not as magically-hot unicorns. Again like Ari explained, when you get expertly good you stop putting anyone, despite their looks/status/reputation, on a pedestal, but realistically it will take some time to get to that point.

That's why top-tier professional athletes practice more than they play. They recognize that if the drills, skills and physical conditioning necessary for success aren't in place when the stakes are low, they don't have a hope in hell when the game is tied and the clock is running down to its bones.

Similarly, to be a good dater it's not enough to know the tricks. You have to understand the principles thoroughly, plus practice them so frequently that they become second nature.

The five experiments that we were going to conduct through one-on-one dates and the people who were going to test them were:

Interrogation (G)room: Deshawn

Can you ask bold and important questions on the first date
and still land a second date?

Dangerously in Love: Stephanie

Does doing an adrenaline-boosting activity on a date result
in a stronger, faster bond?

Me Mind So Horny: Courtney

Can you avoid the friend zone by infusing sexual tension into a date
without the other person being fully aware of it?

You, Instantly New Boo: Maya

There are five words that researchers have determined are the most
influential in marketing, but will they work in dating as well?

Hell Nah/Fuck Yeah: Pricilla

Is there a perfect balance to being agreeable and disagreeable
that people should be mindful of?

Deshawn came into this group touting how bad she was at small talk, so I thought it would be appropriate to push her right into the deep end for some big chat (that's West Indian slang for bold conversations).

 EXPERIMENT ONE

The Interrogation (G)room

QUESTION

How are you supposed to get to know someone when you can't get too personal while you're getting to know them?

HYPOTHESIS

If people began relationships with total honesty and invited their partners to do the same, then awkward small talk would be extinct.

RESEARCH

Psychologist Arthur Aron's research on ways to accelerate intimacy found that mutual vulnerability fosters closeness: "one key pattern associated with the development of a close relationship among peers is sustained, escalating, reciprocal, personal self-disclosure."[1] This work created the popular 36 Questions to Fall in Love. In addition, it inspired my own rendition, called 13 Questions to See if This Is Going Anywhere.

APPARATUS

The researcher goes on a date with a list of questions they must find the answer to by the end of the encounter. Questions include:

What is your religion?

What are your politics?

Do you live with anyone?

Do you smoke/drink/do drugs?

How's your relationship with your parents?

What was your last relationship like?

Do you still talk to your ex?

What would your friends say your weak areas are?

Do you have a criminal record?

What do you think about sex on the first date?

Do you want kids?

Are you in any debt?

Where is this going?

Deshawn and I game-planned for success before her date with a young man who happened to be an Olympian.

"What if he starts to figure out what I'm doing?" she asked nervously.

"He won't. Start with the easy ones about his family and politics then keep an open ear for natural ways to bring the others up without going into rapid-fire mode."

We spent the remainder of the call going over what we'd learned thus far. After analyzing his profile, we agreed that using the Oprah seductive technique, in which you try to inspire the best in someone, would be most effective, given his dedication to a competitive sport. We also agreed that the only way this experiment would be successful is if she was relaxed.

"Talk slow, take pauses when you need them and picture him naked if need be. Given that he's an Olympian that shouldn't be too unpleasant."

We disconnected the call and off she went. The date was supposed to last one hour so when the two-hour mark came and she had yet to respond to my texts, I began to worry. I kept calm by reminding myself I knew the man's Instagram account and phone number. The buddy system is something that I swear and abide by. In my single days I *never* went on a date if someone close to me wasn't aware of all the details. Yes, some of my meetups were spontaneous and in those cases, I'd spontaneously text a friend screenshots of the guy's dating profile and contact information.

But before I considered plastering the community with posters, Deshawn thankfully phoned back.

"Yay me," she said as soon as the line connected. "I think I got them all."

"Tell me everything!" I grinned.

1. *What is your religion?* Grew up Catholic, but the only time he goes to church now is if he goes with his mom back home.

2. *What are your politics?* Fuck Trump.

3. *Do you live with anyone?* He lives alone in an apartment.

4. *Do you smoke/drink/do drugs?* He has never drank or smoked in his life.

5. *How's your relationship with your parents?* He texts his mom good morning every day, but he doesn't talk to his dad often because he didn't grow up with him.

6. *What was your last relationship like?* His last relationship? He didn't have time for her so they broke up because #athleticsIsLife

7. *Do you still talk to your ex?* Not really.

8. *What would your friends say your weak areas are?* That he's not very social.

9. *Do you have a criminal record?* Hell no, could never do that to his parents, plus he already upset them enough when he chose to be an athlete versus a doctor.

10. *What do you think about sex on the first date?* As someone who travels he wished he was more sexually aggressive, but it's not his thing. He's not opposed to it, but it's never happened before.

11. *Do you want kids?* Not now, but he also doesn't know what he'll want in ten years. He used that as an opportunity to make it clear that he had no intentions of settling down for at least ten years.

12. *Are you in any debt?* No.

13. *Where is this going?* He has only had two relationships in the past decade because he'd rather focus on sports and most women seem to be a distraction. So probably nowhere, at least not for a while.

Just imagine the world of good that knowing all of this about someone after one date could do!

Deshawn went on to explain that she kept waiting for him to get upset or catch on that this was some kind of experiment, but he never did. With each question he answered she got more comfortable, until asking if he had a criminal record felt like asking him to pass the salt. She also shared how proud she was of herself for having a conversation that flowed so easily, without the help of alcohol. She admitted it helped a lot that she didn't have to stress about what to say next, since she had a checklist to get through.

"I mean, sure, he gave me a look of 'why are you asking this' and I just smiled and played it off like there was nothing behind it. I think my tone made a massive difference! I spoke slowly and with a hint of friendliness. I was playful and curious, not probing for answers."

We chatted some more about a few other things—What did he wear? How much did he talk about sports? Did he get the bill?—before I asked the only questions that really mattered: Had the experiment worked? Was there a closer connection as a result of getting the important questions out of the way?

"I'm not sure about the connection part, although he did invite me to a beach concert next Friday. So I would say that it worked, it definitely made the date easy and he even asked me a lot of the questions back so I had fun regardless. Actually, I'm going to try this experiment on the guy from London when we FaceTime later . . ."

Conclusion

You can get away with saying almost anything if you say it with a smile and that includes asking intrusive questions—even on a first date.

Dangerously in Love was the one experiment that I was most excited about because it was the only experiment that I hadn't done in the past myself. When I thought, who'd be the perfect person to pull this off, one name came to mind: Stephanie. She was an adventure-loving fiend who had a tough time letting her wild side out on dates or in social settings. And if free-falling didn't shake her loose, I was all out of ideas.

 EXPERIMENT TWO

Dangerously in Love

QUESTION
Where should you go on a first date if you want to create a strong bond, quickly?

HYPOTHESIS
If a new couple participates in an adrenaline-boosting activity on a date, then it will result in a faster bond.

RESEARCH
Dates that include risky behavior have proven to create stronger ties among people than those that don't. Psychologists Donald Dutton and Arthur Aron found that sexual attraction can transpire from arousal in the form of fear.[2]

APPARATUS
The researcher will go on a first date at an indoor skydiving venue then be mindful how her date flirts with, touches and opens up to her.

HOW TO DRAW A CONCLUSION
Do you feel the activity brought you closer? Was there more physical touch than on conventional first dates? Did they want a second date?

"I just realized that this is the first time I've gone on a date where alcohol wasn't involved," said Stephanie from her car as she drove to iFLY at Universal CityWalk. "But I'm excited, actually. I really am."

We went over the principles of flirting and how to be an exceptional conversationalist but in all honesty, there was only one major thing that Stephanie needed to be reminded of: do not downplay yourself. "People will believe what you tell them, so choose to tell them what's great and hopeful in your life," I said. "Even though you don't love your job right now, there are aspects that you do like, so focus on those in conversation."

Around eleven that night she phoned me from her car. "Well, that was a different experience. It wasn't awkward at all and having an activity really loosened up the experience. I have to admit I didn't hate spending time with him."

Stephanie went on to reveal something incredibly powerful, but based on her cavalier delivery, I wasn't sure if she understood the magnitude of her words.

"I felt like I had more power on the date. That was my first time feeling like the power was shifted in my favor and it made me realize I need a partner who appreciates how much I know. It also made me realize I've been superficial about my partner selection in the past. I need to be with a guy who allows me to talk and feel cool!"

I asked her how the indoor skydiving portion of the night went, and she explained that it created an "us versus the world" vibe that brought them closer together. They cheered each other on, hugged in support, high-fived and made a lot of eye contact that felt vulnerable—a side that she wasn't accustomed to seeing in men. She also admitted that her racing heart and the excitement of the new experience definitely made her date seem far more interesting than he actually was. Thus, when they went to dinner after, the spell quickly wore off. At that point she started to notice his flaws and in a shocking turn of events, Stephanie revealed, it was *her date* who downplayed himself way too much. In her words: "In life it's about having your story and your narrative and being happy about whatever that is at the time. He just didn't seem happy at all, which made it hard to look at him like an equal."

I asked her what she thought about the experiment's success and if she would recommend an adrenaline-inducing activity for others to consider when planning a first date.

"I can totally see how an experience where you're in danger can heighten the connection faster than a normal date would. Because it was new and exciting for both of us, we bonded. But there was no chemistry, so there's that too."

"How do you think the date went from his perspective?" I asked.

"I think he was into me and he kept trying to extend the date. I agreed to go to dinner after, but then he wanted to go out more, but I said no. Let me tell you, saying no to the next step of the date felt so good because usually my dates drag on and on! I think this power thing kind of suits me."

Conclusion

If you want to get close to someone in a short amount of time, suggest a date that has an element of danger to it. (I mean, now that I think about it, the movie Titanic *is based on this psychological technique. Luckily for you, no icebergs are required for similar results.)*

Up next we had to tackle the Mind So Horny experiment and coincidentally, the one person who had the nerve to pull it off was also the one person who needed it the most. The last time I saw Courtney she confessed that she had no problem finding dates, but securing a second was proving to be extremely difficult. I had a hunch why based on her recounts: Courtney seemed to be failing to find a healthy balance between heavy conversation and light flirting. What makes functional romantic connections so rare is that there is a ridiculously long list of extremes Eros must swing between: exciting while familiar, available while scarce, confident while modest, sexy while classy, thought-provoking while goofy . . .

and the list goes on. Esther Perel does an incredible talk on the difficulties of balancing these dichotomies in her must-watch TED Talk speech, "The Secret to Desire in a Long-Term Relationship."[3]

The Mind So Horny experiment was designed to help women like Courtney strike a balance between being intellectually and sexually stimulating.

EXPERIMENT THREE

~~The~~ Mind So Horny

QUESTION

How do you create sexual tension without giving off the impression that you're all about sex?

HYPOTHESIS

If you infuse sexual innuendos into a serious conversation, then this will create a subtle sexual bond that results in sparks on a date.

APPARATUS

On the date the researcher will ooze and insinuate sex without ever mentioning the word. This includes stroking bottles, rubbing round objects, thinking of sex while making eye contact, wearing glycerin to appear in heat, eating aphrodisiacs and suggestively drawing attention to the mouth.

HOW TO DRAW A CONCLUSION

How effective was using subtle sexual behaviors/signaling as a means of creating a connection? Did you notice a lusty look in your date's eyes? Did they seem to shift as if in heat?

Courtney's date was scheduled walking distance from my apartment, so she decided to stop by first. Luckily in this circumstance, instead of talking her through what she needed to do, I showed her. I pulled up my episode from *Shan Boody Is Your Per-*

fect Date when I did this same experiment and played it for her. I watched with delightful horror as I welcomed my date looking like I just stepped out of a baby-oil shower. Then I proceeded to caress the decorative oranges at the table, stroke my glass, squeeze lemon all over myself, suck the sauce off my food and gawk at his groin like it was a pharaoh's treasure.

"And you never mention sex?" asked Courtney with one of her gel pens in hand.

"You can make some innuendos but other than that, it's business casual convo."

She jotted some things down then went to the front hallway to get ready. I handed her a bottle of glycerin and two avocados. The glycerin she had heard me speak about before; it's used in fashion shoots to give off a dewy look, so I used to apply it all over before going on a date to give off a fertile look. But the avocados were new. I explained that, according to urban legend, when the Aztecs discovered the avocado, they named it after their word for testicle because of the shape, and the fact that it grows in pairs.

"So just, like, have them on the table and casually play with them during the date," I instructed.

"And how in the hell am I supposed to explain why I have these fruit testicles?"

I shrugged and waved. "You'll make something up!"

When Courtney phoned a couple hours later her tone was different, but not in a I-just-made-this-guy-cum-in-his-corduroys kind of way.

"Well, that was a bust," she confirmed.

I wanted to make the pun probably as bad as you do, but I resisted so we could get to the bottom of what went wrong. Apparently, her date had just moved to L.A. fresh off a divorce and that's all he could talk about. She stroked, squirted, caressed, triangled, teased and licked to no avail as he told her the details of his split.

"I really liked the techniques and I do think I'll use them, but this definitely was not the date," she said, defeated.

This wasn't the first time in recent memory that this *exact* thing happened to Courtney. Another guy she had met online a couple of weeks before who she said was a potential high-interest playmate, had spent the entire evening talking to her about his ex-girlfriend. What's worse is that Courtney ended the disastrous night by letting him know if he needed to vent some more, he could call on her. (**Insert facepalm here.) But I didn't bring this up because now wasn't the time to dig, it was a moment to uplift. Courtney had been pouring her heart out during this whole process and I was disappointed on her behalf for the dismal response she was getting in return. As a black woman, the odds were statistically against her, but I knew she could pull through because attitude determines altitude. Some have a higher climb than others, but I believed she had the determination to overcome this challenge.

Conclusion: Inconclusive

There were a number of reasons I could not wait for Maya to test out the You, Instantly New Boo! experiment. But the biggest one? This was going to be Maya's first official date with a woman.

⟶ EXPERIMENT FOUR ⟵

You, Instantly New Boo!

QUESTION

What do you say on dates so that you don't get awkward silence in between topics?

HYPOTHESIS

If someone uses the five words that researchers have determined are the most influential in marketing, then it will also help them have better conversations on dates.

RESEARCH

According to marketing expert Gregory Ciotti, the five most persuasive words in the English language are: *you, because, free, instantly* and *new*.[4]

APPARATUS

During a date the researcher will use these words as much as they reasonably can. The researcher will make a special effort to use the word *you,* since everyone's favorite topic is themselves, and *because,* since it provides the listener with clarity while promoting additional discussion.

HOW TO DRAW A CONCLUSION

Were there any awkward silences during the date? Was there an increased flow as a result of putting the five words in play frequently?

I chose this experiment for Maya because she was often at a loss for words after getting too many caught in her head. By attempting to use one of the highlighted five (you, because, new, free or instantly) as much as possible, she would always have a springboard to jump off that would keep her talking and prompt her date to do the same.

We connected before she and the new woman were scheduled to meet. As soon as Maya got on the line, she said the forbidden phrase: "I'm nervous."

I didn't correct her, I just listened and reminded her that this was a low-stakes date with nothing to lose. All she had to focus on was the words; everything else was just inconsequential details.

"I actually feel kind of awkward knowing I'm doing an experiment," she retorted.

"I can see that, but let that awkwardness slip into purpose instead. You're not doing anything bad; in fact, you're testing out a theory that could possibly help others to find a formula that helps them overcome mental blocks on a first date. Usually, half the battle is knowing what to say, but your only battle is to see how many times you can say it!"

About an hour and a half later Maya phoned back. "Hey, we just finished up."

I leaned forward and waited for her to continue; when she didn't, I slapped on my Captain Obvious hat: "So how did it go?"

"It went . . . great!" She went on to explain that it was a lot less awkward trying to keep the conversation going because she always had a completion lined up. "It's kind of like driving: even if you're not a great driver, you're still in control if you know where you're going."

Maya estimated that she used the word *you* 60 times, *because* 35 times and *new* 15. She admitted that she forgot the other two altogether, which was totally fine since *free* and *instantly* weren't as important in a non-marketing context.

"I was very surprised that something just like *you* would change a conversation so much," reflected Maya. "And using *because* allowed us to find similarities much faster."

For example, if someone asked her what her tattoos were, she usually just answered the bare minimum. But because she had to use *because,* she found herself going into stories that led to deeper conversation.

Now on to the juicy stuff. "So girl, how was your first date with a woman?"

Maya explained that she loved the experience and how relaxed she felt about challenging gender roles with another woman. She felt bolder, funnier and all-around sexier without feeling any pressure to perform. "I honestly feel so dumb for putting it off for this long because it was so easy, a lot easier than any other date I've been on. I am proud of myself. I feel weird saying it but I am. I was reflecting during this because I could never, even six weeks ago, see myself doing this, and when we started, I would have been clear that I absolutely could never do it. But I did and it went well!"

Conclusion

The word you *promotes conversation about others, which is a bonus since peo-ple like to talk about themselves. The word* because *promotes more sharing and prevents conversations from fizzling out too quickly.* New *is a great way to instill a sense of excitement,* instantly *gives a sense of urgency and* free *is just a word that I dare someone not to love. All in all, whether you are a budding or pro conversationalist, infusing these words into your discussions will work at promoting dialogue.*

Last, but not least (or as I should say *usually* last, but never least) was Pricilla and the experiment that she needed the absolute most: Hell Nah/Fuck Yeah. As someone whose greatest fear is making others uncomfortable, this experiment was perfect for her to prove to herself that she could be bold—hell, maybe even wrong—and still be liked.

 **EXPERIMENT FIVE**

Hell Nah/Fuck Yeah

QUESTION

How do you prevent yourself from coming across as too safe or too contrary on dates?

HYPOTHESIS

If someone is disagreeable followed by agreeable in perfect balance, then their date will believe they've won them over, thus creating a stronger attraction.

RESEARCH

Psychologists found that if you go on a date with someone and agree with ev-erything they say, they will see you as uninteresting and inauthentic. On the flip side, if you disagree with everything someone says, you are deemed unpleas-ant to be around. So researchers found there needs to be a perfect balance of going with the flow and against the grain. In this experiment the dater will disagree with everything their date says for the first half of the encounter, then agree with everything for the second half. Studies show, this particular formula will make the target most fond of the researcher because the target will be on a high from feeling like they had to won the researcher over.[5]

APPARATUS

On a twenty-minute date set your phone timer to ten minutes. For the first ten disagree with everything the person says, then once your alarm goes off switch to agreeing with everything the person says.

HOW TO DRAW A CONCLUSION

Pay attention to the person's body language during the first versus the last ten minutes. Do they begin to mirror you once you are agreeing? Does their attitude shift toward the end of the date? Do they want a second date?

I set Pricilla up on a date with my good friend Rome Green Jr. from the popular YouTube channel Dormtainment. Rome is successful, mega-handsome and family oriented, which made him a high-interest playmate for Pricilla. I know I suggested low-interest playmates for this phase, but I had to find a volunteer in the 11th hour because Pricilla's first attempt at this was unsuccessful. For that date, she never called me for coaching prior but reported back that she wasn't able to execute the experiment because her date wouldn't stop talking. Her inability to take control of the conversation in practice was more reason she had to get back in there and try again.

I walked Pricilla through the official instructions:

1. As soon as Rome arrived, she needed to set her timer for ten minutes then disagree with everything, no matter what he said during that time.
2. Once the timer ran out, she needed to set it for a second ten minutes then agree with everything he said.

3. After that, she could end the date or stay to practice other flirting and seducing techniques.

"Got it!" said Pricilla, keeping it short as usual.

A couple hours later Pricilla phoned me back, this time with a lot more to say. "I can't believe I actually did that!"

"So, I'm assuming it went pretty well because the twenty-minute mark was a long time ago."

"We had a blast," she said.

When they first got to the restaurant there was a massive lineup at the place, so she started the timer before they were seated. She made sure to keep her body language closed off by crossing her arms and pointing her feet straight ahead as they sat side by side. When she asked Rome why he had agreed to go on this blind date, he responded that he loved meeting new people.

She shot back, "I hate meeting new people."

She asked him about himself: what he did, where he lived and where he was from. He straightened up when answering the last question and revealed that he was born in Germany. In fact, he had dual citizenship and spoke some of the language, which he then demonstrated.

Pricilla replied, "I really don't like the German language. It's ugly."

Pricilla laughed when recounting that part and said that he seemed shocked when she said it, in truth she had shocked herself on that one. The rest of the ten minutes pretty much followed that same pattern: He said he likes to experiment with his hair, she hated guys who experimented with hair. He said he travels to the East Coast a lot for work, she hated the East Coast. Then the alarm went off and like clockwork, Pricilla opened her body up then commenced with the agreement portion of the date. From there they spoke about everything from travel to marriage. Pricilla found that they had a lot in common, and once the second timer went off, she was in no rush to leave.

"All right, so it went well and you did great. Do you feel a little crazy now for making this into such a big deal?"

"I know, it's just that I don't like making people feel awkward, so it was really scary for me to think about an entire date of disagreeing with someone. I just don't want to make anyone feel like crap, so I'd rather just say what I need to, to make the time go easy. But honestly this was such great practice because I thought it would make someone so uncomfortable, but in the end, it was the exact opposite."

I asked Pricilla what surprised her the most about the experience and she said she was most amazed by how easy it was to get into her relaxed, funny self. Being a little aggressive gave more space for her sarcasm to come out and play. Before the date she described herself as super-nervous but once Rome arrived, something switched, and she went into mission mode.

"Who would you recommend this experiment for?"

She laughed, knowing that this question was a setup. "I would recommend this experiment to someone like me—someone who is so agreeable and afraid that conflict will hurt way more than it could help. But a lil conflict keeps things interesting and it keeps everyone's ego in check."

Not that I didn't believe Pricilla, but since I knew Rome, I thought it would be stupid of me not to confirm. I texted him that evening to ask how his first blind date went.

> It wasn't bad at all. Like we immediately started talking about life and everything. She warmed up after a bit and it was on and popping from there.

I literally laughed out loud. Rome had just explained the experiment in layman's terms. Best of all, the next day I got a random text from Pricilla that confirmed its and her success:

> Rome wants to go on a road trip to San Francisco with me next month so I'm gonna assume he had a good time with me.

Conclusion

Disagreeing with someone then agreeing works because it makes the person feel like they have won you over. This technique also makes it clear, you have an opinion that you're not afraid to voice. I don't believe this formula should be followed to a T, timer and all, but we should be mindful that while great minds think alike, opposing minds can think bigger. There's a reason why there are no movies or books about people who look, act and think the same—variety is the spice of life. So don't be scared to put a little hot sauce on your next date.

And just like that, Phase Four was over. If you're great at math, then you've probably recognized that there was only one phase left. Their final assignment was to find a high-interest playmate to go on a first date with and secure a second. Sounds simple enough, but if you really think about it, this is the step that most people spend their lifetime struggling with. Of course, the group had an edge having made ample progress through phases one to four. But finding a high-interest candidate also has an element of luck to it that no one, except Deshawn and Pricilla, had been blessed with. However, Pricilla's guy was back on tour and Deshawn couldn't exactly meet London Alex halfway across the Atlantic Ocean on Jet Skis. Meaning, they were in the same position as Maya who had zero leads, Courtney who seemingly couldn't get a second date to save her life and Stephanie who confessed to me that this was the driest her love life had been since she was a virgin.

I realized that this program was on the brink of mediocrity. This made me frantic. I didn't want to make concessions and hand out green ribbons; I didn't want a *Well, that's nice for them* ending; and most of all I didn't want it to be all too easy for them to slip back into their old, worn-in selves because evidently there wasn't anyone worth pursuing. Especially since I knew that it didn't have to end that way. If the group just dug deep and poured over everything that we covered, they would stumble upon their feast, finish the program and win the game of desire with enough energy to play again. But, I also recognized that as their coach it wasn't my place to lace up and fight through the fourth quarter with them. They would never fully appreciate what we'd done if they couldn't prove that they could do it themselves.

Phase Five: Be

— ➤ ➤ ◄ —

Be the person you've always wanted to be
in the company of people who excite you.
Apply what you've learned and enjoy your
exceptional transformation. Revisit the
other four phases periodically because this
work is never truly done.

12

A GAME OF HER OWN

*P*hase Five began with a bang.

Matt Barnes finally wrote back and agreed to meet the women in the group. A couple of weeks earlier (after Pricilla mentioned for what seemed like the tenth time that he was her ideal type) I went ahead and slid into his DMs. It was a long shot, but I told him the straight-up truth: I was working on a project to help women fall in love with their love lives. We had enlisted the help of several experts and I believed he'd be a great addition to teach them how to attract high-profile men. He wrote back to say he loved the idea and agreed to participate. I offered a phone call or Google Hangout, but he believed it best to do a workshop in person. Of course, I could not agree more.

As soon as we set a date, I raced to break the news to Pricilla. But when I did, she broke news of her own to me: "Actually, I got up the courage to DM him about a week ago, and he responded. We were even going back and forth for a bit."

I was mortified. This was something we battled frequently when we all went out because strangers that we chose to get friendly with, would glance at our eclectic crew and ask the obvious: *so how do you all know each other?* We'd exchange a series of panicked looks before someone blurted out: *Uh, school!*

"Why didn't you tell me! Do you want me to call it off so that he won't know you're a part of this project?"

"No," she said confidently. "I want him to know that I'm single and actively looking to change that."

That was bossy and I loved it!

When the day arrived Pricilla, Courtney, Stephanie, Deshawn and I convened in the front of Lakeside Cafe. Maya, again, was out of town visiting her parents. Before we entered, I turned toward the group, even though I was really only speaking to Pricilla. "Tonight is a bonus, so I'd rather not talk much. I'd rather you all lead and get from it what you want."

As we approached the table, Matt stood to greet us and as the cliché goes, he was taller than you'd expect. How tall? In another life, his T-shirt could have been a grown-ass woman's funeral dress. I took the seat beside him and hoped that Pricilla would scoot to fill the other vacancy, but instead she chose the chair farthest away. Great.

The goal of the evening was murky for us all, which became evident as soon as Matt launched into his very candid, very unfiltered intro speech. To say the absolute least (because there's zero value in me sharing most of what he said) Mr. Barnes was far from private. I was shocked that even though he knew the conversation was being recorded, he spoke as if we were a group of fellow inmates on death row with nothing to salvage or save face for. Perhaps he just wanted to give everyone a stark look at the underside of love, which I assumed Courtney picked up on too.

"What is the realest lesson you've learned the hard way about relationships?" she asked.

"That there are actual evil people in this world, my ex-wife being one of them . . ."

About thirty minutes into that story, I was ready to call the night, but then quickly realized I had been focused on what Matt was saying rather than how Pricilla was responding. When I switched channels, I saw a clear-as-day picture of a woman who was absolutely crushing it! Pricilla was taking every opportunity to relate, joke, tease and mind-fuck like a pro. Also, upon further inspection, she had not chosen the farthest seat, she'd hoisted herself into the most visible one, directly in his line of sight. I tilted my head to see her from his vantage and noticed how her burgundy top perfectly played up her hazel eyes. She smiled and leaned forward until the candles lit her up like *Mona Lisa* at the Louvre.

"The best lesson I've learned about love, though, is that you can have as much or as little of it as you like," continued Matt. "I say this to my women friends all the time: don't be afraid to go for what you want because you miss one hundred percent of the shots you don't take."

Pricilla heard the message loud and clear: her body was poised in an S shape so crisp she was serving up Z vibes, she had been smiling so much that I was certain her cheeks would remind her tomorrow and, most incredible of all, she took every opportunity imaginable to brag about her son.

"I think the best lessons on love come from our children," she shared. "Having him and raising him and looking at every part of his character, knowing that I instilled that in him as a single mom, reminds me that I am who I am because of him and he is who he is, because of me. I love him so much and that truly serves as evidence of the good in me, that I too often forget about."

That night, Pricilla found then flourished in her triple-threat game: she was smoking hot, take-it-or-leave-it funny and maternal as fuck!

At one point Matt even remarked, "It seems like everyone keeps looking to you, Pricilla, to take the lead."

But in reality, we were just in awe that she finally was.

Matt graciously paid for the dinner (and later followed every-one on social media), which he did not have to do. Granted, his personal life was a bit of a train wreck, but he was an insanely kind man with a great heart and an even better sense of humor. Based on how quickly Deshawn, Courtney and Stephanie got up to leave, I'd say that in spite of his sweet side they too were over the crazy ex-wife tales. But Pricilla still had stamina and better than that, she had a strategy. When Matt went to the bathroom before he left, Pricilla remembered that she had to go too.

The rest is what literal dreams (or at least Pricilla's dreams) are made of. They exchanged numbers, and then Matt made the connection that they'd already spoken via DMs. He apologized for not immediately recognizing her, then invited Pricilla over to play pool to make up for his bad manners . . .

Even though securing high-interest playmates is what this program is all about, I must admit I was ridiculously shocked at Pricilla's manifested success. When I asked for this meetup it was in hopes that she could gain the confidence to start looking for her ideal, and possibly to get a slice of what it would be like to entertain a high-interest playmate. Not once did it cross my mind that she'd leave with the whole damn cake.

Pricilla more than completed the final assignment. She secured several follow-up dates with Matt and the absolute badass sureness that for her, this was only scratching the surface of her potential. Was he her optimal long-term match? Probably not, but she had finally found the courage to jump into the driver's seat of her love life and it paid off.

To prove it, the good news just kept coming. A few weeks later, she also informed me that she'd gotten a new job:

> These last few months have been truly eye opening for me! I am proud to say I charmed my way into a job that's in my field but completely foreign to me experience wise. This position is going to require me to step out of the background and step into owning my expertise to build a new department from scratch. My new boss is literally centering the

entire part of the practice around . . . ME. This would have terrified me in the past but with my newfound ability to connect with people, I'm not going to count myself out this time. And in general, I stop myself every time I catch myself wanting to fade into the background because I remind myself that I am capable, and I've proved that.

MEANWHILE, DESHAWN ALSO MESSAGED ME TO START THE CONVERSATION that I had been waiting for:

"I don't know how to do this assignment, because the only person I want to be with and see is someone who lives on the other side of the world. I'm swiping and smiling and all of that, but my heart just isn't in it."

Deshawn and London Alex had FaceTimed every single day since she got back. Over the month since their last meetup, their conversations had taken them places that people they saw daily had never been. It left her feeling hopeful, alive, desired but defeated.

"So why can't you go to London to see if you really have something?"

"I can't," she retorted defensively. "I don't know. I don't know if I can get the time off work and I don't know . . . if he'd even want me to."

"So ask."

Nothing is more haunting than blank pages. I told Deshawn that this trip wasn't even about furthering their relationship, it was a necessary act to understand it. Speaking from experience, once you finally understand your connection with someone, getting on with it or getting over it, is leagues easier. In other words, Deshawn would not be able to focus on finding local love if her mind kept wandering off with her foreign prince.

"You have to go to London, find that curtain and yank to see what's really behind it!"

Ahead of Deshawn's big trip I wanted to get her a lil something. She had new hair, new swag, new confidence, a new man in her life. But there was one last thing I still felt she needed for her transformation to be complete: a new bra. As per Talya's advice, having the wrong size bra can throw off someone's look and posture. Plus, if London Alex was so lucky to get *lucky*, I wanted her to feel her best! I also invited Stephanie along for the shopping trip, honestly, as a last-ditch effort. I had seen tremendous amounts of change in the others and while Stephanie had made some improvements, they were marginal at best. I hoped that getting her a new outfit that suited the woman she was destined to become would give her the kick in the ass that apparently, all the other work we'd done had not.

We all met on a Sunday afternoon at The Grove, an outdoor mall in L.A. that your fav B-list celebrities go to get "caught" on camera. We hit Nordstrom then split up: Stephanie to shoes, Deshawn to lingerie and I, to clothing. Thirty minutes later we had scored three cute shirts and one awesome pair of black boots for Steph. Meanwhile, Deshawn kept busy with a bra specialist and racked up a fitting room that would've made Dita Von Teese jealous. Because we were long beyond done with our own shopping, Stephanie and I sat on a tiny bench by the mirrors and waited for Deshawn to reveal each look.

"I'm so proud of her," she said. "It's, like, she's come so far."

Sensing this was my moment to check in I asked, "How are you feeling about your progress, Steph?"

"Honestly, I'm really disappointed in myself. But there's so much going on in my life it's hard to make time to date. There just seems like a million things that need my attention."

"You have no prospects?"

"I mean, there's a cute new guy at my job that just started and there's my trainer that I think is so hot."

"So, girl why aren't you pursuing him? And trainers are a part of your ideal-playmate hit list, so that sounds perfect!"

"I can't," she said, making a pouty face.

She looked and sounded like the same Stephanie who walked into my apartment on day one months ago. I nodded and assured her that she didn't have to force some kind of dramatic after-result if she wasn't ready. I realized then that the clothes I bought her, while cute, were not going to be transformative. A cute shirt and some heels can't pump up a deflated sense of self, neither could all the books, quizzes and hacks. Again, Stephanie still had to make a decision about the direction of her destiny. Unfortunately, no matter how much I wanted to guide her, that journey was a one-lane, single-passenger road.

Deshawn stepped out of the changing room in a soft pink number that made her 38 DDDD boobs look like a straight 10. She put her hands on her hips and turned from side to side, so we could see it from all angles. Stephanie and I stared at her body carefully as we discussed the fit of the bra. I noticed that no matter how invasive our stares got, Deshawn did not seem self-conscious or bashful about her boobs, or the body they belonged to. As confident as I am with my body and chest (or my lack thereof) I'm not even sure if I could stand that kind of focused attention without making some self-deprecating quip. But there was Deshawn, bravely and bodaciously soaking it all up.

The following Thursday, Deshawn left directly from work and boarded a plane to the unknown. It was the most terrifying, ballsy and inspiring second date I had ever heard of in my thirty-three years on this planet. Final assignment, complete.

Little did I know, travel had also been on Courtney's mind. She had gone home to Dallas to visit family a few weeks prior, which I knew. But what she hadn't told me is that she had met someone there.

"I'm sorry I didn't share this with you," she said as she held a cup of tea on my porch. "Half of me didn't want to jinx it and the other half just wanted to keep it sacred—something just for us."

When Courtney went home, she reflexively went on her dating apps and stumbled upon River. By this time, she had become a pro at cross-checking playmates with her job listing to see if it was worth her time. This guy seemed to check out.

So, on her last night in Dallas, she met up with River for a quick bite that ended up turning into a long-ass date.

"Can I see you tomorrow before you leave?" he asked. River leaned forward and touched Courtney respectfully but intently, which happened to be her love language.

Courtney smiled while retelling the story and then she cleared her throat and got serious. "So technically, I've already finished the last assignment. I've been on two dates with a high-interest playmate, but nothing is going to come of that, so now what?"

"But you're from Dallas and you go back there often," I said. "So why can't you just keep in touch and see each other next time you're in town?"

She explained that their connection was too powerful and because of that, the distance was already proving too painful. In fact, they had agreed to stop speaking to each other to save themselves the disappointment.

"We unfollowed each other on social media and agreed to be respectful friends. It's crazy, I feel like I've had to break up with someone I never even got to date, and that's also why I didn't say anything, because I don't even know how to feel about it."

I disagreed with Courtney and gave her the speech that I'll gladly give to you, reader: do not save yourself from the disappointment of a great thing coming to an end. Spoiler alert: everything ends! In fact, every single one of you reading this book will die!! Too morbid? Okay, I'll scale back. To me, the joy of being a person lies in our moments of extreme emotions: love and heartache, grief and creation, failure and triumph. These pinch-me moments, when we can't believe our own reality, are really what our whole, crazy lives are all about. As I often say to my clients, "Feelings are an immense privilege and if you're going to avoid them, you might as well hang up the whole people act and become a cupcake instead."

That's a little silly, I know. But, it's the truth. Every single conscious thought you have is a gift! And a special, bold asterisk goes to the feeling you get in the face of potential love.

In your final awesome days of raging on this incredible planet, I fail to see any circumstance where you're going to choke out the words, "I'm so glad that in my twenties/thirties, I chickened out and avoided that person that made me feel alive."

Even today, when I think back on the inconceivable disappointments that love has awarded me with, I smile because that is exactly what those experiences are to me: awards. The award for Puppy Love on Acid went to my nineteen-year-old self who "got engaged" (you know, the kind without a ring) to my boyfriend because I was leaving Coppin State University early and for some reason, promising my forever seemed more logical than saying goodbye (*hey, Ovan*). The award for Most Ridiculous Leap for Love went to the time I spent all the money I *did not* have to fly to Miami to go on a date with a guy who *did not* know it was a date (*hey, Reggie*). The award for Best Cringe-worthy Screenplay Based on True Events went to the countless poems, short stories, articles and unsent texts I wrote to Mark in the wake of our unfinished love story.

These experiences made me into a woman who has boundless respect for intimacy, pools of empathy for others and unbridled hope that there is no such thing as love lost. The heartbreaks were hard, but also they were unavoidable by-products of meeting the right people who were, in hindsight, wrong for me. Now, I'm not going to lie to you and say I don't regret any of my past relationships. There is a much-different-book's worth of experiences about men who taught me lessons that I didn't need to learn the hard way. But in all those cases, whether I would have admitted it at the time or not, I knew the water was too hot before I dove in headfirst. So, it would be one thing if Courtney wanted to avoid River because she heard warning bells, but instead, she was running from the distant but distinct sound of wedding bells. And in my opinion, if you hear them when you're in the presence of a good person, no matter how far or hella far-fetched the idea seems—go toward them.

She stared down at her cup for a long time then said, "I'm scared."

"That's okay, I do tons of shit that I think is scary, this program being one of them! But I still did it."

"All right," she conceded. "But I'm still going to keep looking for someone who's local."

Courtney left my house that day with two things: first, a vibrator that stunt-doubled as a necklace called the Vesper by Crave because I thought she needed a release, and second, she departed with clarity on what to do next. She and River spoke that night until they had to say good morning. They decided to see each other, at least one more time, before the month was up—but true to Courtney's word, that wasn't going to be the end of her story. A couple of days after that, she was at her favorite juice spot when Derek, a firefighter who she had been drooling over for months, walked in. She knew his name because like at Starbucks, they yelled out orders; she knew his occupation because on one occasion, he had arrived in uniform. And today, she decided, was the day that she'd gather much more about the fine fireman than that.

She struck up a conversation with Derek that flowed so effortlessly, the question "Would you like to go out sometime to get to know each other?" seemed as natural as asking for a napkin.

Later that night she called me in a panic: Derek had said yes to a date and River had set a date to come to L.A. to see her. Now what? I smiled in recognition that lack of supply and too much demand yielded the same reaction from her. Courtney, I had come to lovingly learn, was simply someone who needed order and a healthy level of predictability. If she had a process, she would make progress. So, I decided to try something unconventional to help her achieve that for her final assignment.

I created a step-by-step plan, based on everything we'd learned thus far, that she could use on her date with Derek. (Remember their date from the beginning of the book?) Go back and read that now—I promise it will be better the second time around. Courtney went on a second date with Derek the following week and while she enjoyed him, she wasn't consumed by him. This had a little bit to do with Derek being too reserved but a lot more to do with River. With his flight booked, they had no reason to slow things down. Their conversations became more intimate and they had undeniable physical chemistry that could even be felt over the phone.

When River arrived, Courtney and I didn't speak that weekend nor was she posting from her office on social media as she usually did. So Monday night, when I knew he'd left, I released all restraint and made the call.

"I'm dying to know, how was it?"

She sighed in that Disney princess way that's usually followed up with a song led by a crab. "Amazing. It was honestly not a single drop short of amazing."

For the next hour, Courtney and I chatted about things that I responsibly cannot share, not just because it's not my story but because it wasn't completely hers either—it was theirs. I can say for certain, though, that the feelings, firsts and epiphanies she experienced with River broke her, but in the best possible way.

When we had covered the weekend's happenings from every angle, I expressed how in awe I was of her. We then said our good-byes and I realized, with joyful reverence, I had to say one more: it was time for me to step aside as the primary intimate guide in Courtney's life. I've never been a teacher, but I imagine letting Courtney go was a lot like graduating your star student. Half of you is happy to have had a hand in whatever amazing things they will do next and the other half wants to give 'em an *F* so they're forced to take your class again.

There is only so much you can learn about romance objectively and if you really wanna become a masterful seducer, ain't nothing like the real thing, baby. Don't get me wrong, I'm not cuing the graphics guy to etch "Happily Ever After" over Courtney, or any of the women in the group's story: time still had a LOT of telling to do. But the truth is, even if the River did run dry (oh, come on—how could I resist!) and proved to be no more than a single chapter or even just a footnote in Courtney's memoir, without a doubt he was her next great love story.

Deshawn got back from London and texted me that she'd landed safely, but that she was pooped and would call me tomorrow. Nothing else. Not even a shred of a clue how it went.

Damn that tease, I thought.

The next day I got the call that of course I did not miss. And I'll spare you the wait I had to endure; it was incredible: great chemistry, great conversation and yes, people, for the first time in forever, Deshawn had great sex!

When I asked her what she liked most about the experience she said, "I liked that he didn't try to discourage any of my crazy ideas. I told him on Saturday that I wanted to live in a romantic comedy, so he picked me up at nine A.M., we went for a really long romantic walk in south London, we went for brunch, we went shopping, and when it got dark we went back to my Airbnb to watch a movie, then . . ."

My favorite part of all was her ease. Unbelievable, *sorry-who-am-I-talking to-again?!?* ease. The transformation in Deshawn was so dramatic, to this day I'm not convinced she wasn't a plant. When I spoke to her, she seemed mature, calm and wise beyond water preservation.

"What happens now?" I asked.

"I really don't know and it doesn't really matter," she said. "I enjoyed my time, I stand behind my choices and if he wants to keep talking to me, great, I enjoy talking to him. But if the distance is too much, then I'm grateful for everything that it was. As is."

We ended the call shortly after that mic-drop moment. She thanked me and promised she was just getting started. Most miraculously, all of this occurred without any giggling.

I'd like to say that I cried that night in joy for the three incredible women who had exceeded my expectations, as well as their own. But you're more than likely asking the same question that I was . . . what about Maya and Stephanie? Statistically, I was aware that at least one person wouldn't complete the program but Cherise made sure to secure that spot some time ago. Four out of six I could stomach, but a 60 percent success rate just wouldn't cut it.

I texted Stephanie and invited her out for a night of Boba and playmate hunting. After she got off from work, I picked her up from her apartment, then we headed to Equinox. Not to work out, not to hang out at the juice bar, but so we could park outside, open up multiple dating apps and put our search radius on 0. Once we found a good parking spot, we set up shop and tag-team swiped for an hour.

Again, if you do your job listing from Chapter Eight correctly, your final description should reveal an archetype of who you're looking for. For example, Stephanie was looking for a personal-trainer type—hence why we parked outside of Equinox. When I've told people about this strategy in the past, they've often given me a speech about not limiting your options for love. Which is a fair argument, but I counter that by saying you're not limiting, you're *zoning.* Think about it like this: when you choose a major in college, it's because after a certain number of years of education, it's logical that you can make an informed decision about the *kind* of job that you'd like. You're not committing to a career, but you know the subject that you enjoy and understand best. Similarly, in dating there comes a time where you know what type works best with you, so why not honor that knowledge by focusing in on that community?

I'd love to say I made this genius idea up but it's not 100 percent my brainchild. When I went to school for sexology in San Francisco, my school had the craziest library of sex and relationship books. There was endless rows of titles I'd never heard of from people who were probably dead and that's how I stumbled upon a 1969 bestseller that touted itself as "the first how-to book for the female who yearns to be *all* woman." The book is called *The Sensuous Woman,* and it was anonymously written by a person who went by J. I can see why someone wouldn't want their full name attached to it; I'd best describe it as an equal mix of vile ridiculousness and pure delight.

Amidst its problematic parts, it has classic lines like, "Pay attention to his kissing style. If he attacks your mouth with enough force to make you fear he's going to jam your front teeth down your throat, he's going to be even more cloddish in the advanced stages of lovemaking."[1]

Also, the author J offered the story of a woman named Barbra who had a systematic approach to bagging her boo. Barbra wanted to date an engineer because she loved the quiet, solid and introverted nature of the ones she knew. But she currently worked as an administrator in theater. What's a girl to do? Barbra quit her job, found a position at an engineering firm, started frequenting all social events, yada yada yada, married an engineer.

Using the search radius in dating apps is just a version of that system.

As we swiped on a bunch of buff guys with deep quotes in their bio, I had a great time with Stephanie, as I usually did. She always taught me new words, had great books to quote and was an excellent listener. But maybe I hadn't been listening to her, because midway through our session, she casually said, "Like I was saying, things just started to pick up. That one guy, I turned him down because he didn't want to do the first date on my terms, which felt great. And the guy I did go on a date with, Shan, it's crazy but I really liked him. We went to this speakeasy and we just had the most natural, good time. It's been so long since I've been into anyone, I just wanted to bask in that feeling. He clearly wanted to hook up, but I just felt like making out and damn, it was so good! I'm surprised I resisted."

A little while later, we called it a night. But as I had learned, she didn't technically need this night at all. Stephanie was doing fine on her own.

Next, I had to check in with Maya who had yet to report anything new to me in weeks. To get her back in the groove, I asked around my circle for upcoming lesbian nights. Thankfully, my friend Rachel Scanlon had the perfect suggestion: a comedy night called Two Dykes and a Mic. Maya said she was down to roll and I decided to share the flyer with the group in case they felt like tagging along too.

To my absolute surprise and glee, Stephanie wrote back:

I actually wish I could but, I'm going on a date ☺

Pricilla, Maya and I attended Two Dykes and a Mic and laughed until the drinks in our bellies were clapping along. The all-lady lineup just gave the whole night a fresh vibe as each comic got to step on stage as an individual, not as a representation of an entire sex. Rachel of course was a riot. I've seen her perform several times and she never disappoints. There was also one other comic in particular that I strongly suggest you look up: Aparna Nancherla . . . OMG LAHOL (submitting *laugh all hell out loud* to replace LMFAO, which I've never liked). Seriously Aparna, have my babies, you're so damn funny.

After all the acts were done, we hung around for a bit and chatted with other attendees. Rachel approached me and thanked me for coming. We talked about how funny she was, how great the event was and how inspiring it had been for Maya, who surprisingly, but perhaps not entirely surprisingly, had hopes of becoming a standup comic herself. Nothing came of that night aside from light flirting, and a new hint of light in Maya's eyes. I didn't know why back then, but I remember looking at her as she got out of my car and thinking, *Something is definitely cooking behind those circular frames* . . .

After that, I couldn't get ahold of her for a while. Which in truth had become common in our relationship. The first few times this happened, I assumed she was planning on quitting the group. But after getting to know her more intimately, I came to understand that these personal sabbaticals were exactly that: small breaks from the world necessary to preserve her personhood. A couple Saturdays later, she finally texted back and told me she'd call that evening. Two days later, she made good on her word.

"Hey, I'm so happy to finally connect with you," she said, and I truly believed her even though she had been dodging me. "I know I forgot to get in touch with you the other day, but I had a date and it lasted until two in the morning. It's not an excuse, but it also wouldn't have happened without this whole experience. I'm still shook."

"What number date was this?" I asked.

"Two," she said, and I could practically picture her round, smiling face as she said it. "This was our second date; specifically, this was my *first* second date in my entire life. It's been going amazing; they are in an open relationship, which has been great for me because I feel no pressure at all."

I fired off a few follow-up questions: Where did they meet? OkCupid. What did they have in common? Politics and humor. What made this person special? They were securely attached and spoke her love language. Had she been nervous while getting intimate with them? At first, yes, but she worked through her feelings independently until she was able to relax and enjoy it. Did she *truly* enjoy it? Hell yes. Immensely.

But then, because old habits die hard, I went ahead and made the same mistake I'd made when Maya and I first met: "Are they a man or a woman?"

She paused, and I knew in that nanosecond I'd asked the wrong question. "They are trans masculine and they like the pronouns *they* and *them*."

I smacked my forehead and apologized. "It's just as easy to ask as it is to assume. My bad."

Maya laughed. "It's okay, when you make a mistake you have two choices: you can lose, or you can learn. I think you're learning."

And of course, she was right. I too, had gone through an immense transformation because there is something magical that happens when you place yourself in a pressure cooker of change with others. With the stress, heat and discomfort of it all, you lose sight of why you went in to begin with and that confusion is necessary for a richer result. It's best to throw everything you think you know about yourself out the window before committing yourself to change. You can't make predictions on who you will become if you've never been that person before.

To put the cherry on top of this final phase, the next day I got the most wonderful message from Stephanie:

> Yesterday, I saw the greatest manifestation of your work and investment in me. Like no joke I went on my second date with that guy of high interest (lol lingo) and not only that I felt really hot and good about the dynamic. Thank you for your support and for holding a mirror to my negative habits. Love you and your work more than ever today!

A FEW MONTHS EARLIER STEPHANIE AND I WERE IN MY CAR AND I ASKED HER what celebrity pairing was her #couplegoals. She reflexively replied, Ariana Grande and Pete Davidson.

Which naturally begged the question, "Girl, really? Why?"

Stephanie explained her dream was to also meet someone who proposed that quickly. To her, the highest expression of love was when a person knew they loved you practically before they met you. Of course, we all now know how the #Grandson love story ended, but null and void of that, I thought that was the most telling answer to Stephanie's plight: she was in such a rush to get chosen that she was not just willing to, but *dreaming* of, forfeiting her right to choose.

So imagine my surprise when I asked Stephanie for details and she replied, "I think this guy is into me for sure, but it's a bit much. I've never dated such an eager or expressive person before, so that's refreshing. But I think I want more time and to date around."

I pried a little more, about her second date with the first guy to give her butterflies and dirty thoughts. It turns out she informed him she had time on the weekend, but he wanted to see her sooner. She offered him the time slot after her Thursday spin class, thus making herself seem scarce. I was so proud to hear that she made him work around her plans instead of bending to accommodate anything that included him. This time around, she was definitely more comfortable keeping the ball in her court.

After all that damn work, I finally caught my first glimpse of the woman I had been searching for since we began this journey— the one who understood that the goal wasn't to be taken, it was to be *taking* more than what she was offered. To me, that was the real winning result in Stephanie's Game of Desire. Not the man, not the make-out, not the chemistry or even his affection toward her—the prize was in her acknowledgment of her own power and infinite potential.

I echoed this sentiment along with care instructions: "The most important thing at this crucial point in your life, Steph, is to surround yourself with people who see you for your highest potential and want to help nurture that! Now is your time for growth and personal discovery, and just like a plant, you can't do that alone; you need sun, water and healthy soil. This dude, or anyone you give your time to, better be one of the three."

Assignment complete. Except, it's worth noting that Stephanie was not at her "after" point; instead she was just beginning to distance herself from the "before." Trust is a result of consistency over time. In plain words, you gotta do a lotta good before someone can give you a lil benefit of the doubt. This formula also holds true for our most important relationship of all, the one we share with self. And that was Stephanie's next great assignment: rebuild that bridge between who she wanted to be and who she'd settled into becoming.

I was happy but also nervous about this new guy being in the picture at this crucial time. If he was loving and honest, he could accelerate this next phase for her, but if he was brutish, he could obliterate much of her progress. But I supposed this is where I had to start trusting that Stephanie had the skills, knowledge and confidence to watch her own back; she didn't need me there anymore.

"Knowledge is power and power is the luxury of doing things your way. I hope you find what your is way, Steph, but more than that, I hope you have a blast looking."

SO THERE YOU HAVE IT: SIX WOMEN WHO CAME INTO THIS PROGRAM ACHING with rejection and disappointment that all left with very different, but also all very powerful, outcomes:

Cherise showed that there is no one-size-fits-all solution here. Her story also exemplifies the power of manifestation: if you go into anything, be that a program or a relationship, believing to the point of *knowing* that it won't work, you're going to be right 90 percent of the time. So who's to say the exact opposite can't be true too? Faith is free and if you're gonna choose to do something, you might as well choose to believe in it or else what's the point in trying? A question that Cherise both began and ended with.

Maya showed that you can prove yourself wrong if you give yourself a chance to do something unexpectedly right. When I really thought about her journey, I realized she had the most dramatic but least obvious change. In other words, Maya got bangs. All she truly needed this entire time was a simple snip across the forehead that allowed her to see her natural beauty clearly and her hard-earned capabilities fully. She came into this workshop as a smart, self-aware, witty, sexy, anxious and terrified young woman in a scrunchie. She left a smart, self-aware, witty, sexy, anxious and confident woman with bangs. Moral of the story is, sometimes, yes, you need to reinvent the wheel to make it work for you. But other times, you just gotta remove the rock you wedged in front of it.

Stephanie showed that there is no such thing as a lost cause. There is no un-pretty sister, undecorated Ivy League graduate or unfit community member. You are not destined to make the wrong choices and to never be chosen—that reality has never existed, but you do. And who are you? You are a one-of-a-kind creator with infinite possibilities during your finite time on this planet. You, my dear, are whoever you consistently decide to be. And I know this sounds like some hokey shit, but despite not knowing you personally the way I know Steph, I absolutely know that you are an exceptional creator for one simple reason: someone created the English language I am typing in; a single person out there designed every item of clothing you're wearing; the place you call home, someone constructed; the job you rush to, someone founded; and even the sauce you put on your french fries—another human being no different, no greater, no more capable or awesome than you Made. That. Shit. Up. So, if you're not currently happy with what you have, what's stopping you from making your own shit up?

Deshawn showed that you don't have to naturally have what it takes. You just have to be willing to learn the habits that can take you where you want to go. She came into this program looking, sounding and believing very different things about herself than when she left. It had been months since I heard her proclaim her awkwardness, aloofness or tendencies to anxiously chatter—and she was much better for it. While I'd like to take credit for the shedding of her old skin, in truth her outcome is the fruit of a decision she made long before we met: "My lips are beautiful, my nose is cute, my job is cool, I give great blow jobs and it's time that I helped people to recognize all this greatness as well!"

Courtney showed that hard work pays off. Fuck yes. I'm elated her story went well, not just for her sake but for ours. We live in a world that advertises that the best, brightest and most capable people don't always win (*coughs* Trump). But from the ashes, once in a while we get a story like Courtney's. A woman who came, who saw, who mimicked, who studied, who tried, who lost, who got back up, who triumphed and still kept her arms outstretched with her palms facing up, excited, but most important, well prepared, for whatever was to come next.

Pricilla showed that you make your own luck, even when you feel like you have no resources or favor to gamble with. Regardless of how life has let you down, you can't let it keep you there. And if you are there, remember, you aren't down because you can't do any better, you're there because you've allowed critical voices to speak louder than your true purpose. Dig deeper and fight because only you know the awesome things you're capable of manifesting. It's your time to run towards—not hide from—your unclaimed greatness. And I get it: change isn't easy, but being stagnant hasn't been all that simple either, has it? So, how much harder can it be to act on the chance that you do have what it takes to be with who you want—and to be who you want?

— EPILOGUE —

THIS SH*T WORKS!

*I*t's been three months since the group had their final assignment, but the work has far from stopped. We still keep in touch and swap books, videos and memes that help us to continue to sharpen our skills as expert connectors. While many of the women initially had an aversion to the idea of *more* homework, after seeing the ripple effect of their new capabilities in multiple areas of their lives, their passion for mastery took over just as mine did when I first started years ago.

As mentioned in the intro, if you too choose to devote yourself to this craft, the work will never see its final days. Even after you've wooed an ideal high-interest playmate and moved on to mastering the skills of maintaining the fire you've built, once in a while you'll have to come back to these foundation-building principles. And when you do, I promise you'll always be repaid for the time you put in. To this day, I'm still learning things about the Game of Desire that blow me away. For example, I just read that the most effective way to communicate to someone that you understand them is to put yourself imaginatively, in their shoes. If someone is telling you a tragic or exciting story, picture yourself in their exact position as they're speaking. This will alter your facial expressions and communicate that you truly empathize and relate to their experience, which as we learned in Chapter Six can be the difference between an inconsequential and a life-long bond. If you want to see this tip in mind-blowing action, watch an episode of *The Oprah Winfrey Show* or analyze Jada Pinkett Smith in action as she interviews guests on *Red Table Talk*—their mannerisms in themselves are a master class.

In my first book, *Laid,* I wrote, "In school, we spent several units learning about dinosaurs and only two classes learning about sex. Well, since that time, I've never encountered a single T-Rex, but I have been confronted by plenty of dicks." In the same vein, I've never found a practical use for knowing how to sing "O, Canada!" in French, but everything I've ever learned about the psychology of attraction has made my life and relationships richer. I also happen to know that the group who completed my five-phase program would say the same.

Courtney and River are still going strong. So strong that she's requested a job transfer to Dallas. It actually hurts a little to type that because we have grown so close, but as she said, "I've always known L.A. wasn't my home, but I was determined not to leave without one dream come true. You gave me that, Shan, so thank you."

But if you're impressed with her blooming love life, you'll be thrilled to hear about her explosive self-love. In the past months Courtney has taken herself on numerous vacations, redecorated her place, made peace with past abusers and embraced her natural hair in the process. Best of all, in dedication to the joy she has found in her transformation, she has begun to work on a series of online workshops called "Home Court Advantage" that will help other women who were once bullied to find their strength, and use it.

Deshawn and London Alex still talk daily—crazy, I know! Also, after months of being unhappy at her job under the leadership of an antagonistic boss, she found the courage to stand up for herself and file a formal complaint. That act of self-love led to a powerful ally, a job transfer, a promotion and her being able to live her best life by continuing to doing what she loves for a living. We thank Deshawn with all our hearts for tackling the water crisis in California one noble day at a time, but me personally? I'm insanely grateful that she now owns up to that greatness.

Every time I speak to her now, I have to double-check the caller ID to make sure it's the right person. Her voice is different, her look is different and her energy is totally transformed. With her newfound confidence, she formally began STEMming Upward, a tutoring company specifically designed to help young women of color excel in STEM and social skills, as she has.

Maya still calls me two days after she says she will, but she always has an exceptional excuse. Sometimes she's busy spending time with her cool-ass family, others times she's in Palm Springs with friends, often she's in the throes of writing and occasionally she's been up way past bedtime getting freaky with a fling. Now who could possibly take issue with that?

The bond she and I have grown to share is special and, in many ways, very different from what I have with the rest of the group. I'm proud of that, but moreover, I'm proud that those closest to her have seen a change in her too. Maya told me that on one of her friend trips to Palm Springs the person who told her to sign up for this program to begin with, pulled her aside and said, "I've seen you change in every possible way since you started working with that group and all of it has been positive."

In line with that positive change, Maya is currently in a four-month intensive writing class and as a result, now feels confident in referring to herself as a comedic writer. In the beginning Maya came to me desperate to build a life that was no longer centered around her chronic anxiety, and I think we would both agree, she has successfully accomplished that. She still has her moments but in situations when she is overcome, she privately acknowledges her feelings, takes a step back and then when she's ready, moves forward with renewed confidence and certainty.

Pricilla is just incredible. Like Deshawn, she had troubles with her boss at her job. This served as a great source of bonding for them and from which sprang one of the many accidental miracles of this project, because they leaned on one another. She too put in a formal complaint but when nothing was done about it, she began to look elsewhere and landed on a job that paid better and gave her greater responsibility. She is now the face and personality of her workplace, managing the company's content for social media and heading up all consultations. Given how hard Pricilla once fought me to be left in the background, I was elated that this new job also saw what a crazy waste of greatness that would be.

In addition, within a couple of months of this new role she began to realize she could practically run the business, so she decided to start her own! She found a couple of investors and opened up a scalp micropigmentation salon called Camouflage. Currently, she is decorating and marketing in preparation for a launch this year. She also kept her job, which she still loves, but Pricilla realized through this process that she's ready to make the transition to being a boss. Which leads us to her love life.

No longer content with just being an employee, she got rid of anyone around her that she felt didn't see her as a leading lady. So, she no longer sees Matt romantically, although they do still keep in touch. She is, however, becoming increasingly involved with that multiplatinum artist who she says has a heart of gold and treats hers like it's made of glass.

But as she told me, her favorite improvement as a result of our time together occurred in the most unexpected place: "It wasn't until this project that I started to see my motherhood as a strength rather than something I was low-key ashamed of because I'm young and unwed. But my perspective has changed so much and all I want to do is to show my son that having him young was NOT a mistake. I want to be a leader now."

As for Steph, she's just getting her whole life together and I couldn't be prouder. She is still seeing the same guy and has been enjoying the process of getting to know herself in the presence of someone who adores her. Throughout their months of courtship, he has been persistent and forthcoming about his feelings for her, which, she admits, has taken getting used to. But the guy she's seeing is probably the only thing that hasn't really changed with Stephanie. She decided to move back home to save money and with that, she's been able to hire a career consultant to help fine-tune her course, and a therapist to further explore the roadblocks that have prevented her from stepping into her greatness.

She has always been a lovely woman but now, she's absolutely striking. Best of all, this change has been noticed by everyone around her. Namely, one of her exes, who recently texted her, *I just wanna say, I can see your growth, your confidence, the way you carry yourself. You're more sure of what you want, it high key makes you even more sexier/attractive on top of what you naturally are. I like the new Steph.*

I must admit, so do I. But clearly, I love all the women from the group, and moreover, they feel the same about each other. Stephanie and Deshawn have been looking for a place to live together and Courtney and Pricilla have become accountability partners.

What began as the biggest project of my career has somehow become even bigger than I could have imagined. I knew at the outset I would see change in the participants, but if you asked me back then, "Do you think this work could spark a dating revolution?" I would have said, "I hope so." If you asked me now? "Hell yes. This shit works!"

But before I send you off into the world to see how my five-phase program can transform you, it is worth noting under what circumstances I believe this program will not work:

First, this can't work if you really think that it won't. I am a firm believer that whatever you think is true, is. For example, if a kid believes there's a boogie man in their closet, they might develop a set of rituals around that theory: the closet must be kept closed, no walking on the floor cracks and no going to the bathroom after lights out. Thus, after a while of consistently centering your habits around a belief, it stops mattering if it's actually true or not because you've changed your behaviors to accommodate it. In the same way, if you think you are unlovable, chances are you've begun to respond to the world in a way that has made your fear real.

A lot of people subscribe to the scarcity model of love: an idea that there is a finite number of people who could be a match and even less time in which one must find them. But, with globalization, far less restrictions on who can love who and a roster of single people at your fingertips with dating apps, I just don't see how you can possibly make that argument. That's why I can say with absolute confidence that you are not excluded from finding romantic love. Despite having never met you, I don't just think, I *know* there are several someones out there for you. And now that you know the secrets to making yourself desirable, that goes tenfold. So no matter how persuasive of an argument you can muster, do yourself a favor and stop allowing fear to get in your way. If you want this to work, start acting like you're on your way to the feast. Again, I assure you that there is a chair vacant, just for you.

Second, this will not work if you try to use this system while surrounded by toxic individuals. As you just witnessed, one of the greatest strengths of the workshop was the community of encouragement, empathy and accountability that it was based in. Now, I'm not suggesting that you must surround yourself with a support group centered around your transformation as we had, but you do certainly need support. This work can be challenging, and it may lead to drastic changes that initially will feel kind of uncomfortable to you. If those closest to you are discouraging, poking fun or outright doubting your efforts, that makes it increasingly difficult to see things through.

Yes, on a microlevel, this program is about making you more attractive. But on a macro scale, it's about becoming your absolute best, most vibrant, forward-thinking, flirtatious, positive, chemistry-concocting self in all that you do. And a large part of that has to do with surrounding yourself with people who are excited about the new you and accepting of the current one. I know the process of cutting people off is complex, but to simplify things, negative people are a lot like thongs: you don't realize how far up your ass they are until you remove them. Trust me, you'll thank me later for giving you that extra nudge to put space between you and anyone that makes you feel undesired.

If you don't know where to begin to find a small community that will champion you on this quest, go to TheGameOfDesire .com for a ton of additional resources that can help you.

Finally, above all else, remember that when it comes to The Game of Desire, you were born to win (literally, we're biologically engineered to create pair bonds). All I've done in this book is give you the tools and strategy to enjoy and have better, quicker results while playing. But there are no tips or tricks that can substitute or imitate that special magic that only you possess. Courtney, Deshawn, Maya, Pricilla, Stephanie and even Cherise all came into this with the same natural spark that they left with. The bulk of the work I've done was in cleaning up the debris around that light so it could shine as bright as it was meant to. No, this is not the part where I backtrack and tell you that the secret ingredient is in fact to *just be yourself.* But, I do believe that if you know who you are at your core, what you want and who you deserve, you're more than ready to become one of the few who master this game and have a blast while playing it.

Skillful seduction is not a gift bestowed on the beautiful, it's a series of learned behaviors acquired by the bold. So now that you've completed this book, what's stopping you from getting out there with your bold, bad self?

ACKNOWLEDGMENTS

In October 2017, I sat in Drake's penthouse that was so damn close to Toronto's CN Tower he could've set up a zip line. We chatted about the usual stuff you'd want to talk to *freakin' Drake* about, but then, midway through my line of questioning (that was probably about Beyoncé), he cut me off and asked one of his own: "Where is your book, Boody? Like, why haven't you written something yet that empowers women to play their cards?"

For a second, I was stunned. Then I shrugged it off and switched the topic because little did he know, this was a tender spot for me. My first book had been released in 2009 when I was twenty-four. Back then, I'd told myself I'd write three more before thirty. But, there I was at thirty-two, with no additional books or intentions to start one. The next day I told my manager Adam Krasner about the conversation and said something along the lines of, "Maybe this time next year, if my numbers grow substantially, we can start brainstorming."

But little did I know, Adam's wheels had already been turning, and he used this latest bit of info to go full steam ahead, behind my back. A few weeks later he set up a meeting with my now literary agent, Brandi Bowles from UTA. Then, after a couple months of persistent peer-pressuring, I came up with an idea that we all felt confident enough to take out to publishers.

So I'd like to kick off my acknowledgments by saying thank you to faith and vision. Although in this case I can't take credit for it; Adam, I'm pretty sure you can. They say people are the sum of the five individuals they spend the most time with, but I am the product of twenty times that number of great minds who have collectively thought twice about me. Thank you to all the agents at UTA, teachers, mentors and lawyers who have helped to clear the path toward my purpose, even when my fear had other plans. Your positive impact on my life was my constant inspiration for what I wanted to offer others with this book.

Speaking of this book . . . my freakin' girls! Courtney, Deshawn, Maya, Pricilla and Stephanie—I know we have had a billion lovefests where this has all been said, but I love you so much and thank you for all the lessons I have learned through your trust, vulnerability and wisdom. I don't believe that I will fully comprehend how special our time together was until all of my hair is gray, but in short, know that I had the best year of my life and that is in large part to you. I leave this experience with a body of work I am so insanely proud of, and a group of friends I am proud to stand beside, and behind, whenever need be.

Also big thanks to all the experts who devoted their time to changing these and so many other women's lives: Dr. Barry Goldstein, JT Tran, Daniel Hyun Kim, Ari Fitz, Nina Ross, Crystal Greene, Nicole Thompson, Laura Jane Schierhorn, Makeba Lindsey, Meredith Davis, Melissa Hobley, Talya Macedo and Matt Barnes! You brought something so special to this program that transformed this into a one-of-a-kind powerhouse dating book. Big up, yourselves, I owe you one or two!

When this book was in its infancy stage, a sentence I repeated to whoever would listen was, "I want this to be the greatest thing that I have ever done!" Thankfully, HarperCollins was one of those who listened. I could not have asked for a more passionate and thoughtful partner on this project. Never once did I feel like this book wasn't as important to Lisa Sharkey and her team as it was to me, and that is saying A HELLUVA LOT! Thank you to my editor, Anna Montague, for her thoughtfulness, expertise and patience. This book came from my heart, found its legs with the participants, but only hit its stride thanks to you. I also wanna shout out everyone on Dey Street who gave their time to making this great, including Lynn Grady, Ben Steinberg, Nyamekye Waliyaya, Maria Silva, Kendra Newton and Maddie Pillari.

In that vein, I HAVE to show love to my crew of junior editors: my sister, Lauren Morrison; my mom, Olivia Boodram; my dad, Brian Boodram; and my OG L.A. homie Margarita Rozenbaoum. I legit do not know how I would have finished this without you.

At one low point (which every storyteller I'm sure has) I said to my sister, "Read it and when you're done, lie to me and tell me that it's the best thing you've ever read. Please."

Two days later she phoned and said, "It's the best thing I've ever read."

Of course, I knew she was lying (my sister has read at least half of the Pulitzer Prize list), but the off-chance that she wasn't, was a good enough boost of encouragement for me!

Oh, and you know I can't talk about encouragement without shining the light on ALL of my luvas and friends out there. To every stranger who has ever clicked a video, turned up the volume on their TV to hear me out, liked a post, or most of all to YOU who bought this book (if you're just borrowing it from someone, please stop reading . . . kidding), THANK YOU! I know people thank their fans all the time but that isn't what you are to me; you are life-givers and teachers. Everything I've been able to accomplish is because you said yes to me first and not a moment goes by that I don't forget that. I hope that the knowledge you've gained from this book is a suitable token of my undying appreciation for your sexy ass.

On that sexy note, J, shout out to you again. I already gave you the dedication at the front, so I'm not gonna go overboard, but honestly, you're the shit. Plus, you're sitting right beside me as I type this and I'm probably gonna ask you to read it in a second, so I figured a second thanks can't hurt. Maya Washington you slayed my author photos and served as my accountability partner throughout, I'll never forget that. Thanks Kevin Wade for your incredible makeup artistry, Makeba Lindsey for hair and Talya Macedo, as always, for styling.

A final nod goes to Neil Strauss, a man who I have never met but whose life's work has made a profound impact on me. Neil is famously the author of *The Game,* but his work that really rocked my world was *Rules of the Game.* Never before had I seen such a clear-cut and spot-on guide to finding and keeping a romantic life that is worth its weight in gold. Thank you for sharing your knowledge. If this book makes a tenth of the impact that your books have, I'll give up orgasms for a year. Well, maybe not . . . but for sure, I'll be pretty chuffed.

REFERENCES

Aron, Arthur, Aron, Elaine N., Bator, Renee J., Melinat, Edward, Vallone, Robert Darrin, "The Experimental Generation of Interpersonal Closeness: A Procedure and Some Preliminary Findings." *Personality and Social Psychology Bulletin,* Vol. 23, 363–377. 1997.

Ashmore, Richard D., Eagly, Alice H., Longo, Laura C., and Makhijani, Mona G., "What Is Beautiful Is Good, but . . .: A Meta-Analytic Review of Research on the Physical Attractiveness Stereotype." *Psychological Bulletin* 110, 109–128. 1991.

Birger, Jon, *Date-onomics: How Dating Became a Lopsided Numbers Game* (New York: Workman Publishing Company, 2015).

Boodram, Shannon. Interview with Barry Goldstein.

Boodram, Shannon. Interview with Crystal Greene.

Boodram, Shannon. Interview with Talya Macedo.

Boodram, Shannon. Interview with JT Tran.

Bowlby, J., *Attachment. Attachment and loss: Vol. 1. Loss.* (New York: Basic Books, 1969), 180–198.

Brooks, David, *The Social Animal: The Hidden Sources of Love, Character, and Achievement* (New York: Random House, 2011).

"Sexually Transmitted Diseases Surveillance 2017," Centers for Disease Control, last reviewed October 15, 2018. https://www.cdc.gov/std/stats17/default.htm.

Chapman, Gary, *The Five Love Languages: The Secret to Love That Lasts* (Chicago: Northfield Publishing, 2015).

Chapman, Gary and Thomas, Jennifer, *The Five Languages of Apology: How to Experience Healing in All Your Relationships* (Chicago: Moody Publishers, 2006).

Cialdini, Robert B., *Influence: Science and Practice* (Boston: Allyn & Bacon, 2008).

Department of Justice, Office of Justice Programs, Bureau of Justice Statistics, National Crime Victimization Survey, 2012–2016 (2017).

Greene, Robert, *The Art of Seduction* (New York: Viking, 2001).

"Survey Finds Nearly Three-Quarters (72%) of Americans Feel Lonely," Harris Poll on behalf of American Osteopathic Association, conducted September 19–21, 2016. http://admin.osteopathic.org/inside-aoa/news-and-publications/media-center/2016-news-releases/Pages/10–11-survey-finds-nearly-three-quarters-of-americans-feel-lonely.aspx.

"Anxiety and physical illness," Harvard Women's Health Watch at Harvard Medical School, last revised May 9, 2018. https://www.health.harvard.edu/staying-healthy/anxiety_and_physical_illness.

J, *The Sensuous Woman* (Lyle Stuart, 1969).

Karney, Benjamin R., McNulty, James K., and Neff, Lisa A, "Beyond Initial Attraction: Physical Attractiveness in Newlywed Marriage," *Journal of Family Psychology*, Vol. 22, No. 1, 135–143. 2008.

El Khouly, Ghada, Hassan, Ashraf, and Mostafa, Taymour, "Pheromones in sex and reproduction: Do they have a role in humans?" *Journal of Advanced Research*, Vol. 3, Issue 1, 1–9. January 2012.

Kinsey, Alfred C., Martin, Clyde E., and Pomeroy, Wardell B., *Sexual Behavior in the Human Male* (Philadelphia/London: W.B. Saunders Company, 1948).

Kolenda, Nick, *Methods of Persuasion: How to Use Psychology to Influence Human Behavior* (Kolenda Entertainment, LLC, 2013).

Maslow, A.H., "A Theory of Human Motivation," *Psychological Review* 50, 370–396.

Moore, Anna, and Pan, Landyn, "The Gender Unicorn," Trans Student Educational Resources.

"Emerging new threat in online dating: Initial trends in internet dating initiated serious sexual assaults," National Crime Agency, published February 7, 2016. http://www.nationalcrimeagency.gov.uk/publications/670-emerging-new-threat-in-online-dating-initial-trends-in-internet-dating-initiated-serious-sexual-assaults/file.

OkCupid, "A Woman's Advantage," March 5, 2015, https://theblog.okcupid.com/a-womans-advantage-82d5074dde2d.

OkCupid, "Race and Attraction, 2009–2014" Sep 9, 2014. https://theblog.okcupid.com/race-and-attraction-2009–2014–107dcbb4f060

Perel, Esther, "The Secret to Desire in a Long-Term Relationship." YouTube (TEDx Talks), February 14, 2013.

Persaud, Raj, "The Psychology of Seduction." YouTube (TEDx Talks), July 7, 2016.

Rock, Chris, *Kill the Messenger,* HBO, January 2009.

Sales, Nancy Jo, "Tinder and the Dawn of the 'Dating Apocalypse,'" *Vanity Fair,* September 2016.

Sales, Nancy Jo. Swiped. Documentary. Directed by Jo Sales, Nancy. New York City: Consolidated Documentaries. 2018. 21:40

Stop Street Harassment, "2018 Study on Sexual Harassment and Assault," February 21, 2018. http://www.stopstreetharassment.org/resources/2018 -national-sexual-abuse-report/.

Tashiro, Ty, *The Science of Happily Ever After: What Really Matters in the Quest for Enduring Love* (New York: Harlequin, 2014).

"America's Families and Living Arrangements: 2014," United States Census Bureau, last modified May 4, 2018. https://www.census.gov/data/tables/2014/demo/families/cps-2014.html.

"Anxiety and physical illness," Harvard Women's Health Watch at Harvard Medical School, last revised May 9, 2018. https://www.health.harvard.edu/staying-healthy/anxiety_and_physical_illness.

— NOTES —

Introduction

1. Nancy Jo Sales, "Tinder and the Dawn of the 'Dating Apocalypse,'" *Vanity Fair,* September 2016, https://www.vanityfair.com/culture/2015/08/tinder-hook-up-culture-end-of-dating.

2. David Brooks, *The Social Animal: The Hidden Sources of Love, Character, and Achievement* (New York: Random House, 2011), xii.

3. "America's Families and Living Arrangements: 2014," United States Census Bureau, last modified May 4, 2018, https://www.census.gov/data/tables/2014/demo/families/cps-2014.html.

4. Jon Birger, *Date-onomics: How Dating Became a Lopsided Numbers Game* (New York: Workman Publishing Company, 2015), 3, 54.

5. Nancy Jo Sales, *Swiped.* Documentary. Directed by Nancy Jo Sales, featuring Tim MacGougan. New York City: Consolidated Documentaries. 2018. 38:00.

6. Sales, *Swiped,* 38:00.

7. "Emerging new threat in online dating: Initial trends in internet dating initiated serious sexual assaults," National Crime Agency, published February 7, 2016, http://www.nationalcrimeagency.gov.uk/publications/670-emerging-new-threat-in-online-dating-initial-trends-in-internet-dating-initiated-serious-sexual-assaults/file.

8. "Sexually Transmitted Surveillance 2017," Centers for Disease Control, last reviewed October 15, 2018, https://www.cdc.gov/std/stats17/default.htm.

9. "Survey Finds Nearly Three-Quarters (72%) of Americans Feel Lonely," Harris Poll on behalf of American Osteopathic Association, conducted September 19–21, 2016, http://admin.osteopathic.org/inside-aoa/news -and-publications/media-center/2016-news-releases/Pages/10–11-survey -finds-nearly-three-quarters-of-americans-feel-lonely.aspx.

Chapter 1: I Tell It Like It Is

1. A. H. Maslow, "A Theory of Human Motivation," *Psychological Review* 50, 370–396.
2. Ty Tashiro, *The Science of Happily Ever After: What Really Matters in the Quest for Enduring Love* (New York: Harlequin, 2014), 27–45.
3. "Anxiety and physical illness," Harvard Women's Health Watch at Harvard Medical School, last revised May 9, 2018, https://www.health.har vard.edu/staying-healthy/anxiety_and_physical_illness.

Chapter 3: How Do You Like Your Love?

1. Gary Chapman, *The 5 Love Languages: The Secret to Love That Lasts* (Chicago: Northfield Publishing, 2015).
2. Chris Rock, *Kill the Messenger*, HBO, January 2009.
3. Alfred C. Kinsey, Wardell B. Pomeroy, and Clyde E. Martin, *Sexual Behavior in the Human Male* (Philadelphia/London: W.B. Saunders Company, 1948).
4. Landyn Pan and Anna Moore, "The Gender Unicorn," Trans Student Educational Resources, http://www.transstudent.org/gender/.
5. Gary Chapman and Jennifer Thomas, *The Five Languages of Apology: How to Experience Healing in All Your Relationships* (Chicago: Moody Publishers, 2006).
6. J. Bowlby, *Attachment. Attachment and loss: Vol. 1. Loss* (New York: Basic Books, 1969), 180–198.
7. Amir Levine, Rachel Heller, *Attached: The New Science of Adult Attachment and How It Can Help You Find—and Keep—Love* (Penguin, 2010), Chapter 1, Decoding Behaviors, 8.
8. *Personality Traits*, second edition by Gerald Matthews, Ian J. Deary and Martha C. Whiteman, https://web.archive.org/web/20141205103724 /http://elib.fk.uwks.ac.id/asset/archieve/e-book/PSYCHIATRIC-%20 ILMU%20PENYAKIT%20JIWA/Personality%20Traits%2C%20 2nd%20Ed.pdf (Cambridge University Press, 2003).
9. Tashiro, *The Science of Happily Ever After*, 174.

Chapter 5: The Power of Bangs

1. Nick Kolenda, *Methods of Persuasion: How to Use Psychology to Influence Human Behavior* (Kolenda Entertainment, LLC, 2013), 17–18.
2. James K. McNulty, Lisa A. Neff, Benjamin R. Karney, "Beyond Initial Attraction: Physical Attractiveness in Newlywed Marriage," *Journal of Family Psychology* Vol 22, No. 1, 135–143. 2008.

Chapter 6: Don't Just Be Yourself

1. Robert Greene, *The Art of Seduction* (New York: Viking, 2001), 5–15; 133–136.
2. Andrew Newberg, M.D., and Mark Robert Waldman, *Words Can Change Your Brain* (New York: Penguin, 2013), 15–17.

Chapter 9: The 6-Figure Flirt

1. "Race and Attraction, 2009–2014," OkCupid, Sep 9, 2014, https://theblog.okcupid.com/race-and-attraction-2009–2014–107dcbb4f060.
2. Department of Justice, Office of Justice Programs, Bureau of Justice Statistics, National Crime Victimization Survey, 2012–2016 (2017).
3. "2018 Study on Sexual Harassment and Assault," Stop Street Harassment, February 21, 2018, http://www.stopstreetharassment.org/resources/2018-national-sexual-abuse-report/.

Chapter 10: Scrambled Eggs and Blow Jobs

1. "A Woman's Advantage," OkCupid, March 5, 2015, https://theblog.okcupid.com/a-womans-advantage-82d5074dde2.
2. "How to Get From the Match to Matrimony," The League Blog, February 14, 2018, http://www.theleague.com/how-to-get-from-match-to-marriage/#are-you-in.
3. Taymour Mostafa, Ghada El Khouly, Ashraf Hassan, "Pheromones in sex and reproduction: Do they have a role in humans?" *Journal of Advanced Research* Vol. 3, Issue 1, 1–9. January 2012.
4. Alan R. Hirsch, M.D. and Jason J. Gruss. "Human Male Sexual Response to Olfactory Stimuli," *American Academy of Neurological and Orthopaedic Surgeons*, March 3, 2014, https://aanos.org/human-male-sexual-response-to-olfactory-stimuli/.
5. "The 50 things that put the 'Feel Great' in Great Britain," Bupa (April 12, 2015), https://www.bupa.com/newsroom/news/the-50-things-that-put-the-feel-great-in-great-britain.
6. "Don't Let Scent Insufficiency Take Over—Join Gain® and Renowned Smell Expert Dr. Alan Hirsch to Bring Back the Pleasant Aroma and Freshness You May Be Missing in Your Life!" *Business Wire* (June 4, 2013),

https://www.businesswire.com/news/home/20130604006458/en/Dont
-Scent-Insufficiency–Join-Gain.

7. Alice H. Eagly, Richard D. Ashmore, Mona G. Makhijani, Laura C.
    Longo, "What Is Beautiful Is Good, But . . . : A Meta-Analytic Review of
    Research on the Physical Attractiveness Stereotype," *Psychological Bulletin*
    110, 109–128. 1991.

8. Tashiro, *The Science of Happily Ever After*, 102, 135–143.

9. Tashiro, *The Science of Happily Ever After*, 102.

Chapter 11: Fight-Flight Or Fruit Testicles

1. Arthur Aron, Edward Melinat, Elaine N. Aron, Robert Darrin Vallone,
    Renee J. Bator, "The Experimental Generation of Interpersonal Closeness:
    A Procedure and Some Preliminary Findings," *Personality and Social
    Psychology Bulletin,* Vol. 23, 363–377, 1997, https://doi.org/10.1177
    /0146167297234003.

2. Dutton, D. G., Aaron, A. P. "Some evidence for heightened sexual attrac-
    tion under conditions of high anxiety," *Journal of Personality and Social
    Psychology*, 30(4) 1974: 510–517.

3. Esther Perel, "The Secret to Desire in a Long-Term Relationship." You-
    Tube (TEDx Talks), February 14, 2013, https://www.youtube.com
    /watch?v=sa0RUmGTCYY&t=29s.

4. Copyblogger, "The 5 Most Persuasive Words in the English Language,"
    by Greggory Ciotti, December 6, 2012, https://www.copyblogger.com
    /persuasive-copywriting-words/.

5. Raj Persaud, "The Psychology of Seduction." YouTube (TEDx Talks), July
    7, 2016, https://www.youtube.com/watch?v=3E46oWB4V0s&feature=yo
    utu.be&t=6m15s.

Chapter 12: A Game of Her Own

1. J, *The Sensuous Woman* (Lyle Stuart, 1969), 104; 169–170.

ABOUT THE AUTHOR

Shan Boodram is a certified sex educator and intimacy expert with over 35 million YouTube views alongside her mainstream coverage across ABC's *The View*, MTV, *The Steve Harvey Show*, CNN, the *New York Times*, *Entertainment Tonight*, *Cityline*, *The Rachael Ray Show*, *Forbes* and *Time* magazines.

Known by her community as "Shan Boody," she was the relationship-expert host and a consulting producer for Facebook Watch's *Make Up or Break Up*, and the host and executive producer of the Fullscreen series *Your Perfect Date*. She has produced content for MTV, the U.S. military, OkCupid, *Esquire* magazine and the CBC. Boodram is the author of *Laid*, was a contributing writer for Freeform Network's *The Bold Type* series and has written articles for *Teen Vogue* and *Cosmopolitan*.

Boodram is an ambassador for AIDS Healthcare Foundation and WomensHealth.gov. She is a member of the American Sexual Health Association and Trojan's Sexual Health Advisory Council. She is a certified sexologist and currently lives in Los Angeles with her husband, where she is a full-time vocal advocate for healthy intimacy.